Data Mining Explained

Data Mining Explained: A Manager's Guide to Customer-Centric Business Intelligence

Rhonda Delmater
and Monte Hancock

dp

Digital Press

Boston • Oxford • Auckland • Johannesburg • Melbourne • New Delhi

Butterworth–Heinemann supports the efforts of American Forests and the Global
ReLeaf program in its campaign for the betterment of trees, forests, and our environment.

Library of Congress Cataloging-in-Publication Data
Delmater, Rhonda
    Data mining explained : a manager's guide to customer-centric business intelligence / by
    Rhonda Delmater and Monte Hancock.
        p. cm.
    Includes bibliographical references and index.
    ISBN 1-55558-231-1 (pbk. : alk. paper)
        1. Data mining. I. Hancock, Monte. II. Title.
QA76.9.D343 D45 2000
006.3—dc21   00-047511

British Library Cataloguing-in-Publication Data
A catalogue record for this book is available from the British Library.

The publisher offers special discounts on bulk orders of this book.
For information, please contact:
Manager of Special Sales
Butterworth–Heinemann
225 Wildwood Avenue
Woburn, MA 01801-2041
Tel: 781-904-2500
Fax: 781-904-2620

For information on all Butterworth–Heinemann publications available, contact our World Wide
Web home page at: http://www.bh.com.

10   9   8   7   6   5   4   3   2   1

Printed in the United States of America

Contents

Foreword

What a ride the 20th century has been! Within that relatively brief span of one hundred years it seems as if everything blossomed at once. And business participated in the adventure just as much as anyone else. While a bit patchy and uneven in places, with some people missing out almost completely, still the daily life of almost everyone on the planet was directly affected by the vast and sweeping changes that reached out to embrace them.

Companies started the century with the maturing of the Industrial Revolution. Most of the time they were getting to grips with problems of production and scale—problems that only arose because the adolescent Industrial Revolution rushed heedlessly on into the new century. Two main themes preoccupied corporate attention for most of the century's span—organizing people and organizing material. In fact, for most companies, at least at first, there wasn't much difference between organizing people and organizing physical material. Frederick Winslow Taylor, with his theory of "scientific management," organized people to be "efficient"—but mainly it was efficiency of people handling material. After a while, large parts of companies were dealing with activities other than material handling, and these efforts also needed organizing. Bureaucracy had already been invented, of course, but was honed to a fine and powerful business tool for organizing people. So prevalent was corporate bureaucracy that a popular notion was that of "The Organization Man," which prompted a well-known book of the same name. These seem to have been main themes that preoccupied businesses for a hundred years. But just as the coming of the 20th century brought new themes and problems for businesses, so too does the dawning of the 21st.

Today "The Organization Man" is no longer the reigning image, and time-and-motion studies are not viewed as the best way to achieve business efficiency. Furthermore, narrowly drawn concerns with shareholder value and organizational control seem to have broadened to include two new and different themes—customers and knowledge.

Companies have always been concerned with customers to some extent, of course. However, in the past, customers were always assumed to be available if you could get your product to the market at some appropriate price. Markets provided customers, and companies could assume that customers would, at least in principle, always be available. And given that products would flow into the marketplace as a river flows to the sea, corporate value was viewed as based mainly on the quantity of the flow and the value of each unit. The triumph of the Industrial Revolution, achieved at the end of the 20th century, is that of plenty. There is still much crushing poverty in the world, but it isn't due to the lack of the means of production. However, companies now face the fact that, with such a cornucopia pouring plenty into the marketplace, customers are becoming—even in principle, and in a world where more humans live than ever before—a rare resource. One basic fact, therefore, becomes apparent: customers are the foundation of the value of a company. In some sense, a company is only worth what its customers think it is worth. A company without customers is not a viable entity. Companies are finding it increasingly necessary to be responsive and reactive to the needs of their customers—not just as a good business practice, but also as the crucial tool for keeping competitive advantage, indeed, as a necessity for staying in business over the long haul.

The essential ingredient in responding and reacting to customer needs is managing knowledge. Knowledge of the market, of individual customers, of competitors, of internal capabilities, procedures, practices, customer needs, reactions. Knowledge, in fact, in all its forms and guises. But the idea of managing knowledge is something new. Until the dawn of the 21st century, knowledge management was viewed primarily as a mode of collecting and cataloging information. Individuals alone possessed knowledge, although it might have been applied in methodologies, practices, and procedures. It was enough to manage people who had knowledge and, of course, to have people with the right knowledge. Knowledge was synonymous with people, and people with knowledge. How could a thing be known without a knower? But again, the early 21st century reveals a new truth. Knowledge resides in places other than people's heads, and companies suddenly need to manage, organize, and use that knowledge. Manufacturing and organizational efficiency are still crucial for corporate survival, but those are now common (although hard won) skills. They are not in themselves enough for maintaining competitive advantage. The struggle has moved on to new ground, new capabilities, new skill-sets, new understanding.

Corporate knowledge is found in three places—the formal and informal processes, procedures, practices, and policies of a company; the experience of employees, staff, and managers (currently called intellectual capital); and the data that any sizeable modern company collects and stores about its activities. The three pillars of corporate knowledge are procedurally-, intellectually-, and data-based. Modern business practices are grappling with the issues of managing knowledge in all three areas, but one of the most difficult is that of data-based knowledge.

Data, particularly in the vast diversity and enormous quantity that it is available to modern business, was until very recently almost intractably hard to understand. Yet understanding data is the one crucial step to extracting the knowledge that it contains. Today, technology offers business managers powerful new tools for gleaning knowledge from data—the tools of data mining. But just as business managers shortly after the turn of the last century wrestled with the time-and-motion studies pioneered by Taylor and the unfamiliar practices of assembly lines pioneered by Ford, so too are they now wrestling with the unfamiliar tools and concepts of data mining. But it is on these tools and concepts that the foundations of the new century's business will be erected.

Yet what is to be done with this new and hardly won knowledge? Customers—managing, relating to, working with, understanding, reacting to, responding to—and the crucial relationships with them will become more and more a preoccupying theme as the century advances. The 20th century preoccupation was with managing customers—influencing customers to behave in ways that best served the corporate interest. In times of scarcity of consumer choice, and of mass consumer need, standardized products at low cost were welcomed. Indeed, the 20th century culture spawned the ethos of "keeping up with the Joneses." The metaphorical "Joneses" had some latest-and-greatest mass produced consumer item without which the not-having consumer wasn't to be satisfied. Today, the overt idea that some consumers should "keep up" with others is but a faint shadow of its former self. If there are Joneses, they have morphed into folk who expect unique consumer experiences, and who expect to be treated as unique individuals with individual needs. This challenges all companies: How are masses of customers to be treated as unique individuals, and how can it be done profitably?

One answer to this conundrum is Customer Relationship Management, or "CRM" as it is commonly abbreviated. CRM, as the embryonic business practice it is today, is not directly concerned with managing customers' relationships with a company. Its ethos is to manage a company's relationships with its customers. It is not a tool for manipulating customers, but a tool by which a company manipulates itself so that it achieves what the customer wants. It is a feedback mechanism, a transformational tool, and a sanity check. It is the business process by which a company manipulates itself to get to the goal of treating customers as individuals.

However, CRM isn't a method, or even a tool-kit, that can be "bolted on" to an existing company. CRM uses methods and tool-kits, but is itself a philosophy, an approach, and an organizing principle. Learning the methods and tools of CRM, while powerful and promising, isn't in itself enough. Success requires the principled application of these powerful tools, for the days of manipulating consumers and marketplaces are now over, and the new "Joneses" resent overt manipulation.

The challenge is for business managers and practitioners to come to grips with, and learn to use, the tools that help extract and manage the knowledge enfolded in data, and then to apply it to self-management for facilitating each customer's purposes, hopes, and desires. Cultural mores evolve in concert with business practices, both influencing and modifying the other. Where they will ultimately lead is anyone's guess, but what is certain is that the powerful, new, and ever-evolving methods and tools at our disposal have changed the face of the consumer society forever.

Dorian Pyle
July 2000

Acknowledgments

We wish to thank all of those who have contributed to our writing of *Data Mining Explained: A Manager's Guide to Customer-Centric Business Intelligence*. Particular thanks are due to the management of Computer Science Innovations (CSI, Inc.) and especially George Milligan, CEO. Thanks are also due to Phil Sutherland and Pam Chester at Digital Press for critiquing the manuscript and improving the text with their suggestions, and to Katherine Hancock for assistance in producing many of the technical illustrations contained herein. The numerous case contributors as highlighted in Chapters 15 through 23 are deeply appreciated.

What Is Customer-Centric Data Mining?

As we embark on the twenty-first century, the business climate can be characterized by two foremost challenges: fierce competition and rapid change, each amplifying the effects of the other. Change is both fueling and being fueled by the Internet explosion. It is one of the forces driving brutal competition to gain and retain customers. E-commerce, whether business-to-business (B2B) or business-to-consumer (B2C), increases consumers' options in the competitive landscape. Responding to this environment inspires organizations to search for answers, both internally and externally. At the same time, companies are accruing massive amounts of data, which is sometimes at minute detail (such as click-stream data generated by Web-page accesses).

Data mining is becoming increasingly important to mainstream organizations because these major trends are converging. Data mining is of great interest because it is imperative for organizations to realize the competitive value of information contained within their data repositories. This book is devoted to data mining topics: why it's important, the technologies involved, management of the process, and numerous success stories.

Now that companies have finished celebrating the fact that the year 2000 began with all of the much-anticipated celebration and little, if any, inconvenience, they can again begin looking to the future. With the concomitant emphasis on preparing back office or traditional Enterprise Resource Planning (ERP) applications systems behind them, organizations now have the opportunity to undertake *strategic* information technology projects in support of the integrated front office applications of Marketing, Sales, and Customer Service. Such initiatives are essential to developing advantages in competitive markets. Such customer-centric applications are now widely referred to as Customer Relationship Management (CRM).

As computer *generation* of data outstrips human ability to *assimilate* data, organizations become "data rich and information poor." The goal of data mining is to provide the ability to convert high-volume data into high-value information. There are many definitions of data mining, even among the experts. Most definitions agree that data mining involves discovering patterns of information within large data repositories. As would be expected by the term "mining," such patterns are often obscured and difficult to uncover, so advanced pattern recognition and mathematical techniques are applied. Data mining accomplishes two things: it discovers enterprise knowledge from historical data and combines historic enterprise knowledge with current conditions and goals to reduce uncertainty about enterprise outcomes. Customer-centric data mining is a collection of techniques and methods that enables businesses to engage and retain their share of the market.

1.1   Customer Relationship Management

A wide-range of application systems that support the processes of *finding*, *reaching*, *selling*, *satisfying*, and *retaining* customers are included under the CRM umbrella. The widely available, off-the-shelf, or "shrink-wrapped" applications, such as customer service, contact management, or sales force automation, that have until very recently been "stand-alone," are now giving way to more powerful integrated applications that support several, if not all, CRM processes. These applications are more than Sales Force Automation (SFA) systems merely concerned with finding, reaching, and selling. They are focused on satisfying and retaining customers, as well. Similarly, "Customer Interaction Centers" are not only concerned with satisfying and retaining customers, but with every single contact and selling opportunity. Such systems provide unified data regarding all of the interactions with each customer, regardless of what channel their contact occurred in. The CRM application umbrella now encompasses the strategic applications that emphasize, appropriately so, optimization of customer relationships.

Optimizing customer relationships means not only maximizing the financial value of each customer over time, but may require optimizing the mix of customers based on critical resource constraints, such as sales or support personnel or other staffing levels.

Organizations that identify their most valuable customers are able to prioritize their activities so that they spend their own scarce resources on customers and prospects in order of their *value*. Although "canned" CRM applications typically provide essential processing and record-keeping (database) functionality, true CRM optimization requires analytical functionality that is beyond the limitations of such general-purpose application system "products." Therefore, many organizations find it necessary to complement their CRM, as well as their ERP systems, with Business Intelligence (BI) tools. BI tools are software that support decision-making. BI includes a range of tools such as query and reporting, business graphics, online analytical processing (OLAP), statistical analysis, forecasting, and data mining. These tools are often packaged into cohesive groups. Several vendors attempt to cover the BI spectrum by offering BI tool suites. Business Intelligence functions are discussed along with other Information Technology considerations in Chapter 5.

1.2 The Strategic Information Imperative

At the same time the focus of Information Technology (IT) departments is shifting from ERP or "back office" to "front office" CRM emphasis—more and more business processes are being automated, resulting in accumulation of vast amounts of transactional and performance (e.g., financial) data. Some of the "super-sized" information system vendors are even working on the integration of enterprise-level ERP and CRM systems. The costs associated with collection, processing, and storage of such vast data resources can be quite significant. Even so, many "data rich" enterprises retain their valuable historical information in vast formless archives. They miss the opportunity to exploit the core of precious strategic information that is buried within their huge archive libraries.

Some examples of such strategic information that might be exploited are the following:

- A financial institution holds data describing all products launched in the last five years, along with sales performance data. Could such data be used to predict the performance of new products or target marketing programs to the best advantage?

- A utility company has historical information regarding power utilization based on day of week, time of day, weather, etc. Could such information be used to develop demand forecasts?

- A cellular communications provider has information on pricing plans, call volumes, payment history, and other data including demographics. Could such information be useful in customer retention programs?

All of these objectives can indeed be accomplished. The key is to identify the small number of critical influencing factors that enable each problem to be solved from the vast array of hundreds or thousands of data attributes for each customer. Often, consistent patterns of the critical factors are discovered, which conform to customer "profiles." Such problems are difficult, if not impossible, to solve with the use of ad hoc query, analysis and reporting packages: the basic BI tools. While such tools can be very useful for monitoring activities, they seldom provide optimal support for the business decision-maker.

The "glass-house" data centers, which house the powerful mainframes and disk farms that hold organizational information resources, must serve the information and analytical requirements of a spectrum of information consumers and producers in order to satisfy a variety of key objectives. Today's Business Intelligence tool suites support a large portion of the information retrieval and analysis needs for these users. These tools are discussed within an information technology context in Chapter 5.

Beyond general-purpose BI tools, which support clearly beneficial standard and ad hoc business reporting and analysis, there remains a need for "high-end" analytical capabilities including the exploitation of data patterns for applications involving identification and prediction. Such capabilities are called data mining. Many experts consider part of the data mining process to be the development of predictive models based on the patterns discovered through data mining discovery. The authors subscribe to such a "mine and model" definition.

A *model* is a formal description of a system. These descriptions may take many forms, depending upon the purpose of the model. The purpose of the model is to describe the relationship between the system's inputs and outputs. "Inputs" may be thought of intuitively as "current conditions," and "outputs" as assessments or predictions.

Consider a retail sales model. The system is a population of customers for the product. The input could be unit price, and an output could be the number of units that will be sold next month. An example of a model would be a mathematical expression that estimates the output as a function of the input (i.e., estimates the number of units that will be sold next month at a given price).

Data mining analysts develop models of two kinds: predictive models and descriptive models. These will be discussed at length later (Chapters 8–10). In general, *descriptive* models provide information about the *current state* of a system (e.g., "you are bankrupt"); *predictive* models provide information about *future states* of a system (e.g., "you will be bankrupt in three months").[1]

As formal descriptions, models don't have to be mathematical. Models can be collections of descriptive statements (see rule-based models, Chapter 10). Your checkbook is an historical model of your spending behavior. A GANTT chart depicting a software project schedule could be considered to be a model of the software development process. Data mining analysts use models as a means of:

- providing an integrated representation of discovered knowledge about a system and

- making discovered knowledge actionable.

Data mining, as it relates to customer relationships, is the focus of this book. In Part I, the importance of data mining is discussed. In Part II, the science and technology framework that supports data mining is focused on. Data mining management issues are presenting in Part III. In Part IV, data mining applications and case studies are discussed in various vertical markets. The appendixes include a glossary, a bibliography, references for business intelligence company directories, and a basic statistics tutorial.

1.3   Distilling Knowledge from Data

Data mining provides the tools and techniques that are essential for optimization of customer relationships. Data mining enables organizations to use data actively for very powerful impacts, rather than

---

1.   It has become common in practice to use the term "predictive model" even though no time element is involved. This will be discussed in Chapter 10.

just passively storing it. Such applications can leverage large corporate IT investments with true business benefits.

Today's analysts need automated assistance to focus their attention on the "information-bearing" aspects of their data resource. They need help to discover the hot spots and interrelationships that are worthy of further investigation. Common to all users is the need to maximize the amount of useful information extracted, while minimizing the loss of productivity that results from the information retrieval effort, prohibitive access, communications difficulties, or retrieval of meaningless, incorrect, or corrupted data. In order to satisfy the needs of analysts, data mining systems can be designed to represent associations in large data sets, extract and transmit material across a distributed multi-user network, and analyze, interpret, and display information in a variety of meaningful ways.

It isn't unusual for data repositories to contain millions of data attributes, whether they are ERP or CRM databases, decision-support repositories, data warehouses, data marts, or some other form. Consider, for example, a retail establishment collecting data on consumer purchases, which may only be feasible for customers who carry credit accounts with the store. Demographic data for each customer may include: age, gender, marital status, family size, employment, income, credit history, etc. Each customer may periodically purchase a variety of products. With tens of thousands of customers over a multi-year history, it's easy to see how data volume and complexity can grow beyond the ability of humans to comprehend trivial details, much less identify subtle and meaningful patterns that may be very valuable.

Complicating the data volume picture, is the number of distinct pieces of information (which may be called attributes, elements, fields, or features[2]) that relate to each entity or object that the data describes. How do conventional Business Intelligent tools exploit this rich environment? They enable users to generate reports and graphs and manually test "hunches." This can be very useful for analyzing profitability, product line performance, and so on. The means to identify and calculate such information are well-known and understood. Data mining techniques can be applied when users don't already know what they are looking for.

---

2.   "Features" is the name mathematicians and data miners typically use for these distinct pieces of information. The number of attributes or features is sometimes referred to as the "breadth" of the data.

For example, a bank might make the assumption that sales of safe-deposit boxes and Certificates of Deposit (CDs) are related. An analyst equipped with BI tools could probe historic data to determine whether this assumption is true. The result would be an analysis that is limited to the scope of the original assumption; unsuspected trends in customer behavior would almost certainly be missed. While the assumption-driven approach does often find important information, it is inherently limited. Using data mining techniques, analysts can extend their capabilities with discovery-driven analysis.

Data mining provides an automatic method of discovering patterns in data. Data mining applications ingest and correlate data comprehensively, unlike human analysts, who are prone to pursue their intuitive hunches in a sequential manner. Even so, to reach its full potential, data mining must be a collaborative effort between machine and human being. The machines do what they can do best—perform many thousands of brute-force correlations, while the humans do what they do best—assess the value of mechanically discovered regularities in the data. It is this alliance of the best of human and machine capabilities that enables effective data mining projects to ascend to higher capability levels, by analyzing data sources that are too large for manual browsing, and too intricate for unaided human intuition.

Discoveries don't only answer questions. Often, they raise them. This begins a sequence of data mining cycles, with each discovered pattern driving the next rounds of analyses. It is this cyclic engagement of the data that gives data mining its "rapid prototyping" characteristic. Of course, it remains the responsibility of the data mining analyst to select the most promising lines of investigation, because not all discovered patterns will provide organizational value.

Data mining tools can identify the relationships that are actually present in historical data. The tools also have the capacity to uncover new, unsuspected hunches to be tested. Such lines of investigation are based on real, historical data patterns representing actual business experience in the user's market. This becomes the starting point for focused, in-depth analysis. The results may be surprising. Combining discovery-driven analysis with the more pervasive assumption-driven methods will ultimately produce the most comprehensive analysis for the greatest business benefit.

1.4   Who Benefits from Data Mining

Organizations who are most likely to benefit from data mining:

- have large volumes of data;

- have communities of knowledge workers that need to under-stand data, but are not trained as statisticians;

- have organizational data which is complex in nature; i.e., detailed and multifaceted, with complex data relationships; and

- exist in competitive markets.

Small enterprises with less robust data resources can also benefit from data mining technology, but may not have the computing and analytic resources needed to yield the greatest benefit from data mining projects. It is not necessary to have a vast, enterprise data warehouse to perform data mining, but it may well be the best vehicle for returning value on the data warehouse investment.

In the early stages of data mining market evolution, technology was a major emphasis of software vendors, who designed products for the innovative, early adopter. Since data mining approaches are based on combinations of rule-induction systems, neural networks, and advanced regression statistics, early adopters themselves were highly technical. They understood the details of these sophisticated methods well enough to utilize them effectively, and communicate their results to others in their organizations.

During the same time frame as data mining technology and applications have evolved, the computing and communications environment has changed dramatically, shifting tremendous power to the desktop platform. This technology shift coupled with broader demand to perform analytical functions requires a less technically burdensome approach. Today's data mining tools must provide greater analytical capabilities and performance within an easy-to-use framework. Current data mining environments make extensive use of graphics for both user interface and representation of results.

Data mining tools are no longer targeted to the relatively small market of mathematicians employed in operations and market research. They are becoming increasingly easier to use by a spectrum of knowledge workers, such as marketing and financial analysts. The knowledge acquired through data mining activities can be captured by computing professionals and implemented within applications systems to serve a full spectrum of application users, from call center representatives to Chief Technical Officers (CTOs).

To further understand how organizations could benefit from the application of data mining techniques to their market share and risk mitigation, consider the answers to the following questions:

- What is the predictive phenomenology of healthy accounts versus accounts in arrears?

- Moderately in arrears versus accounts ending in severe arrears?

- Regional variations in arrears and arrears according to other definable characteristics?

- How do we increase sales of collateral and secondary products?

- Target new markets?

- Design new offerings?

- What discriminates us from our competitors?

- How do these discriminators affect market share?

Several case study vignettes are included in Chapter 3, and detailed case studies are included in Chapters 15 through 23.

1.5 Past Experience Can Be Used to Predict Future Events

Although significant value lies in the better understanding of historical business experience, many companies can achieve significant benefits by using past experience to predict future outcomes. For example, knowledge of the characteristics of historically profitable products can be used to design new offerings. Or, knowledge of return-on-investment in past direct-marketing efforts can be used for better targeting of future efforts.

Databases facilitate the manual analysis and reporting of data, but they do not prognosticate. Data mining techniques can be used to build models of past business experience that can be applied to achieve benefits in the future. Ultimate business insight is achieved as a combination of accurate hindsight and thoughtful foresight.

1.6   Data Mining Builds Customer Relationships

Magnifying the impetus for data mining tools and techniques is the Internet phenomenon. As we are all experiencing, the Internet is transforming the competitive landscape at a breakneck pace. With the phenomenal growth-to-date and clear expectation of accelerating growth for the foreseeable future, Web-enabled customer interactions will certainly increase. Estimates of the number of North American Internet users during 2000 range between 60 and 100 million. Annual growth rates are estimated at about one-third each year.

The World Wide Web is fueling the growth of electronic commerce. During 1999, the U.S. Department of Commerce reported that electronic commerce had grown by more than 700 percent during the previous 5 years. There is no end in sight to this continued tremendous growth trend. The U.S. Department of Commerce also projected Internet sales to surpass $300 billion by 2002. This is comprised of both business-to-business and business-to-consumer e-commerce. Some projections expect the e-commerce market to surpass the one trillion dollar mark during the next five years.

How do CRM and data mining relate to the Web? A familiar example is Amazon.com of Seattle, Washington. In its own words, "Amazon.com opened its virtual doors in July 1995 with a mission to use the Internet to transform book-buying into the fastest, easiest, and most enjoyable shopping experience possible." Since its inception, the company has grown to be a leading online shopping site, selling to over "20 million people in more than 160 countries" and offering millions of titles in books, audio, video, games, and electronics categories.[3] Its convenience and aggressive pricing has put pressure on retail outlets for similar products, and it continues to grow.

Amazon makes effective use of customer profiling techniques. Whenever a Web customer conducts a search of the Amazon.com site, Amazon.com offers additional products, using phrases such as "Customers who bought this book also bought," "Our auction & zShops sellers recommend," "Customers who bought titles by [this author] also bought titles by these authors." For each, several additional selections, or authors are offered. Amazon.com also offers the opportunity to "Look for similar books by subject" with a list of

---

3.   www.amazon.com/exec/obidos/subst/misc/company-info.html/ref=gw_m_b_aa/002-3695658-1015216

check boxes for several additional subject areas. All of these offer opportunities for consumers to add value to their shopping carts.

Amazon.com provides a rudimentary example of customer profiling that does not require the type of advanced algorithms which are needed for more sophisticated profiling applications, such as those involving prediction or classification (categorization), as will be described in Chapter 10. Far more precise or specialized applications can be developed with today's technology and applied to e-commerce.

Another familiar example is the growing number of sites to match job-seeking candidates with open positions. There are thousands of such sites, with some of the more notable examples being Monster.com and Jobs.com. There are also sites that specialize in particular industries, like ComputerJobs.com; or locations, like career-finder.cincinnati.com. These sites are generally free to job seekers, and may be funded by advertising and recruiting organizations.

A final familiar example is the travel industry, where there is a growing number of sites offering the capability for individual "consumers" to make their own arrangements without the need for intermediaries. Priceline.com provides an innovative capability that allows consumers to submit travel "bids" at their desired price point. Priceline.com automatically identifies and books the travel provider that best satisfies the bid, based on price and other selection parameters, and then notifies the buyers of the details of their travel arrangements. Leading transportation and lodging companies, as well as sites offering services from multiple providers, are not alone in offering information and online reservation services. Many independent "Mom and Pop" service providers are also taking advantage of the Web to promote their offerings.

Again, the "profiling" that takes place within job or travel "matching" applications could be considered primitive compared to the advanced mathematical techniques to be described later in this book, but the pervasiveness and momentum are noteworthy. Further, as the Web continues to grow, we can clearly expect more advanced effective techniques to be applied to enhance the experience for the Web shopping public.

All three examples above were based on "customers" interactively accessing the Internet, which ultimately results in selections or purchases being made. Imagine the impact on competition! What are the barriers to entry? A well-crafted Web-site from an independent or start-up company can offer a similar online shopping experience to the established "brand names."

How then, can a company differentiate its offerings in such a competitive climate? In a single word: *relationship*.

Undoubtedly, some consumers will not only want, but will be willing to pay a premium to companies that have earned their loyalty. Earning such loyalty will require companies to adopt tailored programs (both on the Internet and "in person") based on a variety of customer, or prospect profiles. Priceline.com is not for everyone. Some buyers prefer to shop from a selection of best options.

Thus, the Internet not only increases the need for data mining, but also provides new information to be the subject of mining activities. Some companies are applying data mining to find patterns in "click-streams," (the paths that Web-surfers take) while yet other Web customer characterization applications loom on the horizon.

1.7   Data Mining Yields Customer Knowledge

In the authors' own experience we have recently experienced increasing demand for development of customer-centric data mining applications. Our book is based on actual experience. Business Intelligence continues to grow both in terms of capability and in the extent of implementation. The reason is because Business Intelligence, and more specifically data mining, provides key insights that can be used to:

- enhance competitive position;
- enhance products and services;
- focus business processes on high-value customers;
- solve difficult problems; and
- overall, improve customer relationships.

Principal competitive advantages for next-generation enterprises stem from the application of Business Intelligence to customer relationships. Data Mining is the key technology to provide such competitive advantages. It provides payback opportunities for the significant investments in collecting information into data ware-houses or data marts.

Along with the benefits of offering "immediate" access to a huge worldwide base of prospects, the growing Web offers unbounded competition, and ease of comparison shopping for your customers. Therefore, customer satisfaction is paramount. The winners will be those who offer a rich, interactive, and targeted experience to Web customers and prospects. How can such a well-targeted approach be offered without data mining?

While the preceding customer profiling examples represent recent innovations, they are far from high-tech. Their importance here is that they illustrate a few ways that the business climate, and sheer competition, is being impacted by the Internet. Such competitive pressures will drive organizations to move quickly toward any capability that offers competitive advantage. High-end data mining offers such promise.

1.7.1   An Illustration . . .

You graduated from a first-class business school. You had the right contacts, a good business plan, adequate startup capital—every-thing the conventional wisdom said was necessary for success. The first year was tough, but that was not unexpected. Revenues were slightly higher than projected, resulting in nearly a break-even net profit. During years two and three, the business experienced con-trolled growth, and by year four, began turning a solid profit. In accordance with your business plan, you added a second office, arranged for a line of credit to provide expansion capital, and con-tracted for a regional advertising campaign. Outsourcing reduced costs associated with selected business operation components. But revenue plateaus in year five. You analyze your plan, spend days with your accountants; even bring in a business consultant. As far as anyone can determine, yours is a textbook example of the well-managed small business.

It is at just such a moment in its history that many well-run busi-nesses falter, and begin the slow descent into failure. The conven-tional wisdom of just a few years ago held that the hinge upon which corporate success turns is management's complete and accu-rate knowledge of the business. "Know thyself!" was law number one. The working out of this business-centric model of management is seen in the massive enterprise data repositories of the late 1990s—large corporate IT organizations tend disk farms containing gigabytes of legacy data of uncertain value. "You have to know your business to manage it!" and computers and communications links have made it possible to know everything, right down to the color of the last lipstick sold. And what manager, after having paid to collect and store all this data, is not going to want some of the impressive reports that can be produced from it?

Perhaps it is possible to "know thyself" too well, if such knowledge comes at the expense of losing sight of what's most important. We have used our burgeoning computing capabilities to bury decision makers under an avalanche of bits. You are too smart to continue "navel gazing" for long. You know your business inside out, and it's spiraling downward. What else is there to know?

1.7.2   The Market! (Also Known as Customers and Prospects)

Like it or not, successful business today is driven not by management, but by customer behavior. Managers who believe they can drive their market in this new millennium will lose out to managers who learn to be driven by their market. The market will not announce its needs and wants. It won't provide a written plan. But markets do express their "plans," so to speak, in the subtle behavioral patterns of many customers over time.

The data that represents an orderly business enterprise can also be used to analyze its disorderly market. The same data that indicates how much of products A, B, and C were sold last month can also indicate that big-ticket customers bought products A and B together, while small-ticket customers bought products A and C together. The same data that indicates sales on premiums advertised through different media also indicates which customers can or cannot be reached by each vehicle or program.

Improved communication and market access are removing market inefficiency. Individual low-volume customers now have direct access to manufacturers and basic service providers. Third-millennium customers have direct access to producers. Only those who understand their markets will survive. As stated earlier, customer-centric data mining is a collection of techniques and methods that enable businesses to engage and retain their share of the market. In other words, if you're going to "navel gaze," make sure it's the navel of your customer.

1.8   Data Mining as Part of Your CRM Strategy Can Enhance Your Competitive Position

The business that knows its customers best will serve them best. Customer-centric data mining provides insight into customer attributes and behaviors. This understanding is the basis of any sound business forecast.

Retaining customers costs less than acquiring new ones. The rapid expansion of e-commerce and highly efficient markets has made it easy for customers to change service providers. Many business relationships beyond 2000 may only last for a single transaction. Businesses must realize that "marketing" includes customer retention. The best-spent marketing dollar is the one that keeps the customers you already have.

Operational efficiency is the key to keeping costs under control. Business forecasting is fundamental. Estimation of lifetime value of customers is a high-return activity. This forecasting is more than planning and developing cash-flow models. It includes market projections grounded in real business history. It can answer questions, such as "How much revenue is each current customer expected to generate over the next twelve months?"

Recently, a major fast-food chain began to do hourly demand projections for its outlets so they could have the right number of burgers warming in the bin (e.g., Thursday afternoon at 1 p.m. in a specific location). Such projections result in fresher product to the customer with less waste. Everybody wins. Forecasts with this level of detail and specificity cannot be born out of someone else's experience, they must be based on specific relevant information. For example, the fast-food restaurant at Hibiscus and Babcock Streets experiences different traffic patterns than the one at Wickham and Ellis Roads. Information about your customers' interactions with you exists only in your own data.

Market share isn't everything, because not all customers are created equal. Some customers are profitable, and some are not. Some might be more trouble than they are worth. Data mining is central to optimizing return-on-investment (ROI), because it offers objective,

quantifiable insight into what's "driving the numbers." Market deregulation and improved communication infrastructure have enabled
customers in many markets to go directly to any supplier they wish.
Turnover, also called "churn" or "attrition" in certain industries, has
become a serious problem. Data mining can help by answering two
questions:

- Which of my high-profit customers are most likely to leave? *Be
  proactive to retain them*.

- Which of my low-profit customers are least likely to leave?
  Raise their price and make them more profitable.

Data mining can identify high-potential customers in each market. It can help determine which customers are most likely to make
big-ticket and collateral purchases. Data mining can extract "profiles" of these customers, which can be used to identify business
opportunities. What is really going on when we engage in data mining is allowing the data to speak for itself.

The conventional approach to data exploitation is to build models of business and customer behaviors based upon human intuition
and experience. These models are descriptions of how we have
come to see the business, and are based upon experiences aggregated over long periods of time; such wisdom will, by definition,
never be "up-to-the-minute." Because these models are based upon
our own experience, they'll contain no surprises. Integral to such a
view will be all of our hidden assumptions about what the data
really means. In the conventional approach, we describe for our-
selves what we already believe to be true about our enterprise. This
inherent limitation prevents the conventional approach to data analysis from ever making any truly revealing discoveries.

1.9   Data Mining Is Not Magic

There is always hype when a promising new technology appears.
Data mining is no exception. There are a growing number of data
mining products and vendors with emphasis on market share. The
pressure is on to gild the lily. Market talk notwithstanding, there are
some limitations to data mining technology.

Data mining cannot ingest your noisy data and tell you what it
means. Data mining applications do not understand your business;
they cannot deliver ready-to-use business strategies based on analysis

of raw data without intelligent interpretation. Data mining applications cannot find information that is not actually present in the data. "Garbage-in, garbage-out" applies. If business rules are not present in your data, no worthwhile technology will find them there.

The information produced by data mining engines requires intelligent review by a knowledgeable human expert. Discovered patterns are regularities in the data; whether they are significant and useful, still must be determined by a person who knows the business and can turn knowledge into action.

Data mining does have application to developing real business intelligence. Fundamentally, it provides a systematic way of finding and exploiting useful information latent in large, complex data sets. But, data mining is not magic. Real data mining is *methodology with technology support*. "Hype" data mining is mythology with marketing support. Both are available in the marketplace.

1.10 Summary

Markets are changing now more rapidly than ever before. The fortunes of every business hinge on meeting the market when it arrives at its future manifestation. Data mining can help uncover trends in time to make the knowledge actionable. In data mining, models of experience are driven by the data itself—without hidden assumptions and without simplifications that hide the unsuspected truth. This assumes that the data mining practitioner is honest and does not discard selected parts of the data or "salt the mine."

Every organization's enterprise data has a story to tell. Data mining is the search for that story. Each story explains how a business has *actually* operated in the recent past. It provides detailed accounts of customers' behaviors, not as they are perceived, but as they have *actually* occurred.

Given the high value of enterprise data and the great utility of its information, one could question why every organization is not involved in data mining. The truth is, most companies are to some extent. Every analyst that looks for patterns in a spreadsheet of enterprise data is mining the data—looking for information that is present, but not obvious. Modern data mining techniques, however, make it possible to look at complex enterprise data in ways that exploit relationships that just cannot be managed using naive manual techniques. They automate the correlation and analysis of bulk data in many dimensions and in ways that a person armed with only a spreadsheet cannot. Modern enterprise data warehouses often consist of many gigabytes of uncorrelated data—data that is incomplete, error-laden, and multifaceted. Only sophisticated algorithms leveraging high-speed computing machinery can even begin to discover and exploit the more subtle patterns present in such a data repository.

How Data Mining Can Enhance Your Services and Products

While some organizations offer only services and no products, the converse—offering products without services—is seldom true. Even buyers of commodity goods have questions and quality issues that require interaction with customer service personnel. Data mining can be useful for enhancing a company's sales and service Customer Relationship Management (CRM) processes as well as its product offerings. This chapter discusses a range of computer applications that support these CRM functions, with emphasis on customer profiling, customer interaction centers, and product improvement.

2.1   Improved Sales and Service

Data mining can be used to improve the performance of many sales and service functions by identifying critical circumstances or significant trends. Many organizations maintain multiple application systems that retain customer information. Companies may utilize some, none, or all of the systems selectively from the following list:

- Contact Management System or Lead Management System

- Sales Force Automation (SFA)

- Customer Service Automation, also called Customer Care, Help Desk, Call Center, or Customer Information Center (CIC)

- Order Fulfillment

- Field Force Automation

- Marketing Automation, which may include Relationship Marketing and/or Database Marketing

- Electronic Commerce

The Customer Interaction Center, or its predecessor—the "Help Desk," has historically been viewed as the focal point of the CRM program for many organizations. Customer satisfaction is essential to retaining market share. Effective customer care can result in very happy customers—especially if those customers have had less than stellar service in the past. Customers who are treated courteously, professionally, and fairly in an expeditious manner will appreciate the effective customer care your company has given them. Even businesses that are commodity-based must provide effective customer care in today's competitive environment. Whether their customers are businesses, consumers, or some other type of customer, managing relationships is critical.

The days of "fire-and-forget" sales are over. Vendors can't expect their customers to lay dormant until they're ready, if ever, to place another order. Customers expect to be able to pick up a telephone, send a Fax or electronic mail message, or visit their vendor's Web page to submit an information or service request. They expect immediate access to up-to-date, consistent, correct, and comprehensive information pertaining to a vendor's business, products, and services. They also expect information on their own account (order status, etc.). As we embark on the new millennium, many view the mission of CRM as providing a comprehensive view of all customer interactions—Web, telephone, support, sales, etc. Isolated Sales Force Automation (SFA) systems that don't integrate with marketing and customer service are clearly inadequate. The comprehensive enterprise CRM systems that are emerging today are intended to keep track of all such customer interactions, as well as each customer contact by a company representative. Such representatives may be in the form of sales, support, training, customer interaction center, other personnel, or even by automated means.

Providing such a capability manually would require a very large CRM workforce—if it could be done at all. For businesses with geographically broad markets covering multiple time zones, CRM is a "24 hours a day, seven days a week" (24, 7) endeavor. Servicing international markets adds complexity by introducing linguistic, logistic, and cultural requirements for the human and automated systems.

Many organizations have tried to address staffing and skill levels, as well as other issues with automation, resulting in both well- and poorly implemented Interactive Voice Response (IVR) systems. Some of these systems could be accused of erecting a wall of aggravation between frustrated customers and disinterested businesses. In the current competitive climate, a Web-savvy market will not tolerate such ineffective customer interfaces. One answer is to provide automation of intelligence within customer service systems; in other words, customer service systems with embedded intelligence.

Such rich, comprehensive CRM systems as described previously are relatively immature. And some of the large enterprise software vendors have an even more ambitious comprehensive vision that involves melding Enterprise Resource Planning (ERP) and CRM so that all business transactions, be they front office or back office, share information resources (data and processing). Such a rich repository will both fuel, as well as be fueled by data mining.

Customer Relationship Management (CRM), as discussed in Chapter 1, is a critical element for any business venture, whether or not it employs "CRM terminology." CRM covers the complete life-cycle of the customer relationship, from lead generation to on-going service, support, and growth of an account. Every organization has "customers," even though they may be called "patients," "members," "partners," or by some other name, depending on the market in which they exist.

Data mining techniques, as will be further explained in Part II, can be applied throughout the complete customer relationship life-cycle. The following table identifies several examples.

Table 2.1

CRM Life-Cycle Stage	Activities	Data Mining Example
Finding	Lead Generation	• Customer acquisition profiling • Web-mining for prospects • Targeting market
Reaching	Marketing Programs	• Customer acquisition profiling
Selling	Contact Selling	• Customer acquisition profiling • Online shopping • Scenario notification • Customer-centric selling

continues

Table 2.1   *(continued)*

CRM Life-Cycle Stage	Activities	Data Mining Example
Satisfying	Product Performance Service Performance Customer Service	• Customer retention profiling • Scenario notification • Staffing level prediction • Inquiry routing
Retaining	Customer Retention	• Customer retention profiling • Scenario notification • Individual customer profiles

The capabilities of data mining that are useful in building these examples to enhance CRM performance include:

- Learning patterns that allow rapid, proper routing of customer inquiries.

- Learning customer buying habits to suggest likely products of interest.

- Categorizing customers for focused attention (e.g., churn prediction and prevention).

- Automating intelligent responses to customer "events" (inquiry, purchase, churn).

- Providing predictive models to reduce cost and allow more competitive pricing (e.g., fraud/waste control).

- Assisting buyers in the selection of customer-centric inventory.

2.2   Customer Profiling

Customer profiling is the process of identifying consistent patterns within customer or prospect data that provides information that can be used to make business decisions and take appropriate actions. For example, customer profiling might be used to identify which prospects are most likely to respond favorably to a certain type of selling campaign or offer. It is a very useful technique that can be applied in all phases of the CRM life-cycle. Customer profiling may use advanced data mining capabilities, or less sophisticated methods. The Amazon.com example, described in Chapter 1, provides an initial example of customer profiling as used for cross-selling.

Customer profiling can also support campaign management and other selling objectives.

Advanced customer profiling applications utilize powerful data mining techniques to build predictive models based on common profiles within a customer base. This approach requires adequate historical data, which is discussed further throughout the book. Briefly, for data to be adequate there must be a sufficient sample size to support development of mathematical models. The data must have adequate predictive salience to support the application. Typically, the number of attributes used for customer profiling models is reduced to those key attributes that are most effective in identifying the differences between profile groups. An attribute is an element of information with a value that describes or measures a property about an entity or object. An attribute may also be called a data field, element, property, feature, column, or cell. Once the profiles are defined, they can be identified with their most prevalent result or "outcome." This information can be stored in a repository, provided as a computer file, a report, or incorporated within an automated process. The information can be stored within an enterprise application system, such as the systems that support CRM.

Customer acquisition profiling utilizes predictive patterns to identify which prospects are most likely to make a particular type of purchase. It is useful in identifying the best prospects (some may consider this to be an aspect of lead generation) and in determining which marketing programs will be most effective to reach the customers that conform to particular profiles. As an example, a financial services provider may target a specific market and geographic region for market penetration programs, such as the merchant credit processing market consisting of thousands of small businesses in greater Cleveland, Ohio. The size of this market is likely to preclude effective, comprehensive, one-on-one marketing at a reasonable cost. If desirable, prospective customers most likely to move their business to this particular financial services provider could be identified based upon available indicators, then marketing could be focused for best return-on-investment.

Customer purchase profiling is similar to customer acquisition profiling in that purchasing patterns are used to identify additional selling opportunities for customers or prospects that are already in a buying mode. Similar profiles can be used to identify or optimize cross-selling opportunities and processes.

Customer retention profiling is similar to customer acquisition profiling in that predictive patterns are utilized to identify which customers are likely to remain loyal to the business and which ones are in jeopardy. All businesses expect to experience some customer turnover each year. Many departing customers do not give detailed explanations of the basis of their decision to leave. This makes it difficult to determine how business practices must be modified to increase retention. If customers who are likely to move their business could be identified before a decision to leave has been made, the vendor would have a greater opportunity to take action to retain their business. Similar to customer acquisition profiling, data mining techniques can be constructed to determine effective indicators of retention likelihood and identify those customers whose "retention profile" indicates high "retention risk." Customer profiling is discussed further throughout the book.

Someday, CRM data mining applications will likely develop to the point that individual customer profiles can be developed and retained to enable individual customer behavior (i.e., purchasing) patterns to be realized and used in CRM programs. For example, seasonal buying patterns and individual market-basket analyses of gifts or particular sporting goods could be quite useful in business promotions. The market-basket analyses would identify which categories of products the customer tends to purchase together. For example, if Franco is buying vermicelli, he will need to purchase marinara sauce and wine. Conversely, if Franco never buys sauce or wine (because he always makes his own), he might appreciate it if the purchase suggestion is not made in favor of those items he prefers. This type of individual buying-behavior profiling could be particularly powerful in e-commerce (Web-based) applications.

Web-mining is another emerging application of customer profiling. One example is an intelligent agent that searches corporate Web pages looking for prospective clients that match a vendor's customer acquisition profiles.

Customer profiling can also be used to support scenario notification. Scenario notification triggers information or action-based recognition of specific patterns of data within or among application systems. Data mining can be used to identify the patterns of interest for each scenario. Such data patterns can result from customer behaviors or other processes. The scenario notification can implement notification via a variety of means, such as e-mail messages or submitting actions to customer service queues. Scenario notification can be useful in a variety of selling, service, and retention activities.

Additional information on customer profiling is contained in case studies throughout Part IV.

2.3   Customer Interaction Center (CIC)

Data mining can be used to drive Customer Interaction Center programs through the application of customer profiling techniques. It can also be used to support inquiry routing and staffing level prediction applications. Depending on your industry, your "customer care center" may have more contact with your customers on an on-going basis than anyone else in your organization. For this reason, those who staff your "customer care center" play a key role in determining the satisfaction, additional sales, and ultimately the value of your customers to your bottom line. Customer profiling techniques can be applied in multiple points of service within the Customer Interaction Center, as described below. Both customer profiling and scenario notification, as described above, can be useful for a variety of programs within the CIC to enhance the level of customer satisfaction and retention.

A common complaint of customers seeking assistance from CICs is the inefficiency of the triage process. When people go to a hospital with a medical problem, they expect a knowledgeable expert (triage officer) to expeditiously match them with an appropriate caregiver. Customers with product or service problems have come to expect the same thing. Quite often, though, they find themselves talking to a marginally functional robotic voice telling them to choose among options they don't want. Or, they are "referred" from one modestly trained customer representative to another, leaving them ultimately bereft of confidence in the vendor. Given a choice, customers forced to play "help desk roulette" won't call or buy from that company again.

Data mining can help by offering intelligent support for the triage process. This support can be effective in automating certain types of customer routing, being able to determine when human intervention is essential, providing automated information services to customers, giving intelligent support to service personnel, and automatically monitoring the entire CIC process for later analysis.

As an added side benefit, "call center" data that has been objectively and consistently collected provides a source of mineable data (as in data that can be mined) for CRM applications, such as churn prediction. Customers dissatisfied with a service often call a help center at least once before taking their business elsewhere.

Effective predictive models can be developed to determine the optimal staffing levels of the customer interaction center. The best models would predict the number of staff members of each job function and level that would be required at certain times of the day, week, month, and year. Since new products and services may be introduced sporadically, the model needs to adapt based on recent variations. For example, a model that accounts for seasonal variations may also need to reflect the actual variances experienced during a preceding period, in both number and staffing skill levels. Such a predictive model not only provides customer service benefits, but can provide efficiency improvement and thereby reduce costs.

2.4 Data Mining Can Help You Improve Your Products

The preceding examples clearly demonstrate that data mining can enhance sales and customer service. It may seem more challenging to apply data mining techniques to improve products, but, in fact, several opportunities exist to improve products, such as design, performance, safety, warranty, delivery, and packaging

The authors were recently engaged by one of the "big three" automakers to perform a data mining study of customer satisfaction based on industry-standard survey data. The goal of the exercise was to identify the critical components or features of an automobile that have the most influence on customer satisfaction ratings. The results of this data mining study could influence product design and development investment in the areas that are most critical to increase customer satisfaction levels, as well as the grouping of options into packages that result in the best satisfaction levels.

Extending the automotive industry example to the data mining of warranty and safety data could again ultimately influence product design and development investment, thereby resulting in improved products.

Data mining can be used to optimize delivery of products and services by optimizing the delivery infrastructure (e.g., placement of ATM machines).

2.4.1 Just In Time (JIT)

Having all the elements of an activity come together at the last possible moment (Just In Time) keeps costs low, but requires deep insight into the process. Inaccurate estimates of required resources or timing can lead to substantial loss. The ability of predictive models (see Chapter 10) to enhance these estimates can bring about substantial savings.

Data mining offers great promise for enhancing the product offerings of businesses engaged in JIT sales, such as volume retailing of perishable or hard-to-store merchandise. These businesses must meet the market with exactly what it demands at the demand rate. Hamburgers are a good example. Leave a burger to harden too long in the "ready" bin, and repeat business will suffer. On the other hand, leave a customer to harden too long at the register and the effect is the same.

Just In Time manufacturing is another area in which data mining can reduce inefficiency. The case study for energy (see Chapter 22) contains an excellent example of a JIT model that precisely forecasts the hour-by-hour demand for a perishable product: electricity.

2.4.2 Embedded Intelligence

Systems are said to have *embedded intelligence* when they automate functions that require decision-making and/or adaptation. This "machine intelligence" can be implemented in a number of ways. The most common ways are conventional rule-based systems, fuzzy logic systems, and black-box regression systems, such as neural networks. Black-box regression systems are models that operate according to mathematical rules not explicitly stated; The parameters governing these rules are derived (usually automatically) from sample data. An example is a neural network that has been trained to predict a specific outcome.

Using embedded intelligence, smart systems can carry out some decision-making tasks that previously required human involvement. The potential for cost savings, consistency of results, and improved enterprise efficiency is large. "Intelligent behavior" corresponds roughly to properly sequenced actions—it consists of patterns and can be the subject of data mining activities. Discovered patterns can provide the algorithms and rules by which embedded intelligent systems make decisions.

2.5   Summary

Data mining can be useful for enhancing both a company's services and its products, which can benefit virtually every business entity. In addition to supporting a wide range of CRM functions, data mining supports customer service, as discussed in more detail in Chapter 15. It can also support direct marketing activities, as is discussed in Chapter 16.

3

Data Mining Can Solve Your Most Difficult Problems

Every mature business has some seemingly insoluble problems—difficult judgments about customers, resource allocation, business strategy, or organization. Niche careers are sometimes built entirely upon insight into some arcane problem associated with an essential business process—insight the possessors can't or won't share with anyone else. These are the "five-percent problems": the intractable residue that remains after years of work has solved the other 95 percent. These five-percent problems are the principal targets of data mining.

In a sense, most of today's enterprise problems are no more difficult than those of fifty years ago. Managers in the 1950s faced many of the same problems that decision-makers face today. But, there is one very important difference—scale. In terms of the number of customers, variety of products, array of marketing channels, speed of commerce, churn, fraud, etc., *everything* today is much bigger. So big, that unaided human decision-making processes are losing their ability to keep up. There may be nothing wrong with the processes themselves, other than their inability to scale up.

Further complicating the modern decision-maker's problem is a reduction in the time available for deliberation. Fifty years ago, slower communication and distribution channels gave managers time that they just don't have today. Enterprise management is a sequence of decisions. Managers must evaluate current conditions in light of past experience and future expectations and choose among the available courses of action that will lead to the best result. Data mining techniques can be used to learn about the factors bearing on a decision and construct an application that uses those factors to help the enterprise make those decisions in an objective, consistent way.

As managers grow in experience, they develop and refine decision-making methods well suited to their enterprise. These methods formalize important knowledge about how the enterprise operates. Good decision-makers are often successful because of the knowledge they possess. If intelligence is the engine, then knowledge is the fuel.

As enterprise operations become more complex, however, decision makers are forced to make compromises in the application of these methods simply because there is a practical limit to the number of factors the human mind can objectively consider. The fine distinction being made here between knowledge and intelligence is important to achieve an accurate understanding of what data mining does.

3.1   What Data Mining Does

Computers are not at all intelligent, but through the application of data mining and other intelligent software techniques, they can discover, store, and apply knowledge. Since knowledge is at the heart of effective decision-making, data mining techniques for the discovery and exploitation of knowledge can aid humans in many aspects of enterprise management. Computers are easily capable of correlating 50 subtle factors as part of a decision-making process. This is something that human beings, no matter how intelligent, simply cannot do.

Enterprise knowledge falls into three categories:

1.   knowledge about the past, which is stable, voluminous, and relatively accurate,

2.   knowledge about the present, which is unstable, compact, and relatively inaccurate, and

3.   knowledge about the future, which is hypothetical.[1]

---

1.   "future" here is broadly understood. A "prediction" can mean estimating next quarter's revenue. It can also mean assigning a credit score to a potential customer. This latter application is a "classification" activity: An entity is categorized based on current and past information. In data mining, this kind of classification is often referred to as prediction. It completely loses its temporal connotations, for example, when a mammogram image is classified as "normal." A system with this function would still be called a predictive model, even though its purpose is to classify, looking back in time to the creation of the image, rather than forward.

Some readers who are particularly process-oriented may want to read Chapter 4, before they read the condensed case study examples that follow. As with any methodological process, care should be taken to adjust the process to fit the problem at hand. As analysts gain experience with data mining applications, they are able to make beneficial adjustments to the process within the context of a particular application or problem. The steps of the process are:

- Step 1: Problem Definition
- Step 2: Data Evaluation
- Step 3: Feature Extraction and Enhancement
- Step 4a: Prototyping Plan
- Step 4b: Prototyping/Model Development
- Step 5: Model Evaluation

As part of a rapid prototyping sequence, some or all of these steps may be repeated as knowledge is gained about the subject data being mined and based on desired and actual levels of performance. For production implementation of data mining application systems, there are two additional steps in the process:

- Step 6: Implementation
- Step 7: Return-on-Investment Evaluation

Since this chapter is focused on problem solving, the final two steps are omitted from the following discussion.

In the first case study, the data mining example is described followed by a discussion of how the steps of the process apply to the case in detail. Three additional case studies follow with the process described at a higher level. The four case studies represent the four types of data mining solutions described earlier in this chapter: discovering relationships, making choices, making predictions, and improving a process. All of these are drawn from the authors' experience, illustrating how data mining can solve your most difficult problems. Through these examples, the "flow" of the process is described in several different contexts. These examples are intended to give insight into the process whereby data mining activities are conducted. Additional case study examples are provided in Chapters 15 through 23.

3.4.1 Case Study 1: Discovering Relationships (Detecting Collaboration)

In this case study, data mining techniques are applied to determine whether computer programs written by university engineering students are the product of collaboration (a "no-no"), or are original single-author works. The major points illustrated are:

- items being analyzed (e.g., computer programs) can be represented by abstract "features" (in this case, numeric facts about the programs);

- data mining can automatically discover unsuspected patterns in the abstract features; and

- the discovered patterns carry actionable information about the original items (the original computer programs).

Plagiarists copy the work of others and represent it as their own. Plagiarists are betting that the recipient of the copied work will not be familiar with the original. Just to be sure, the plagiarist may make subtle modifications in the work to mask its association with the true source. If there are many possible sources for a work, and the work has been subtly modified, checking it for originality can be very challenging.

This case study recalls Monte's first encounter with data mining, which occurred in the early 1980s. He was on the adjunct faculty in the computer science department at a large university, teaching a combination Fortran/numerical analysis course. He taught this course three times, each time to a class of about 120 students.

The course culminated in the execution of a major computing project by each student, which involved substantial amounts of both mathematical analysis and software development. It was made completely clear to the students, both orally and in writing, that there was to be no collaboration on the final project. This was an engineering school, and the competition for grades was intense. Naturally, this gave rise to a tremendous pressure for students to perform; and some mechanism was needed for verifying that each student's work was original. Each semester that Monte taught this course, he was faced with a massive problem at the end of the semester: insuring the integrity of the grades on the final project.

But how can one instructor possibly compare all possible combinations of 120 substantial computer programs? Manually comparing each pair of projects, it was estimated, would require about 3,000 hours. These students were smart enough to change variable names, and do other things that would make two software source-code listings look different, even if they were essentially the same. The best that could be done manually was to compare a subset of papers selected at random, relying on the unseen forces underlying a just universe to help expose errant scholars. These unseen forces never produced any results.

What was needed was a way to automatically identify subtle patterns present in the programs submitted to determine whether two very different looking source code listings actually represented the work of a single person. The third time Monte taught the course, he decided to try automating the integrity check. He resorted to data mining.

In order to collect the necessary data features to support an automated analysis, students were required to submit their computing projects on a single unbursted listing. This ensured that important numeric job statistics prepared by the computer itself would be included with each project. These statistics included things such as the length of time it took for the program to run, the number of instructions the program generated, the number of symbols that the creation of the program produced, and so on. The students were sophisticated, but it was suspected that they were not sophisticated enough to perpetrate deceptions which would withstand formalized mathematical pattern analysis.

Seven statistics from the project computer listings were selected as features for the analysis. Because patterns could not be revealed by merely plotting the seven numbers, data mining was used to look for patterns among the seven-dimensional points representing the 120 projects. Any groups of points that were tightly "clustered" identified suspicious sets of papers to be compared by the instructor. The data mining application routine found only two suspicious clusters of points: One consisting of a single pair of points and the other consisting of five points, tightly grouped (see Figure 3.1).

On the day the graded projects were to be returned to the students, the seven suspicious papers were withheld. One hundred thirteen students cheerfully left the auditorium, leaving two young

Figure 3.1
*Clusters of
collaborating
college kids*

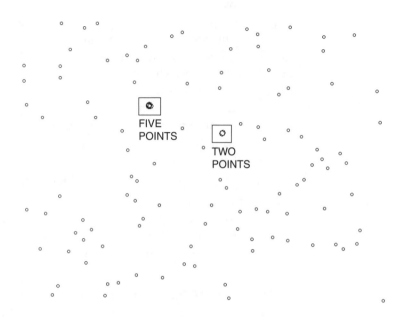

men sitting together in the front of the room, and five young men sitting together in the back. Although there are additional human-interest details to this story, for our purposes it's enough to say that when confronted with the evidence, all parties admitted their duplicity (save one, whose work had been secretly copied by a roommate, who confessed).

Although this example may not be data mining at its best, it illustrates what is possible when given a clear problem statement and adequate data. It also suggests that patterns occur in all sorts of interesting places and their imaginative exploitation can produce useful, and sometimes surprising, results.

This case study also demonstrates that data mining can be very useful in cases where there isn't much data involved. The collaborating college kid problem has only 120 records, each with 7 attributes. The whole data set was less than 4,000 bytes. The problem is difficult not because there is voluminous data, but because the matching process is complex. In Chapter 4, the amount of data required for success in general data mining applications is discussed.

human reason and experience are still the final arbiters of enterprise truth.

At each step in the analysis, specific objectives were satisfied, allowing systematic progress toward a successful conclusion. As the investigation proceeded, these steps were repeated as necessary, and the investigation focused on areas showing greatest promise.

3.4.2   Case Study 2: Making Choices (Telecom Subscription Fraud)

This is a business problem characterized primarily as one of "making choices": The choice is between a good customer and a bad customer. In the "telecom" (telecommunications) industry, service providers enter into service agreements with customers who may or may not pay their bill. Service providers assume an advance risk, because they don't bill for service until the end of the billing cycle (typically a month). Subscription fraud occurs when customers subscribe for service with fraudulent intent (no intention to pay for services rendered). This example deals with subscription fraud for cellular telephone subscribers. Specifically, the enterprise goal is to discover patterns in historical business data that can be used to limit loss due to this type of fraud.

The major points illustrated are:

- data collected for one purpose can sometimes be used for another;
- intuitive concepts like "good" and "bad" can be mathematically expressed; and
- data mining can be used to build algorithms that predict complex behaviors.

To develop deeper insight into how data mining helps managers "make choices," we now consider a case study involving one of the most difficult business choices: "Do I want this customer, or not?" The following discusses the approach to this problem.

3.4.2.1   Problem Definition (Step 1)

The subscription problem is faced by all businesses engaged in providing service for credit. Such businesses don't know in advance who is going to pay their bill. Many businesses operate at-risk for some period of time because they are providing service and incurring cost under the assumption that the customer will pay for services rendered. Different types of losses can often be quantified based on historical data. Knowing the relative size of the cost of an incorrect decision can be very helpful in making business decisions about how to manage them. An essential part of problem formulation for the subscription problem is estimation of the various error costs.

After consideration of all these factors, the data mining problem might be stated as:

> *Identify which customers should be offered a service contract and which customers should not be offered a service contract, based upon the information available at the time an offer decision must be made.*

3.4.2.2   Data Evaluation (Step 2)

Certain information can be ascertained at the time a potential customer walks in the front door. Some of it is helpful in making a credit decision, while some is collected to support administrative processes. Not all of the information collected is relevant to the contract offer decision. In fact, there are likely to be some factors, such as race, gender, religious affiliation, age, etc., which cannot legally be used in a credit decision. These must be excluded from consideration. Sometimes, additional data may be collected from outside sources.

It is desirable to collect information that provides insight into income, payment history, job status, credit accounts, and so on. The foundation could be a standard credit application that the potential customer will fill out. Since the information collected using such a "volunteer" format cannot be expected to be completely reliable and objective, it should be augmented with a second, more objective source, such as a report from a credit bureau. It is determined, then, that information taken from a credit application the provider administers, supplemented by a report from a credit bureau, will be used to estimate the likelihood that a customer is going to be "good" or "bad." In our example, a total of 23 features were extracted from application forms and third-party data sources.

To identify the relevant data (that which is pertinent and of high quality for the credit decision), data mining methods are used to estimate the information content of each available factor. There are a number of data mining methods for determining data pertinence and quality, including Bayesian analysis, visualization, auto-clustering, and so on. These are described in detail in Chapter 8.

3.4.2.3 *Feature Extraction and Enhancement (Step 3)*

It is expected that "good" customers have certain characteristics in common: They have adequate incomes, pay their bills on time, have a good employment history, have successfully carried other credit accounts, have a checking account, etc. When these factors are present in combination, confidence that this will be a "good" customer is increased.

It is also expected that "bad" customers have certain characteristics in common: They have marginal incomes, a spotty payment history, change jobs frequently, have credit accounts in default, etc. When these factors are present in combination, confidence that this will be a "bad" customer is increased.

3.4.2.4 *Prototyping Plan (Step 4a)*

The service application and credit report contain information that is believed to be relevant to the credit decision. But, what should the provider look for? What single piece of information or set of facts tells her whether to extend an offer of service, ask for a deposit of a particular size, or tell this potential customer to take his or her business somewhere else?

Using information from previously collected credit applications and credit reports, data mining techniques can be used to build a predictive model (see Chapter 10) that ingests this information and produces a classification result of either "good" or "bad." The credit manager will use this classification to support her final decision, a decision that she still makes herself.

Because the goal is to divide the population of potential customers into two groups (good and bad), it makes sense to look at how these two groups have appeared in the past. In the history of the enterprise, there have been good customers and bad customers. Data mining techniques can be used to look for similarities among these two groups of historic customers. Characteristics which are regularly seen among bad customers, but rarely seen among good customers suggest caution be used when observed in a potential customer. Characteristics common among good customers, but rare among bad suggest that the risk is low when observed in a potential customer.

Here data mining is being used to codify real, historical experience. The enterprise wants a decision that is conditioned by actual business history. In this way, even an inexperienced credit officer will have the benefit of the results of actual outcomes for the business collected over time. Of course, the human standing at the service desk will use insight and business policy to make the final determination. A predictive model based upon data mining technology will make this determination more consistent, objective, and consonant with real business experience.

3.4.2.5   *Prototyping/Model Development (Step 4b)*

In this case, what is needed is an application that actually performs a credit score computation. A data mining application that ingests feature information and renders a decision of this sort is an example of a "predictive model." Once the relevant data has been identified, a predictive model based upon the credit application and credit report is built. There are many predictive modeling paradigms currently in use, including rule-based systems (KBES), neural networks, decision trees, etc. One appropriate to the problem will be selected and implemented. Validation will be conducted using blind tests.

The validated system will then be integrated into the operational environment as a new module in the credit decision system, or perhaps as a separate software application. Documentation, online help, and supporting business procedures will, of course, have to be created.

For credit scoring applications, data mining techniques provide decision support to the credit manager who must make a choice: Shall an offer of credit be extended to this potential customer or not? In this example, data mining tools were used to select and condition data that served as the basis for a predictive model. This predictive model makes available to the credit manager the accumulated business history as it might bear on the present decision by directly answering the question, "What has been our experience with customers similar to this one?".

The development of a risk model requires a fair amount of experimentation. Work the authors have done in this area has led to the creation of risk models in as little as two months of prototyping. If the modeled population is fairly diverse, results can be improved by building separate models for different portions of the population.

The development and capabilities of this predictive model is discussed in more detail in Chapter 20.

3.4.3 Case Study 3: Improving the Process (Estimating Future Market Demand)

In this example, data mining techniques are used to make demand predictions, which in turn are used to make a process more effective. Specifically, the goal is to discover patterns in business data that enable estimation of the demand for a product at a future time. Hence, this is a business problem characterized primarily as one using a decision or prediction to improve the process.

The major points illustrated are:

- data doesn't necessarily have to be known precisely; it can be estimated;

- one prediction can be part of the basis for another; and

- data mining can be used to build algorithms that predict time series.

The electric utility industry is being deregulated in the United States. Businesses that were once protected monopolies are, for the first time, facing the prospect of true competition. Because they have held protected markets, utilities are behind many other industries in developing internal processes necessary for successful operation in a competitive environment. This means that utilities will no longer be competitive by doing merely an adequate job of controlling production costs. To the consumer "electricity is electricity" and service is expected to be trouble-free, so the principal market discriminator will be cost.

3.4.3.1 Problem Definition (Step 1)

Utilities are capital-intensive. They have a tremendous investment in their physical plants, which have been designed to specifications with "peak demand" as a primary consideration. Therefore, much of their investment is frequently offline, generating cost rather than revenue. One way to reduce costs due to "capital inactivity" during low demand periods is to generate power for sale to utilities experiencing demands in excess of their local peak capacity. This is called "wheeling power." Electricity is becoming a commodity. Expect the appearance of "power exchanges" similar to stock exchanges.

In order to make a service-on-demand business efficient, it is essential to have accurate near-term predictions of market demand. If periods of high and low demand can be predicted, production can be scheduled more efficiently. Electrical utilities want to generate exactly as much power as they can sell immediately, because electrical power, a perishable commodity, cannot be efficiently stored in quantity.

The ability to predict the price of a commodity can generate a lot of profit. Utilities stand to reap huge gains if they can make these predictions accurately. Specifically, they would like to be able to answer this question:

> *What will be the hour-by-hour demand for power in my service area next week?*

Because there are 168 hours in a week, 168 predictions must be made. If the predictions extend many hours into the future, each prediction must be accurate enough to be used in the prediction of the hours following it, since errors will be compounded.

3.4.3.2   Data Evaluation (Step 2)

What information is available for making predictions of this type? Because of the tight regulation of electric utilities, they keep detailed histories of their power generation. These histories are typically load values on the half-hour or hour.

To determine what features to use for load prediction, the factors that most affect the end-users' consumption behaviors will be of primary importance. Industrial users have very regular profiles of consumption and tend to be very predictable. Commercial users have consumption profiles which correspond to their business hours; they are somewhat less predictable than large industrial users, but fairly consistent nonetheless. It is the behaviors of the millions of residential consumers that are difficult to predict. It is also residential consumption that is the lion's share of the market for most utilities. The most difficult part of this problem is also the most important.

3.4.3.3   Feature Extraction and Enhancement (Step 3)

Analysis of the historic usage patterns indicates that there are two types of consumption drivers for residential users: Temporal and environmental. Temporal factors are those related to time. Residential consumption patterns vary in regular ways according to month, day of the week, and time of day. Environmental factors relevant to the prediction of residential electric consumption relate mostly to the weather (as opposed to spatial factors such as ZIP code, elevation, etc.). Hourly measurement of temperature, humidity, barometric pressure, precipitation, wind speed, and so forth, are all potentially relevant to load prediction. Finally, interviews with the human experts that utilities retain to make these predictions manually reveal that they use these same factors: Typical loads for similar month, day, hour, temperature, humidity, etc. These are the features to be mined for patterns and used in a predictive model.

3.4.3.4   Prototyping Plan (Step 4a)

Because of the way the data is stored, the most natural way to make load predictions is in 24-hour blocks: a day at a time. This could be regarded as 24 separate predictions, but a review of the data shows that the load at any given hour is highly correlated with the load during the few previous hours. The load at 2 p.m. is not independent of the load at 1 p.m., but related to it. This suggests that there is benefit in building a predictive model that produces a block of 24 hourly predictions as a group, rather than 24 separate, unrelated predictions. This "block prediction" methodology provides predictions that are consistent with historic load profiles.

3.4.3.5   Prototyping/Model Development (Step 4b)

The actual load predictions are made in two stages. First, a data mining technique is used to find a 24-hour period in the past which is "most similar" to the 24-hour period for which a prediction is to be made. This gives a block of 24 consistent predictions for the month and day of week corresponding to the prediction period. Second, a predictive modeling technique (multiple nonlinear regression) is used to make corrections to this "load profile" to adjust it for the weather forecast for the prediction day.

Once the proper set of predictive features has been constructed, the development of a prediction model can sometimes be completed in a month or two of prototyping experiments. Much of this time is spent refining the feature set and validating the model. To see a detailed technical paper on this project, visit http://www.csi.cc.

3.4.4   Case Study 4: Making Predictions ("Churn")

In this example, data mining techniques are used in another customer-related application: predicting "churn." Simply stated, "churn" is turnover in a customer population. Specifically, the goal of this study is to discover patterns in customer relationships to predict which customers will leave so prophylactic measures can be undertaken to reduce customer loss. Hence, this is a business problem characterized primarily as one of "making predictions."

The major points illustrated are:

- features about what's changed (revenue-then vs. revenue-now) help with prediction;

- data mining can be used to explain aspects of complicated business relationships; and

- multiple data mining models can be combined into a single model.

To gain additional insight into how data mining assists people in "making predictions," we now consider a case study involving a critical prediction: "Which of my current customers I am about to lose?"

3.4.4.1   Problem Definition (Step 1)

The churn problem is of great interest to any business driven by market share. Many pieces of data indicating customer behaviors and various aspects of the business-client relationship can be stored in a database or data warehouse. To retain market share, businesses need to detect and remediate problems in their customer relationships. To gain insight into this detection and remediation problem, it is natural to look at the enterprise data warehouse for indications of customer dissatisfaction, and behaviors that are characteristic of customers at risk of taking their business elsewhere. The problem could be stated as:

> *Identify which customers are at greatest risk of terminating their business relationship within a specified period.*

3.4.4.2   Data Evaluation (Step 2)

There is usually a wide range of features available for investigation. Demographic, financial, temporal, and other indicators may be expected to bear information about the quality of customer relationships. Ultimately, to make this information actionable, the exploitation of these indicators would be integrated into the business processes (in Step 6).

3.4.4.3 Feature Extraction and Enhancement (Step 3)

In some cases, it might be expensive for customers to change service providers, due to business, hardware, software, and infrastructure costs associated with making such a change. Hence, such changes are not made without good reason, at least in the mind of the customer. How might these reasons show up in enterprise data?

A number of factors might drive such a change. For example, if a customer leaves the market (for example, by going bankrupt), it is expected that the business relationship will terminate. Or, if a competitor changes its price structure, or the quality of the service/product provided no longer meets the customers needs, the enterprise might lose its business.

Overt indications that a customer relationship is becoming "brittle" might include a decrease in the frequency of purchases, reduced sales volume in total dollars, increasing frequency of complaints to a customer service representative, extended periods where no purchases occur, and so forth. More subtle risk factors might be the type of customer, costs and fees the customer incurs as a result of doing business with the company, and the complexity of the business relationship (simpler is usually better). Even the time of year is likely to be relevant: Business relationships are more brittle at the end of a quarter or fiscal year. Using data mining techniques, we will extract and analyze these indications to build a churn prediction model.

It is quite possible that there are other indications of brittleness that we have not yet recognized; indications that could be complex combinations of seemingly unrelated facts. Data mining techniques such as Bayesian analysis, auto-clustering, regression, and rule induction are applied to look for any such indications. These techniques are discussed in Part II.

3.4.4.4 Prototyping Plan (Step 4a)

Many large organizations have customer relationship managers, specialists who are responsible for preserving good relationships between the business and its customers. These managers will be the primary audience of the predictive churn model. As in any information system, identifying the audience or users of the application and their requirements is critical to the success of the project. Such business specialists and are not likely to be expert in the details of complex data analysis. For this reason, the churn model will have to be constructed to provide risk assessment, along with an explanation of the factors believed responsible for the elevated risk. In the best of all possible worlds, the model will also provide suggestions for corrective action. These will presumably be drawn from historic business experience.

Churn prediction is a complex, multi-factor mathematical process. An adequate solution will probably consist of a combination of heuristics based on business knowledge and black box regression methods that exploit complex historic customer behaviors. Such a hybrid predictive model should be designed and built by specialists.

It is not uncommon to build multiple predictive models and allow them to vote on what the final prediction will be. Each predictive paradigm has its own peculiar strengths and weaknesses. By constructing an appropriate hybrid, we exploit the strengths of each while mitigating the weaknesses of all. Chapter 10 contains descriptions of several of these paradigms.

3.4.4.5 Prototyping/Model Development (Step 4b)

Churn models are very complex because the factors that drive customer relationships are many and difficult to quantify. The prototyping of churn models devotes most of its schedule to properly coding the feature data.

In churn models built by the authors, "then and now" features have been found to be useful: "The revenue *then* was so-and-so, but *now* it's thus-and-so." This pairing is useful because it provides an historical reference. Prototypes that select various combinations of the many available features can be expected to lead to a set that supports the prediction.

3.5   Summary

Every mature business has some seemingly insoluble problems—difficult judgments about customers, resource allocation, business strategy or organization. These are the "5-percent problems." The intractable residue that remains after years of work has solved the other 95 percent and are the principal targets of data mining. Data mining techniques can be used to learn the factors bearing on a decision and construct an application that uses those factors to help the enterprise make those decisions in an objective, consistent way.

4

The Data Mining Process

As indicated earlier, a myriad of perceptions about data mining exist with some variance regarding the scope of data mining activities. Some consider data mining to consist only of "knowledge discovery" endeavors, while many others (including the authors) consider data mining to include predictive modeling as well. There is also disagreement about the proper context for data mining: whether a data warehouse is essential or an integrated suite of tools is required. However, there is general agreement among practitioners that data mining is a *process* that begins with *data* in some form and ends with *knowledge* in some form. This chapter describes the data mining process. The goal is to describe the steps and the activities of this process at a high level without becoming lost in the details of relevant tools or techniques that will be addressed in the next section.

4.1   Discovery and Exploitation

Knowledge discovery, the process of discovering knowledge in data, includes the data analysis that must be performed to discover the most powerful and relevant select factors for a specific problem. Model development could entail developing a single or series of models, with each attacking a specific aspect of a complex problem. Thus, data mining is conceived of as a process having two components: *Discovery*, during which meaningful patterns are detected in data and characterized formally (descriptive models); and *exploitation*, during which meaningful patterns are used to create useful applications (predictive models).

This inclusive view of data mining may be a broader definition than currently held by many, who reserve the term *data mining* for what, in this text, is called the *discovery* component. Those same people refer to our *exploitation* component as *predictive modeling*. The broader view is taken here for several reasons.

The Business Intelligence (BI) market as a whole appears to support the broader concept of data mining. This is perhaps driven in part by tool vendors who continually increase the scope of their integrated environments.

Several of the same tools and techniques are used for both discovery and exploitation, making discrimination between them somewhat subjective (i.e., at what point is the data being "exploited" to achieve an objective).

Analysts increasingly want to engage in both discovery and exploitation using data mining tools and methods, going back and forth between the two during a project. Distinctions between discovery and exploitation blur in such situations.

Although an inclusive view of data mining is used here, it should not be inferred that the distinction between discovery and exploitation is unimportant. The purpose of managing a data mining project, selecting the right techniques, and keeping track of "what we're doing now" is extremely important. In this chapter, the data mining process that was introduced in Chapter 3 is described as a sequence of steps, where each has a specified purpose. The purpose, order, and content of each step are expressed in terms that are general enough to encompass those outlined in several existing process standards. More thorough discussion of the applications and methods supporting the discovery process are treated in Chapters 8 and 9. More thorough discussion of the applications and methods supporting the exploitation process are covered in Chapter 10.

Data mining projects are undertaken to solve enterprise problems. Some of these problems can be considered solved when insight is gained (e.g., "What are the indicators of impending default?"), others are solved only when such insight is "made actionable" by incorporating the knowledge into an application system (e.g., "Default is predicted—decline the application!"). It's the difference between a question mark and an exclamation point: The discovery phase of data mining produces "descriptive models" that address the "?". The exploitation phase of data mining produces "predictive models" that bring about the "!".

It is the enterprise goal that determines whether both discovery and exploitation are pursued for a particular data mining project.

Typically, analysts and researchers want to *discover*, while managers and practitioners want to *exploit*. Discovery is a prerequisite to exploitation; however, sometimes sufficient knowledge of the domain exists to enable exploitation (modeling activities) to be conducted without the necessity of undertaking a full-blown discovery effort. This is the approach taken, for example, by expert system developers who build intelligent applications using the knowledge already possessed by domain experts. As illustrated below, every well-planned data mining initiative includes an inquiry into what is already known about the domain.

4.2   Ontologies as Models

A good way to develop an understanding of data mining as a process is to look at the two kinds of models that it produces: descriptive and predictive. This brings us to the idea of *ontology*. For philosophers, ontology is a "theory of being." It is an attempt to answer questions encountered in Philosophy 101 such as, "What is reality? Do things have meaning? What can be known?"

In data mining, ontology has a similar meaning. Formally speaking, ontology for a data set is a representational scheme that provides a consistent, coherent, unifying presentation of the data in context. Loosely speaking, ontology for a data set is an interpretation of the data that reveals its meaning by explaining its characteristics. These representations are called *models*. Models represent ontologies in various ways: as consistent sets of equations describing data relationships and patterns (mathematical models), as coherent collections of empirical "laws" or principles (scientific models), etc.

When models merely *describe* patterns in data, they are called *descriptive models*. When models *process* patterns in data for the purpose of predicting outcomes, they are called *predictive models*. In practice, models often have both descriptive and predictive aspects. The distinction between the two is not always clear.

4.3   Scientific Basis

The process by which scientists devise physical theories (the so-called "scientific method") provides a good example of a systematic search for ontology. The scientist comes to the experimental data with a minimum of *a priori* assumptions, intending to formulate and test a model that will explain the data. This suggests an excellent intuitive example of the difference between descriptive and predictive models: a comparison of the work of the 17th century scientists Johannes Kepler and Isaac Newton. Both men addressed the same problem of describing the motion of the planets. Kepler produced a model that was primarily descriptive, while Newton produced one that was primarily predictive.

Kepler, whose work preceded Newton's by several decades, had mounds of raw numeric data giving precise locations for the planet Mars over approximately a twenty-year time-span. This data, collected by Kepler's mentor, Tycho Brahe, contained obvious patterns. Kepler sought an ontology that would describe these patterns in the form of a scientific theory: a descriptive model. Kepler tried all kinds of schemes for representing the patterns[1]. *This repeated cycle of selecting data, hypothesizing a representation, and testing the representation is the heart of the data mining process.*

Kepler was engaged in manual data mining of a type not unlike modern analysts working in new domains. Finally, after more than ten years of manually hand-checking numerous candidate models (computers being unavailable in the 17th century), Kepler tried using ellipses. He found that if he selected an appropriate ellipse with the Sun at one focus, he obtained a model that fit the data. The first workable ontology had been discovered[2].

Later that century, Isaac Newton, using Kepler's descriptive model as the starting point for a complete ontology of the solar system, formulated the Theory of Universal Gravitation. Along with that theory, he formed a predictive model for planetary motion. Using the methods of differential and integral calculus (which he invented for this purpose), Newton was able to do more than just describe the shapes

---

1.   He tried epicycles; he tried equants; he tried circles. For each hypothetical model, Kepler laboriously ground out the implied motion and compared it with Brahe's observations. None of these ontologies led to models that were consistent with the data.

2.   Continuing his data mining work, Kepler completed his descriptive model in three statements of principle, called Kepler's Laws of Planetary Motion. Not much text for 25 years of arduous labor, but a stunning intellectual achievement. While the scale of Kepler's model was wrong (his solar system was only 1/7 the actual size) his description of it was correct (the planets move at varying speeds in sun-focused elliptical orbits). Kepler's descriptive model, however, gave no insight into why elliptical orbits should arise and whether others might be possible. Descriptive models rarely explain.

of the planetary orbits. He could explain and predict the motion of individual planets with mathematical precision.[3]

In the business world, data repositories hold latent information in the form of patterns and relationships, much as did Brahe's raw orbital data. Through application of the data mining process, descriptive models can be built that answer descriptive questions: "What characterizes a good/bad customer? What kinds of customers buy which kinds of products and services? What are the early indicators of fraud/churn/default?" The result is a partial ontology that describes enterprise patterns.

These descriptions might be used to enhance the ability of existing business systems to serve enterprise goals. In the case that existing systems cannot directly leverage these descriptions, there might be a need to complete the ontology by constructing predictive models and making the descriptions actionable. "Go through this data base and mark all the good/bad customers! Go through this list and identify the customers that are most/least likely to buy these products and services! Examine this data set and mark the transaction streams suggesting elevated probability of fraud/churn/default!"

4.4   Data Mining Methodologies

Like any process, data mining can be carried out haphazardly or systematically. Today's spiral development methodologies enable developers to carry out development or prototyping cycles that provide incremental improvements and offer frequent opportunities to gather substantial customer input while mitigating risk.

The methodology described throughout this book is consistent with the authors' years of experience participating in data mining and other IT projects. It is also consistent with CSI's Cognitive Engineering Methodology (CEM) six phases (through implementation) and a seventh phase to evaluate the Return-on-Investment (ROI) of a project. This development methodology supports the industry standard spiral approach for building high-end systems. The amount of

3.   He had extended Kepler's partial ontology to a full ontology by adding to the descriptive model a predictive one. Further, Newton's mathematical formulation showed how the gravitational force gave rise to elliptical orbits, and suggested that others (general conic sections) were possible. The modern data mining process can be thought of as the creation of an ontology from data through some combination of descriptive and predictive modeling. Both types of models have important business applications.

effort expended in each phase depends upon the problem. The greatest effort is expended during the fourth phase that constitutes the bulk of the work. Phases may be reordered, repeated, or eliminated, as required. Every problem is a little different. The recommended steps are also consistent with the CRISP-DM methodology, described below.

4.4.1   CRISP-DM Methodology

Cross-Industry Standard Process for Data Mining (CRISP-DM) is intended to provide a general methodology to support the data mining process. The rationale for an industry standard data mining methodology includes that:

- users are not always technology experts;
- the methodology should provide a framework for documenting and reusing the experience gained on data mining projects; and
- business issues are as important as technology and must be addressed by any process model.

Development of CRISP-DM was funded by a consortium that includes the European Commission, as well as corporate members such as: NCR Corporation, a data warehouse supplier; Integral Solutions Limited (ISL), developer of the Clementine Data Mining System (since acquired by SPSS, Inc.); Daimler-Benz, European industrial giant; and OHRA, one of the Netherlands' largest insurance companies. At the time of writing, the development partners are in the process of trying to determine the best way of continuing CRISP-DM as an independent initiative. One possible option is a self-funding special interest group (SIG) comprised of data mining tool and service suppliers, and large-scale commercial users.

According to Colin Shearer, an SPSS employee who participated in CRISP development, "There is no licensing fee required for using CRISP. The developers are pleased to see organizations adopt the methodology. They simply request that people using or presenting it acknowledge CRISP-DM in their materials. The CRISP consortium holds the copyright for the CRISP-DM process model. CRISP-DM is supported by the SPSS Clementine data mining tool."

4.4.2   SEMMA Methodology

Another standard that is competing for the position of informal *de facto* standard is SEMMA (Sample, Explore, Modify, Model, Assess). SEMMA was created by SAS Institute and is supported by its tool, SAS Enterprise Miner.

4.4.3   Common Approaches

A review of the various data mining processes that have been proposed as standards leaves one with the impression that, underneath it all, roughly the same process is being described in different ways. This is largely true. It is a conclusion supported by the fact that proponents of competing process standards rarely debate the merits of their favored process. Instead, they focus on how well their favored process works when applied in conjunction with their favored data mining tool. This makes sense given that the creators of the most popular processes are closely associated with tool developers.

The principal implication is that, in actual practice, most data mining activities conducted by experienced analysts proceed in about the same general way: Data is gathered, conditioned, and analyzed, resulting in descriptive models; then, if desired, the results of the analysis are used to construct, validate, and field predictive models. Each of these activities encompasses multiple steps, requires the application of particular techniques, and has its own "best practice." It is these steps, techniques, and practices that data mining process standards seek to specify.

Rather than sacrifice generality by describing the ad hoc details of just one of the competing standards, or blur the fundamentals by trying to survey them all, the following data mining process discussion is conducted at a higher level of generality.

4.5   Conventional System Development: Waterfall Process

For many years, conventional system development methodologies were based on a series of linear phases generally described as a "waterfall process." Such processes proceed step-by-step through a clearly delineated and distinct sequence of phases. Each phase occurs one time in sequence during the process. The output (resulting product) of each phase flows as input into the next (hence the name). As a sequence of (more or less) end-to-end steps, a waterfall process is inherently "linear." Its phases can be overlaid in an intuitive way on a calendar to produce a program schedule. Tracking a program's progress can be accomplished by marking a position on the schedule. At any given time, it is fairly clear what has already been done and what is to be done next. Estimation of cost-to-complete is (in principle) straightforward.

To develop an information system, the particular phases of the waterfall process could include: analysis/specification, design, development, testing, and installation. Once specification is completed, it is essentially left forever, followed by design, and so on. Once a phase is completed, nothing short of a catastrophe can "turn back the clock."

An odd result of this process has been the segregation of developers into engineering specialties corresponding to the waterfall phases: system architects, design engineers, software/hardware engineers, test engineers, and field engineers, respectively. In practice, this usually means that as the design engineers are starting on a program, the system architects are leaving to begin the next one. This planned loss of technical perspective has predictable results, and probably lies at the base of many cost overruns and loss of accountability for failures of large programs.

The development history of complex systems is rarely "linear" in the real world. One need only look at a PERT (Program Evaluation Review Technique) chart or Gantt chart for a complex program to see how the putative simplicity of a waterfall process actually plays out in practice.

This combination of shortcomings is bad enough on conventional efforts. What happens when a "waterfall mindset" is brought to data mining, which consists of activities for which you can't write specifications? How do you schedule knowledge discovery, given that there is no way to know in advance what the data contain? And when a discovery suggests a completely new line of inquiry, what do you do? A different development process is needed for data mining: a rapid prototyping process.

4.6   Data Mining: Rapid Prototyping

The data mining process has been variously described, but a sequence of steps can be set down that describes what typically happens in practice. Additional information is contained in Chapter 13, "Successful Data Mining Project Management." As analysts gain experience, they can adjust the general process to suit the problem at hand.

At a high level, the steps that constitute the data mining process are:

- Step 1: Problem Definition
- Step 2: Data Evaluation
- Step 3: Feature Extraction and Enhancement
- Step 4a: Prototyping Plan
- Step 4b: Prototyping/Model Development
- Step 5: Model Evaluation
- Step 6: Implementation
- Step 7: Return on Investment Evaluation

The order and content of these steps is kept flexible, and applied according to a *rapid prototyping* (also called "spiral") methodology. Rapid prototyping methodologies are development processes that are flexible in order and content, open-ended, cyclic, and incremental. They consist of steps that can be rearranged, adjusted in scope, and repeated as necessary. Project Schedules based on this methodology serve primarily to allocate time to categories of activity (the steps), but often don't specify when activities will occur, or how often they will be repeated.

The repetition and cycling of steps is what gives data mining a rapid prototyping character. Rather than running through a standard "waterfall" development, data mining analysts build incrementally more powerful versions of the entire model that are tested and enhanced in cycles. This process is perfect for data mining because data mining is a process of discovery where each prototype may serve as the foundation for the next. A self-reinforcing cycle of incremental improvement ultimately produces a final prototype that is fully functional. It's hard to describe this kind of cyclic process in "linear" terms.

We detail the general content of the steps that constitute a generic data mining process, keeping in mind that, in practice, these steps will be dynamically adjusted as work proceeds. Each step can be part of a discovery effort or an exploitation effort. In the task descriptions below, the personnel required for each task are denoted by the following abbreviations:

- CE: Cognitive engineer (the data mining analyst)

- DE: Domain expert (usually a customer/end-user having in-depth *operational* knowledge of the domain)

- DO: Data owners (usually MIS personnel who collect/manage data, but not operational/business experts)

- PM: Program manager (manager who can make cost/schedule decisions for the data mining effort)

- SE: Software/database engineer (application developer)

4.6.1   Step 1: Problem Definition

4.6.1.1   *Purpose: To produce and document the "definition of success."*

For a discovery effort, success might mean completing a systematic analysis of data describing some important business factors ("We are very interested in churn"); documenting answers to questions about the domain ("What are the common characteristics of customers we lose?"); or testing hypotheses ("We think shifting demographics are affecting sales in certain regions"). The purpose of Step 1 is the creation of a list of analyses to perform, questions to investigate, and hypotheses to test.

For an exploitation effort, success usually means the development of an effective predictive model. ("We need an application that detects fraudulent transactions.") The purpose of Step 1, then, is the formulation of a clear objective to be accomplished.

4.6.1.2   *Principal Participants and their tasks:*

- CE/PM/DE   Interview domain experts (usually the "end user" of business intelligence)

- SE/CE/DO   Interview data owners (usually MIS personnel charged with collection and maintenance)

- SE   Collect documentation (white papers, schemas, specifications)

- SE   Select media and hosting mechanisms (how data will be transferred as stored)

- SE/CE   Identify the data mining environment (set up lab/workspace/intranet)

- SE/CE   Identify tools (might include purchase/license and installation)

The problem definition phase generally results in a project definition document that should be signed by appropriate project sponsors. These sponsors are typically a management person, such as the program manager and user/customer manager.

4.6.2   Step 2: Data Evaluation

4.6.2.1   *Purpose: Produce an effective representation of the domain (data ingest and format)*

4.6.2.2   *Principal Participants and their tasks:*

- SE   Ingest data (e.g., plug in JAZ drive, download, spool, etc.)

- SE   Format data (RDBMS, .CSV, etc.)

- SE/CE   Create environment and set up tools

- SE/CE   Validate ingest and format operations

- CE/SE   Randomize record order

- CE/SE   Sample data

- CE/SE   Partition data

During this step, the data is organized for analysis. This includes four activities: randomizing, sampling, partitioning, and hosting.

Randomizing involves establishing a scheme that ensures that the selection of sets of data to be used for analysis will be random samples. (A random sample is a sample selected in such a way that every item has an equal probability of being chosen.) Random samples are used so that results obtained during analysis can be expected to be typical of the population as a whole. For simple "flat files," randomizing for sampling can be accomplished by thoroughly "shuffling" the order of the records prior to sampling. For data in a database or warehouse, randomizing requires the establishment of a sampling interface to ensure that selected samples are random. Some databases support random sampling as an intrinsic function.

Sampling involves selecting a subset of the data (a sample) to be used for analysis. A sufficiently large randomly selected subset should be used to provide a representative sample. The authors use a rule of thumb that we call the 6MN rule to estimate the minimum number of records to select for a sample.

Let the number of categories of data that must be distinguished be N. (For example, if the data will be used to characterize differences between good, fair, and poor clients, then N = 3.)

Let the number of relevant fields in each record be M. (For example, if the fields to be used in each record are total sales, frequency of purchase, time since last purchase, and payment timeliness, then M = 4.)

Then the 6MN rule says you need a minimum of 6MN records to expect analysis to produce meaningful results. In the above case: $6 \times 3 \times 4 = 72$ records.

The rationale for this rule is to provide a mean and standard deviation in each data field for each class: Demanding 3 values for a standard deviation for each of M fields gives $3 \times M$. Doing this for every category gives 3MN. Doubling things for good measure (no kidding!) gives 6MN. (Keep in mind this is an ad hoc minimum size. It is not guaranteed to be adequate.)

Most statisticians would probably be horrified by the naïve reasoning just outlined. But in practice, this rules seems to do a pretty good job of setting the minimum size for an analysis set. For example, the authors worked on a data mining effort for a multi-billion dollar financial services company having two categories of interest (churn vs. non-churn), so N = 2. There were 100 fields in each customer record, giving M = 100. The 6MN rule said that *no analysis should be applied to any data set* consisting of fewer than $6 \times 100 \times 2 = 1,200$ records. This minimum sample size worked pretty well. Of course, larger sets were also used.

The 6MN rule is a crude rule of thumb for a minimum sample size, but other criteria apply. For example, samples must contain an adequate number of examples of every category of interest. Sampling theory is complex and cannot be discussed in detail here. It is an area of ongoing research in the data mining community.

Partitioning involves selecting an appropriate number of samples for particular aspects of analysis. It is recommended that a minimum of four random samples be created. They are:

- *The calibration set.* This set is used only for the estimation of population parameters, such as means, standard deviations, maximum and minimum values of each feature, estimation of data quality (e.g., counting missing values, outliers), and so on. Once used for these general measurements, the calibration set is put aside (but, see Step 4b).

- *The analysis set (also called "the training set").* This set is used for analysis during the discovery phase of data mining and for model construction during the exploitation phase of data mining. For example such a set will be used for rule induction or construction of neural networks or decision trees. Once these activities have been completed, the training set is put aside.

- *The validation set.* This set is used to verify any "discoveries" made during analysis, and to evaluate the performance of any models created.

- *The hold-back set.* This set is held by the "customer," and never seen by the data mining analysts. It is used to evaluate the results of the data mining activity.

It is essential that all four of these sets be sufficiently large representative samples drawn in an unbiased way from the same population. If this is not done, results of the analysis are subject to question on procedural grounds. If good randomizing and sampling schemes are employed, the creation of these partitions can (and should) be automated.

Hosting refers to how data will be physically stored and accessed. Will a database be used? Will all analysts access the same set? Will the data reside on disk, tape, or Web page?

The hosting question, while important to data mining, is not peculiar to it. Conventional system design considerations apply. For the purposes of data mining, it must be remembered that analytic tools will probably have to make many passes through the entire data set, so speed of access is important. In general, this is an indexing, not a hardware problem. Many enterprises address the hosting problem by building data marts or data warehouses.

4.6.3   Step 3: Feature Extraction and Enhancement

4.6.3.1   *Purpose of feature extraction: Produce a "data mining-ready" data set: representative, reproducible, reliable (accurate and complete).*

4.6.3.2   *Principal Participants and their tasks:*

- CE/SE   Data evaluation, cleansing, and conditioning
- CE/SE   Auto-clustering, visualization, statistical regression

In feature extraction, the initial selection of which "fields" to use from each record is made, using the calibration set selected in Step 2. This begins with "data cleansing." The evaluation of data quality, handling of missing values, processing of outliers, registration and normalization of data, coding, and quantization of data. These operations are all discussed in later chapters.

Next, simple analytics (often manual) are applied to validate the representation of the data, develop analyst intuition, assess problem complexity, and choose those fields to be used in the analysis based upon their quality and apparent information content. The chosen fields are called "features." Methods for making this determination (such as auto-clustering, visualization, regression, etc.) are discussed in later chapters.

The purpose of feature enhancement is to select the best set of, and representation for, features selected during feature extraction. Many sophisticated techniques have been created for selecting the best features and enhancing their information content. Some of these are discussed in later chapters.

4.6.4   Step 4a: Prototyping Plan

4.6.4.1   *Purpose: develop working hypotheses for the analysis based upon enterprise goals and construct a plan for testing them (tool selection, experiment formulation, schedule, methodology, etc.).*

During this step, the data mining strategy is finalized, making this a planning step. Based upon the work done in Steps 1–3, the set of analyses, questions, and hypotheses from Step 1 are formalized into a plan for a sequence of experiments. Experiments that can be performed in parallel can be assigned to different members of the data mining team. Because discovery breeds discovery, this step is likely to be executed several times during the data mining cycle.

4.6.4.2 *Principal Participants and their tasks:*

- CE/PM   Formulate descriptive hypotheses and prepare prototyping plan

4.6.5   Step 4b: Prototyping/Model Development

4.6.5.1 *Purpose: Develop models (explanatory, predictive, or both).*

This is the step that constitutes what most people mean when they use the term "data mining." It's the step during which the data is worked by the analyst or model builder. This step uses the analysis set (training set). If intermediate "validation" of a discovery or model is needed during this step, it's fair to use the *calibration set*. Using the *validation set* during this step, however, is an intolerable violation of methodology, and invalidates step 5 below. The details of this step are addressed in later chapters.

4.6.5.2 *Principal Participants and their tasks:*

- CE/SE/PM   Systematic analytics and model construction

4.6.6   Step 5: Model Evaluation

4.6.6.1 *Purpose: Evaluate the results of the last prototyping cycle.*

During this step, the analyst and program manager take stock of the progress in discovery/exploitation, documenting successes and failures against the plan formalized in Step 4a.

4.6.6.2 *Principal Participants and their tasks:*

- CE/PM   Model evaluation and documentation of status

If it is determined that the data mining activity has concluded, the team proceeds to Step 6. If there are still discovery/exploitation tasks to execute, and progress is good, the team may proceed from here to Step 4a. If there are remaining tasks but progress is insufficient, the team might proceed to Step 3 to consider selecting different/additional features and reworking the data. If no progress is being made, the team might need to return from here to Step 2, or Step 1, and rethink the goals of the effort.

4.6.7   Step 6: Implementation

4.6.7.1   *Purpose: package and deliver the final product.*

For a discovery effort, delivery usually includes writing a technical brief documenting the effort and presenting the knowledge discovered. For a predictive modeling effort, implementation may include finishing the user interface, writing technical and user documentation, populating operational data structures, and creating and installing the final product.

4.6.7.2   *Principal Participants and their tasks:*

- CE/SE/PM   Implementation and delivery

4.6.8   Step 7: Return-on-Investment Evaluation

4.6.8.1   *Purpose: Compute the Return-on-Investment (ROI).*

This activity cannot be performed until the data mining activity is complete. Here the financial impact of the data mining activity is computed. For example, if the final prototype can correctly predict fraud in 40 percent of the cases presented to it, the average for each instance of fraud is X, and there are Y instances of fraud per period, what is the value of the savings obtained as a percentage of the cost of the data mining effort itself? (Be sure to include the cost of any errors made by the model. This is discussed in some detail in a later chapter.)

4.6.8.2   *Principal Participants and their tasks:*

- CE/PM   Estimate ROI

    The rapid prototyping methodology allows (and intends) the repetition and cycling of any/all of Steps 1–7.

4.7   A Generic Data Mining Project "Schedule"

For the sake of illustration, this chapter closes with a hypothetical data mining project "schedule." As described above, rapid prototyping efforts aren't linear, so the "schedule" below consists of a list of tasks with total effort allocated to each. Additional information along with a sample graphical schedule is included in Chapter 13, "Successful Data Mining Project Management."

Notice that the amount of effort dedicated to data conditioning (Tasks 2 and 3), *not* model building (Tasks 4A, 4B, 5, and 6) that most people call "data mining," constitute the lion's share of the data mining effort. This is an important point: If lack of time or resources demands that some task be cut short, avoid skimping on Tasks 2 and 3. Cutting these efforts is among the principal causes of failure for data mining projects, because the analysis of poorly conditioned data often leads to poor results. This is a corollary of the "GIGOO Rule," discussed in Chapter 11.

Typical "focused" data mining efforts involve one to five people and take anywhere from one month to one year, depending on the scope and complexity of the problem being addressed. It is not unusual to precede a large data mining effort (e.g., five people for a year) with a small proof-of-concept effort (e.g., two people for four weeks). This allows enterprise managers to estimate ROI for the extended effort based upon some reasonable estimate of what the data will support. If the work done during the small effort is well documented, it can jump-start the larger follow-on.

4.7.1   Task List

4.7.1.1   Task 1: Problem Definition (5%)

subtask 1A:	CE/PM/DE	Interview Domain Experts
subtask 1B:	SE/CE/DO	Interview Data Owners
subtask 1C:	SE	Collect documentation
subtask 1D:	SE	Select media and hosting mechanisms
subtask 1E:	SE/CE	Create the data mining environment
subtask 1F:	SE/CE	Co-locate tools

4.7.1.2   Task 2: Data Evaluation (20%)

subtask 2A:	SE	Ingest data
subtask 2B:	SE	Format data
subtask 2C:	SE/CE	Validate ingest and format operations
subtask 2D:	CE/SE	Randomize record order
subtask 2E:	CE/SE	Sample data
subtask 2F:	CS/SE	Partition data

4.7.1.3   *Task 3: Feature Extraction and Enhancement (35%)*

        subtask 3A: CE/SE   Data Evaluation, Cleansing, and Conditioning

        subtask 3B: CE/SE   Autoclustering, Visualization, Statistical Regression

4.7.1.4   *Task 4a: Prototyping Plan (2%)*

        subtask 4A: CE/PM   Formulate descriptive hypotheses, prepare prototyping plan

4.7.1.5   *Task 4b: Prototyping/Model Development (20%)*

        subtask 4B: CE/SE/PM Systematic Analytics, Model Construction

4.7.1.6   *Task 5: Model Evaluation (3%)*

        subtask 5:   CE/PM   Model Evaluation, documentation of status

4.7.1.7   *Task 6: Implementation (15%)*

        subtask 6:   CE/SE/PM Implementation and Delivery

4.7.1.8   *Task 7: Return on Investment Evaluation (post-project)*

        subtask 7:   CE/PM   Estimate ROI

4.8   Summary

Data mining is worth doing if done well. A rapid prototyping methodology for data mining is similar to the scientific method and can produce both descriptive and predictive models. Data mining requires the involvement of data mining analysts, software and database engineers, and business expertise. The most natural data mining methodology is not a "linear" methodology, but "spiral," and involves repeating and cycling through steps whose order and content is flexible. The flexibility allows the data-mining analyst to pursue the implications of discovered knowledge. Much of the effort of a data mining activity is devoted to properly handling the data itself.

Part II

Pillars of the Data Mining Framework

- Information technology
- Data management
- Mathematics

5

The Information Technology of Business Intelligence

As is apparent in the discussion and illustrations throughout Part I, data mining is not married to any particular information technology. The precious information that is the goal of data mining to discover may be apparent in a minute data source, as illustrated by the "case of the collaborating college kids" in Chapter 3. There, a set of 100 rows by 7 columns successfully identified the population of interest. At the opposite end of the spectrum are data mining applications based on massive and sometimes very complex data stores involving millions of records run on very powerful computing platforms. Two examples of this latter type of application are included in Part IV: Fingerhut's Mail Stream Optimization identifies which of its 120 independent catalogs will be sent to more than 6 million customers (Chapter 16), and United Airline's Orion system for passenger-demand forecasting that processes 350,000 logical flight paths for roughly 120 million possible combinations (Chapter 21).

If data mining applications lack specific IT requirements, why then include a chapter on information technology in a book such as this? The answer is to clarify and hopefully simplify the reader's expectation of the IT infrastructure requirements that data mining entails. Also, to provide confidence that some initial data mining initiatives may be carried out without major investment in massively parallel computers and data silos, or expensive special-purpose software tools, as many vendors would prefer for you to believe.

As in any information system, specific technical requirements depend on the nature (size, volume, and complexity) of the application, data communication and performance requirements, and how the system will operate. For example, the system may run interactively, within another application, or as a periodic process. The IT infrastructure must be adequate to support the capacity, reliability, availability, and throughput requirements to enable an application to satisfy its specific Business Intelligence objectives. Although your specific high-value data mining application may require and may have Return-on-Investment (ROI) justification for major IT infrastructure upgrades, it is often possible to conduct feasibility assessments relating to your objective prior to making a major investment commitment (refer to "gauntlet" discussion, Chapter 11).

Information Technology (IT) discussions are frequently conducted within the context of computing and communications architectures. The central issues for our purposes revolve around data—its acquisition, storage, analysis, and exploitation. Today's Business Intelligence (BI) tools address all of these, and are the primary subject of this chapter, along with related information technology considerations.

5.1   Business Intelligence Tools

BI tools are software that facilitates analysis and decision-making. BI includes a range of functions such as query and reporting, business graphics, online analytical processing (OLAP), statistical analysis, forecasting, and data mining. These tools are often packaged into cohesive groups such as reporting or modeling, but several vendors attempt to cover the full BI spectrum by offering BI tool suites.

Several companies began offering the precursors of today's BI products more than a quarter-century ago. At that time, they were called "end-user computing" tools. Software vendors began by offering basic reporting, charting, or statistical processing capabilities that would be considered quite rudimentary today. Even so, they represent an essential shift of information access control from the so-called "glass house" to the users of information. (A Corporate Data Center, under the control of an Information Management organization was once frequently referred to as a "glass house.")

These users are the people who perform analyses, make decisions, and ultimately make data into information that can become *actionable*. Information that is actionable provides the opportunity to take action that will ultimately result in a business benefit. For example, identifying profitable customers who are likely to take their business to a competitor enables proactive steps to be taken to address each customer's areas of concern. If such proactive programs are effective, the business retains a valuable customer.

Adoption of Business Intelligence tools continues to increase. While products supporting end-users cannot be considered new, a new generation of products became prevalent during the last decade that is most closely associated with the name "Business Intelligence." The key differentiation of these tools over earlier tools is the support of Online Analytical Processing (OLAP). BI adoption will undoubtedly become even more widespread with the OLAP support that is provided in Microsoft's generation of Office 2000 and database products.

As indicated in the Business Intelligence timeline Figure 5.1, BI tools have evolved dramatically since the early reporting and analysis capabilities were first put into the hands of end users. The tools have become increasingly sophisticated over time as indicated by the descriptions below.

Figure 5.1
Business Intelligence timeline

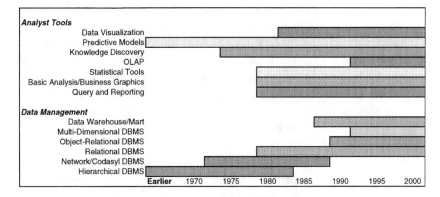

There are more than 500 vendors in the BI tool market. In addition to the software corporate giants, a few of the better-known BI niche companies include Brio, Business Objects, Cognos, IBI, SAS, Seagate Software, and SPSS. Many of the examples used are based on the authors' data mining experience at Computer Science Innovations (CSI, Inc.). For more information on the companies that offer BI products or services, see the reference information included as Appendix C.

5.1.1 Query and Reporting

Query and reporting capabilities provide users with the important ability to combine their data into meaningful displays and reports. Although business applications typically provide standard informational reports, users have the need to answer questions that arise on an ad-hoc basis, so the tools must provide the capability to: combine information from multiple data tables, perform arithmetic computations, and the like. These tools provide the capability to generate files as well as robust capabilities for developing display or hardcopy output of data. Although such tools were initially offered on the host platforms where the data was stored, they eventually migrated to desktop platforms. A migration to Web environments is currently underway.

5.1.2   Basic Analysis

As with query and reporting, basic analysis capabilities began on host platforms. They provided basic statistical capabilities along with rudimentary business graphics (e.g., scatter, line, area, bar, columnar, and pie charts). With the advent of the personal computer, spreadsheets, such as Lotus 1-2-3 and Excel, became quite prevalent as the chosen tools to conduct a great deal of basic analysis. As desktop operating systems and platforms have become more powerful, spreadsheet tools have become more capable. Graphics software capabilities have evolved as well. They now enable a wide array of data representation in graphical displays.

5.1.3   Statistical Tools

Once again, the advent of desktop computing put a larger variety of tools into the hands of more users; statistical packages are no exception. These support basic statistical capabilities as described in Chapter 7 and Appendix D, on up to advanced mathematical modeling capabilities.

5.1.4   Online Analytical Processing (OLAP)

OLAP provides users with multi-dimensional drill-down capabilities. Its functionality is like a hierarchy of spreadsheets within spreadsheets. It enables users to view data from various perspectives (dimensions) as well as the capability to "drill-down" through successive levels of detail. It is an extremely powerful tool for interactive analysis. Products featuring OLAP capabilities typically include query, reporting, and business graphics, as well.

OLAP will undoubtedly become more widespread as it becomes more pervasive throughout the Microsoft product line. Microsoft's database services provide multi-dimensional analysis capabilities on desktop platforms through Excel PivotTable® SQL Server OLAP Services, Access 2000 direct connection to SQL Server, as well as server-side OLAP support in SQL Server.

The OLAP vendors are consistent in the extension of their OLAP technologies to the Internet. This movement provides some key advantages to a large organization that desires to make the same information available throughout its organization without deploying "fat client" (PC software) applications or distributing data resources.

5.1.5 Knowledge Discovery

Knowledge discovery is essentially the application of machine learning techniques to large data aggregations to identify, extract, and exploit meaningful associations. This is sometimes called Knowledge Discovery in Databases (KDD). Discovery methods, which are at the core of the generic architecture for a knowledge discovery application, detect and evaluate groupings, patterns, and relationships.

This activity may be conducted within the context of a specific problem-solving task (e.g., with a classification or prediction goal in mind), or may be to discover unanticipated patterns of interest. These associations or patterns are derived without human intervention from the contents and interrelations of data items. Knowledge discovery incorporates statistical, knowledge-based, connectionist, linguistic, and conventional techniques. Depending upon the discovery method used, the knowledge extracted may be in the following different forms:

- *Data objects* organized into groups or categories, each group representing a relevant concept in the problem domain. Inductive discovery methods in this category are called clustering methods.

- *Classification rules* that identify a group of objects having the same label, or disparate groups of objects having different labels. These methods are termed classification/regression methods.

- *Descriptive regularities* (qualitative or quantitative) among sets of parameters drawn from object descriptions. Inductive methods in this category are called empirical discovery methods.

Information extracted using knowledge discovery techniques may be used to support human decision-making, e.g., prediction and classification tasks, summarization of database contents, and explanation of observed phenomena.

5.1.6 Data Mining Models

As described in Chapter 1, a *model* is a formal description of a system that may take the form of a mathematical expression or algorithm that provides a value based on input variables. Data mining models can be either descriptive or predictive (and are thoroughly discussed in Chapters 9 and 10). Descriptive models provide information about the current state of a subject, while predictive models anticipate future states (outcomes) of a subject.

Models are useful in providing the means to:

- provide an integrated representation of knowledge about a system (subject); and

- make discovered knowledge actionable.

5.1.7 Data Visualization

A myriad of data visualization techniques are available to enable analysts to view patterns and trends and interact with data. The visual images enable their users to develop insights into data that cannot be recognized through other data representations, which equates to interactive knowledge discovery. Visualization is discussed in more depth in Chapter 8, "Data Mining Techniques: Knowledge Discovery."

5.1.8 Business Intelligence Tool Suites

At the present time, many vendors of data mining tools offer fairly diverse suites of applications. Many provide bundled OLAP tools with pleasant user interfaces including extensive drill-down and graphic capabilities. We are still early in the history of BI deployment. As is typical in the life-cycle of new technologies, initial vendor offerings are sometimes menageries of capabilities that are architected as much or more to obtain market share as for capability. Because many enterprises have never utilized tools that are more sophisticated than a spreadsheet for data analysis and modeling, emerging desktop OLAP products may seem like rocket science.

Some vendors are beginning to include more advanced data mining tools within their suites, such as advanced statistical and modeling capabilities. But it is likely to be some time before the general users attain the maximum benefit from desktop versions of the most demanding data mining applications, owing to the expertise required to create and use them. This puts vendors in a bind: Do they immediately offer advanced applications that clients will misuse to their own harm, or do they field products having technology gaps? Most vendors offer their products individually as well as in enterprise suites.

5.1.9   Best in Class Tools vs. Enterprise Suites

Other than potential economic advantages associated with standardizing on enterprise suites and dealing with a smaller number of vendor providers, it is not clear that enterprise suites offer usage advantages over best in class tools. This is primarily because users tend to migrate toward the class of tools with which they are most comfortable. For example, some users make extensive use of query and reporting but are unlikely to delve into advanced analytic or statistical packages. Others are likely to embrace OLAP to the exclusion of other capabilities.

Custom applications that provide excellent value through the deployment of embedded intelligent models are most likely to be based on best in class tools.

5.2   Data Resources

In this "information age" most organizations are totally dependent on automated (computerized) records. Physical media for storing data, while perhaps less fascinating than processing advancements, have also continued to improve technologically while becoming more cost effective. This has provided more alternatives for storing and archiving information as well as the ability to cost-justify large repositories that were previously cost-prohibitive, thus adding more fuel for the data explosion, and a richer field for business intelligence applications. Chapter 6 is devoted entirely to data issues as they relate to data mining. Here we discuss the applicable information technology.

5.2.1   Database Management Systems (DBMS)

Relational databases continue to be the most prevalent means of storing business data. The precursors of relational databases were sequential files (a.k.a. flat files), ISAM (indexed sequential access method), VSAM (variable sequential access method), hierarchical databases, and Codasyl or network databases.

Relational DBMS supports Online Transaction Processing (OLTP) as well as some business intelligence applications. Simply stated, a relational database is a collection of tables (row by column data) that can be logically connected to each other based on data values. DBMS products provide the technical environment that shields the database users (application developers) from the technical complexity (e.g., physical addresses, etc.) of how the data is stored. DBMS typically supports a query language (often based on the Structured Query Language (SQL) standard), as well as reporting, application development, and database administration tools.

Our society's dependence on computing technology and RDBMS has provided commercial funding for on-going product development. Today's most popular databases, such as Oracle and SQL Server, have evolved to support not only simple textual and numeric data, but complex objects (e.g., multimedia) as well, preserving relationships among entities, their attributes and image, audio, and document (e.g., HTML, XML, or other) data.

The underlying complexity of DBMS functionality and relationship is hidden from the user, but can obscure patterns of interest for data mining activities and actually hinder the discovery of undiscovered patterns. It is very likely that the patterns are undiscovered precisely because the conventional representational scheme obscures them. Having to view data through a screen of user-defined patterns imposed in advance can get in the way. Therefore, some advanced data mining tools require that queries of the data and joins (combination) of tables be completed in advance of data mining activities.

5.2.2   Data Warehouses and Data Marts

Data warehouses and data marts are repositories of information that are intentionally separate from the databases used to support OLTP applications. The distinction between warehouses and marts is not of critical significance for our discussion. It is sufficient to say that data warehouses are often meant to provide a comprehensive enterprise data repository, while data marts are generally focused on a specific business functional area.

Both data warehouses and data marts are targeted to support analysis (BI and data mining). Their separation from databases that support production OLTP applications provides two distinct advantages: performance and perspective.

The performance advantage means that high-volume, specifically focused, fast-response transactions (such as those in purchasing applications, for example) do not compete for computing and data access resources with analytic applications that must retrieve or access complete sets of data.

The perspective advantage stems from the ability to view trends over time periods for purposes of analysis. Rather than providing a snapshot in time as generally required for business operations (current balance, current demographics, etc.), data warehouse repositories frequently include a historical time dimension to facilitate analysis. The nature of the business and requirement for trend analysis determine the unit of time for the time dimension. For some applications, monthly or even yearly data may be adequate. Other more dynamic applications may require analysis of trends based on weeks, hours, or even minutes in extreme cases. An example of a case where time in minutes might be necessary would be analysis of purchasing patterns at drive-through restaurants. Detecting such patterns could be useful for a variety of operational improvements including staffing, purchasing, workflow, and so on.

Having information in by-the-minute increments should not be confused with up-to-the-minute information. Gathering, preparing, and storing data in a data warehouse generally involves a several-step process to transform transaction data. Rather than being immediate, the transformation process is usually conducted on a periodic basis.

The dimensional, star-schema or hyper-cube models often used in data warehousing are representation schemes that are well suited to interactive business intelligence applications, as described above. There is a trend toward the incorporation of more advanced data mining tools into data warehouse product offerings. Designing dimensional data repositories is quite a bit different than developing relational databases, but requires a similar level of detailed understanding about the information to be stored and the applications the data will support. The Data Warehousing Institute and DM Review Web sites are both referenced within the Vendor Reference Appendix C. Additional information on data warehousing is available from both of these sources.

As with relational databases, not all of the desirable advanced data mining techniques can be applied effectively, directly against the data warehouse, so it may be necessary to extract data from the data warehouse before using such tools. Intelligent mining agents hold promise to satisfy at least a portion of the need to go directly against a data warehouse, and certainly applications that employ data mining models can operate directly against a data warehouse or an RDBMS. They can do so by directly accessing the data of interest and then call a subroutine that performs that data mining function.

Even so, data warehouses provide some key benefits in support of data mining. They provide a stable, controlled repository from which appropriate segments can be extracted and conditioned for automated mining. It isn't clear that integrated data mining tools within warehouses will become prevalent anytime soon. An analogy might be the expert system shells of the 1980s, many of which lost focus on their key functionality and ended up on the shelf.

5.2.3 Document Data

New database products support complex relational and object queries, and many preserve document tagging (e.g., HTML, XML). This is a rapidly and still evolving area. The ways data mining will be applied in this new arena are not completely clear, although it is likely that pattern recognition among words and phrases will be useful in converting historical documents into XML structures (document type definitions and or schemas).

XML holds the promise to ease data integration problems between applications and organizations over the Internet, so it is already being implemented for e-business applications whose goal is to gain a competitive advantage. At this writing, standards within vertical industries are in a state of flux, so early-adopters can anticipate several iterations of their applications before things settle down.

5.2.4   Data Preparation

Extract, Transformation, and Load (ETL) is a category of tools that is widely used in preparing data to be stored in a data warehouse. As the name implies, this category of tools provides a range of useful operations to prepare source data for storage in a data warehouse or some other target environment. Extraction tools utilize selection criteria (which may range from simple to complex) to acquire subsets of data from source data files. Transformation tools accomplish exactly what their name implies. They provide such capabilities as cleansing, conversion routines for processes such as format conversions, aggregation functions, and so on.

This transformation typically includes a data cleansing process that may consist of several steps. These steps are activities such as validating each data field for compliance with acceptable ranges and values for each specific field, removing "dummy data" (e.g., all 9's), performing cross-field validation (i.e., ensuring that gender or age-related information makes sense), parsing multiple-use fields or other data artifacts into appropriate new single-purpose fields, and so on. Even data that has undergone such a process in preparation for storage in a data warehouse should be regarded with some degree of skepticism for data mining activities.

Feature extraction and enhancement tools provide transformations that are specific to data mining, to prepare a set of features for mining techniques, as explained in more depth in Chapter 6.

5.2.5   The Data Storage Explosion

The current state of the art in data storage technology supports logical address spaces of hectopetabytes (100,000,000,000,000,000 bytes). The *logical address space* of a database or data warehouse is the data volume that can be handled by its logical architecture and access mechanism. The *physical address space* is the data volume that is actually supported by the real system implementation (i.e., with physical storage media, like magnetic or optical discs). There are few, if any, systems in existence that have physical online storage in the petabyte range. Many more repositories of such size exist when extended (e.g., archival) storage is included.

5.3   Business Intelligence Applications

The tools described in the section above can be used to create sub-systems or entire applications. Although, in the authors' experience advanced data mining models are often encompassed within a broader application context.

5.3.1   Decision Support Systems (DSS)

Decision support systems may be used to facilitate or automate the human decision-making process. Computers, therefore freeing knowledge workers for more creative tasks, can perform many tasks that are repetitive or tedious, such as inspection or classification, better. Automated Decision Support Systems can also be used to capture human knowledge through Knowledge Management repositories or Knowledge-Based Expert Systems (see Chapter 10).

5.3.2   Executive Information Systems (EIS)

Before the advent of personal computers, and even today, EISs are intended to provide executive-level personnel with easy access to critical information for use in management decision making. They differ from DSS tools by being generally more narrow in scope, less ad-hoc with predefined responses, and easier to use. Many EISs are based on touch screen or other technologies that don't require keyboard interfaces. In the future, more EIS applications will be based on voice recognition technologies, so the user can tell the computer what information should be displayed, and perhaps answered with a computerized voice.

5.3.3   Web Mining

Applications of data mining to Internet information are predominantly focused on maximizing advertising exposure or revenue. Many such applications focus on "click-stream" data: the path a Web surfer goes through in navigating the Web. When XML replaces hypertext markup language (HTML) as the predominant language on the Web, document data published on Web pages will become far more accessible and provide a rich field for innovative knowledge discovery and other data mining applications.

5.4   Processing Platforms

A discussion of information technology can hardly be considered complete without a discussion of computing and communications technologies. However, for purposes of business intelligence, let us consider the communication network to be "a given." Of course, such a naïve approach would not be used when considering specific application requirements. For example, if data mining services are to be provided within an Application Service Provide (ASP) context, then clearly adequate communications bandwidth, along with privacy and security provisions, are mandated.

Although massively parallel computers are not required to perform knowledge discovery or field advanced data mining algorithms within applications, they do have their place: to support complex operations on massive data repositories. Consider an application that takes weeks to execute, but the information provided is needed on a daily basis.

At the opposite, or bottom end of the spectrum, are personal data mining applications that run successfully in a desktop environment. As in any information system, BI applications can be deployed in a variety of multitier architectural configurations. It is necessary to have a good understanding of the application usage requirements in order to determine the best platform deployment configuration.

5.5   Business Intelligence Philosophy

As discussed in Chapter 1, data mining involves the identification and exploitation of data patterns, for applications such as automated decision support and those based on predictive models. This has some deep implications, which together constitute our technical data mining philosophy. The following considerations provide ideas to keep in mind when approaching business intelligence problems.

1.   The quality of subject data is critical, and of much more importance than the quantity.

"Data" is merely a vehicle for carrying information; the wrapper around the candy. Data mining can be carried out even on very small data sets (e.g., the college kid problem in Chapter 3). What is required is that the data actually contain some actionable information, and this can only be determined by examining it. Small sets may contain gold, and huge sets only garbage.

2.   Useful information is actionable.

Not all patterns are created equal, and there are varieties of inequity. The relative value of a discovered pattern in data depends on many factors. Perhaps the most important is an easily overlooked one: actionability. There is a subtle trap that catches almost every data miner at some time in their career. Data mining applications are usually developed using cleansed and normalized repositories of historical business data. In such a data environment, it is easy to forget that the various fields and dimensions being used in the mining activity come from different sources, are derived using different processes, and become available for use at different times in the business cycle. Building a spectacularly successful churn predictor within a static development environment can be pretty heady, until someone in MIS points out that essential fields used aren't available at the time in the business month that the prediction must be made.

3.   Tools are helpful when appropriately selected and used, but can otherwise be harmful.

Data mining without tools is exactly as effective as coal mining without tools: You'll get dirty hands and a little bit of coal. To increase effectiveness, we use tools. The purpose of tools is to provide focus and leverage. I can't drive a nail with my fingers, but I can with a hammer. The hammer doesn't increase my strength, but allows me to apply that strength at exactly the right spot to accomplish the task. Likewise, data mining tools provide focus and leverage. They direct the attention of the human user to persistent patterns within data sets (focus). And, they allow the human to navigate rapidly through volumes of high-dimensional data (leverage).

Data mining tools fall into several categories including statistical, graphical, inductive, and predictive. Of course, tools are no better than the hand that wields them. Powerful tools, while capable of great good, are destructive when misused. Perhaps the greatest harm is done when misinformation "discovered" by poor data mining is used to poison otherwise sound business intelligence gained from other sources.

4.   The information is in the data.

Information is never created by tools. Tools can, of course, reveal hidden information, and render intractable information accessible. They also make it possible for humans to interact with data in new ways, and so leverage human intuition. Visualization tools, in particular, help domain experts gain new insight into enterprises they thought they understood exhaustively.

Some tools can "concentrate" information in data so that it can be more easily exploited. This is quite important for problems that have information distributed across a large number of data items. The various vantage points that are provided by Online Analytical Processing (e.g., drill-down) can be very useful, as one example. Advanced information concentrating techniques such as principal component analysis (PCA) and independent component analysis (ICA) can often reduce the number of data items that must be analyzed without too much loss of information.

Remember the story of Rumpelstiltskin? He was the evil elf who saved the life of a young maiden by spinning straw into gold. Sometimes data miners forget that this is just a fairy tale. GIGO does *not* mean "garbage in—GOLD out." (It does mean garbage in, garbage out.) Good tools properly used help find information, but they do not create it.

5.   The work is in the data . . .or, it should be.

Because there are two aspects to data mining (the "data," and the "mining"), it is natural to consider a trade between the two. When my data mining isn't working, should I focus on the data, or focus on the techniques being applied?

The answer is almost always to focus on the data. The data mining tools and techniques that are generally available today are so powerful that even in the hands of a novice, they can usually be counted upon to find something if anything is actually there. When *nothing* is found, it's time to consider reconditioning the data, or, more likely, adding some new features to the set being worked. "Algorithm roulette" is much less likely to produce a breakthrough.

If determined application of appropriate tools and optimization of data for mining do not produce results, it might be time to consider retaining some outside data mining expertise. Persistence is important in data mining, but at some point it becomes foolish optimism. There is risk in continuing to apply more and more sophisticated tools to work ground that continually produces nothing beneficial. If no value is being generated, there is probably nothing there to be found. Better to move to another hill and start digging fresh.

5.6   Summary

The selection of a data mining tool set should be based upon the characteristics of the enterprise. The key considerations are those of data size, throughput requirements, domain complexity, and user sophistication. Enterprises with lots of data, demanding performance requirements, highly complex behaviors, and mathematicians or analysts on-staff may elect a set of advanced analytic tools. Those having small data and lower-complexity domains may derive benefits more quickly from simpler tools with a much lower learning curve.

Many of the tools discussed throughout this chapter have been what we would call "conventional." Most require the *a priori* organization imposed by modern database technology. Conventional BI applications access data based upon relationships among objects, records, and fields, so SQL-like query structures must be present.

By contrast, data mining applications whose primary function is to *automatically* discover and exploit patterns present in data are considered to be "advanced." Advanced data mining applications provide adaptive and often non-intuitive visualization, rule induction (non-parametric data summaries), automatic data organization and structuring (e.g., auto-clustering, decision trees), and the construction of trainable predictive models (regression models such as neural networks, radial basis functions, adaptive logic networks, etc.). Advanced data mining applications often don't require underlying data structures. They generally make few *a priori* assumptions about the data, and do not rely on complex linking structures to support relational access. Advanced data mining applications are repeatedly performing many-to-many comparisons among data, and impose much greater access demands than a few human "OLAP'ers" browsing a data mart. Advanced data mining techniques are the subject of Chapters 8 through 10.

6

The Data in Data Mining

As one would expect, data is a critical element in data mining success, a veritable "pillar" if you will. Although organizations have been capturing data for decades, it has primarily been to support mundane record-keeping activities. Advances in computer storage technology have made it possible to save virtually every scrap of data generated by large enterprises. Nevertheless, valuable "nuggets" of information are often contained within vast computer archives.

The fundamental motivation for data mining is the goal of discovering and exploiting such valuable patterns in data. Apparent patterns may be regarded as manifest indications, but not proof of the presence of actionable information latent in the data. Similarly, the apparent absence of patterns can only sometimes be reasonably equated with the absence of actionable information.

It is also the case that poor data preparation or representation and improperly used tools can make existing patterns hard to detect, and make random noise look patterned. Unaided human intuition can be a poor guide in data mining. For these reasons this chapter discusses several important considerations regarding data: meta data, data representation (quantization and coding), feature extraction and enhancement, data quality, relevance, independence, data preparation, and feature selection.

Data miners can expect to be confronted with larger and larger repositories of data to mine. They must realize that actionable patterns are not the result of data volume, but of information content. Patterns don't appear because a megabyte, gigabyte, or terabyte of data have been amassed. Patterns appear because information is present. By data, we mean facts, figures, measurements, and descriptions such as demographic characteristics, and the like. Although information is based on data, it conveys intelligence or knowledge.

It may not be necessary to examine thousands, or even hundreds of transactions to recognize that there are seasonal trends in product-line sales. If a pattern exists in a million records, it can often be expected to appear among a thousand, or perhaps even a hundred. More records can make some patterns easier to detect, and others more difficult. Miners often utilize sampling to extract appropriate subsets of data for experimentation and validation.

Sampling techniques are used to extract a representative portion of the population. Such a reduction may be necessary to reduce the computer processing time, but it could also be necessary to reserve unseen cases for independent testing of a model. (Sampling techniques are addressed in Chapter 7. Blind testing and cross-validation techniques are addressed in Chapter 11.)

6.1   Meta Data

While data describes an individual object or entity, and can be amassed to provide information about a population, *meta data* provides information about that data. Meta data includes such facts as the number and type of data stored, where it is located, how it is organized, and so on. Meta data is essential to data mining because it provides the map for navigation through the data. Meta data may be retained with the data itself, or in a separate structure. Definition and maintenance of meta data are critical issues in the architecture of data warehouses and data marts. In a certain sense, the meta data *is* the warehouse architecture, because it provides the substance upon which all access and applications are based.

6.2   Representation: Quantization and Coding

The process of converting numeric data to nominal data by using codes to represent a range of values is called "quantization." In quantization, sets of numeric values are replaced by a symbolic name. The reverse process converting nominal data to numeric data is called coding. In coding, symbolic names are replaced by numeric values.

Data consists of values obtained from a population sample. Data expresses, in symbolic form, attributes of members of the population being sampled. If the population is "wage earners in New York," for example, data for each wage earner might consist of annual income, number of withholding exemptions, age, ZIP code of residence, etc.

Business data repositories generally consist of both data types: Nominal and numeric. Each data type must be handled differently. Nominal representations give values by names, even though they may appear to be a collection of numbers. A simple distinction is that one would not expect to perform arithmetic on a nominal data item. Examples include names, product identification numbers, Social Security numbers, telephone numbers, product attributes such as color, size codes, expiration dates, and model numbers. They are *names* or identifiers rather than *measurements*. A nominal symbol's numeric value is not related to its meaning. A quick test to determine whether data is nominal or numeric is to ask, "Would the average of these values be meaningful?" If the answer is "no," then the data is probably nominal. It would make no sense, for example, to average peoples' Social Security numbers, or divide individuals' phone numbers by their ZIP codes because these are really names, not numbers.

By contrast, numeric data are numbers whose values are meaningful. A person could be 66 inches tall, 66 years-old, or have a 66-inch waistline. These are examples of numeric data. The person might also be employee number 66, but that data is nominal. Numeric data can be average, totaled, and plotted. Numeric data may be manipulated mathematically in straightforward ways. The numeric value of numeric data directly represents its information content.

The data mining techniques that are applicable to nominal data are basically those of syntactic processing rather than numeric processing. Nominal data can be sorted, arranged in tabular form, parsed, or represented in graphs and trees.

Nominal processing techniques can be performed on numeric data. This is accomplished by quantization, representing ranges of numeric values as appropriate nominal codes. Quantization generally results in a loss of information because different numeric values are assigned with the same symbol and therefore can no longer be distinguished. As illustrated in Figure 6.1, salary ranges could be quantized into "decades." A person with an annual salary of $32,413.00 (or in the fourth decade) might be assigned the symbol D to represent his or her salary (the fourth letter of the alphabet), while another person, with an annual salary of $36,709.00 is assigned the same symbol to represent his or her salary. These individuals can no longer be distinguished from each other using salary, but for many applications, fine distinctions are not important. The simplification accomplished through quanitization can facilitate the model development process.

There are many quantization techniques. This all amounts to putting ranges of numeric values into discrete bins. In the early 1950s, a mathematician with the last name of Max created a statistically optimal quantizer now known as the Max-Lloyd quantizer.

Figure 6.1
Quantization
illustration

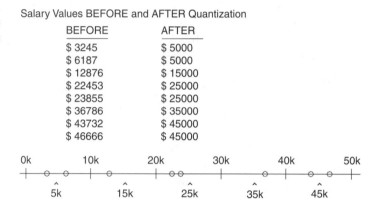

Salary Values BEFORE and AFTER Quantization

BEFORE	AFTER
$ 3245	$ 5000
$ 6187	$ 5000
$ 12876	$ 15000
$ 22453	$ 25000
$ 23855	$ 25000
$ 36786	$ 35000
$ 43732	$ 45000
$ 46666	$ 45000

Ordinarily, coding does not result in information loss. For example, the days of the week can be coded as the integers 1 through 7: Sunday = 1, Monday = 2, and so on. This allows a symbolic name like "Monday" to be used as a numeric value for mathematical operations. This can cause problems, however, if the coding scheme is sub-optimal. The coding scheme would suggest that Saturday and Sunday are as different as days can be because they are separated by the greatest distance (7 − 1 = 6). But, for many purposes, Saturday and Sunday should be regarded as very similar, since they are both weekend days. Poor coding schemes can lead to data mining failure as surely as improper use of mining tools.

For a detailed quantization and coding example, refer to section 7.8.

6.3   Feature Extraction and Enhancement

Quantization and coding are the primary transformations required for typical business or Information System (IS) data. However, there are also many kinds of continuous data that provide a fertile field for data mining, such as audio, video and other types of signal data, and manufacturing or other process control data. In order for data mining to be performed on such data, "features" of the data must be extracted or determined through some mechanism. In some ways, feature extraction is a data compression activity. A large data set, such as an image, is reduced to a small data set, perhaps even a single numeric feature, in such a way that category indicators are preserved. As a data compression activity, feature extraction is distinguished from conventional data compression in that the recovery of the original is not intended. Feature extraction, then, may be characterized as very *lossy* data compression that preserves category indicators.

Viewing feature extraction in such a manner allows the tools and formalism of information theory to be applied directly.

6.4   Data Quality

It is possible to approach data stores without ever thinking about the quality of the subject data. This often leads to the discovery of exciting "nuggets" that later turn out to be "fool's gold." In our experience, we have yet to encounter a substantial enterprise data set that is completely free of quality problems. For one specific problem, a client provided 100,000 records that had been manually classified with a standard identifier, one-at-a-time, by high-level human experts. Their "supervisors" then manually validated the set. The client provided assurance that this data set established a definitive "gold-standard" benchmark for the development of a predictive model. Much to the client's surprise (but not to the authors') automated analysis indicated that approximately ten percent or 10,000 records, were incorrectly classified.

Such an error rate is not unusual. Clients usually know that their data isn't perfect, but they've put a lot of effort into its collection and maintenance, so they tend to overestimate its true quality. Further, data quality is not easily quantified. The definition of "data quality" varies from application to application, and has subjective components. Data that is good enough to land a man on the moon might not be good enough to land a person on Pluto.

Low-quality data frequently occur systematically. For example, a particular month's sales data was corrupted or a certain set of demographic data fields is missing. Systematic problems are the most easily corrected, because they are easy to identify and render a solution. For example, if March sales data is missing or erroneous, an estimate could be reconstructed by extrapolation or averaging from other months. Also, systematic data problems can be discovered and analyzed much more easily than random scatterings of unrelated spurious data.

Low-quality enterprise data is still enterprise data and might be essential to successful data mining. A much better approach is to *cleanse* the data: correct remediable errors and reduce the impact of irremediable errors without introducing spurious information.

High-quality data, for data mining purposes, has five key characteristics. They are:

1.   Accuracy

2.   Consistency

3.   Completeness

4.   Relevance

5.   Independence

Data is *accurate* when it gives a faithful representation of the domain. Data that is collected by sensing equipment (meters, clocks, etc.) are subject to errors arising from erroneous calibration, dropouts due to electrical or network problems, and mechanical failure. These kinds of errors can usually be described unambiguously and detected in the data by appropriate software. Data that is entered by humans is subject to an infinite variety of garbling (misspelling, truncation, transposition, miscoding, or loss of synchrony). Some of these errors can be prevented during data entry (entry by pick-lists), and some can be detected after the fact. If inaccurate data is part of a set being mined, true patterns may be obscured, and spurious patterns induced. Data accuracy cannot be ensured, but it can be measured. This is addressed in Chapter 12.

Data is *consistent* when all of its parts make sense in context. Consistency is very important in data mining because the underlying patterns constituting consistency are part of the information content of the data. Inconsistency occurs when separate parts of the data don't make sense together (e.g., diagnosis = pregnancy *and* gender = male). Formally, data is consistent when it satisfies the rules of the domain (e.g., "Males are never pregnant"). If inconsistent data is part of a set being mined, the usual result is that no sensible patterns are discovered.

Consistency can be evaluated by applying rules to the data. Inconsistent records can then be corrected, or eliminated from the data set that will be used to develop models.

Data is *complete* when all attributes have values (are not null). This is the most frequently encountered data problem in data mining. It is often the case that data sets have records with "empty fields." On a credit application, for example, the applicant might decide not to answer certain questions, resulting in blank data fields.

Data is *relevant* when it carries information about the problem of interest. Clearly, an essential element of data mining success is the availability of relevant data. The relevance of individual features can be quantified in several ways: the correlation of the features with the outcome or category, the presence of meaningful clustering when data is plotted, the utility of the feature in estimating or explaining information in the data. Relevance measures may also be qualitative, for example, when it is noted that fields are only populated a certain percentage of the time on average.

When features are used for predictive modeling, relevance can be defined as "predictive power." This is the relative ability of a model to predict ground truth (the outcome of interest) using only the given feature.

Data are *independent* when the information they impart is not redundant. A frequent mistake is to assemble a collection of features by selecting only highly relevant features to the exclusion of all weak features. The mistakes that highly relevant features may not be independent. For example, "Sales" and "revenue" may be good features for predicting changes in a company's stock price, but they are certainly not independent. There might actually be much more aggregate information content in "sales" combined with a much weaker predictor, such as "total payroll." When each feature is regarded as an information source and two features clearly "get their facts from the same place," only one of them needs to be used for building a model, no matter how "powerful" the features might be individually.

Thus, *the best feature set may not be the set of best features*. Features that function poorly by themselves can produce excellent results when used together. The "best feature set" often consists of a carefully chosen collection of strong and weak features that are roughly uncorrelated to each other. The need to test powerful features for independence is a lesson often learned the hard way by beginning data mining practitioners. Frequently, five or six weak features taken together have more predictive power than two or three powerful features taken together.

6.5   Relevance and Independence of Features

The following examples illustrate relevance and independence in greater detail. Consider a set of six features to be used to predict whether a particular stock (traded on NASDAQ) would go down, go up, or remain the same during the next 60 seconds. A statistical analysis of the features used was performed that determined their relative "predictive power." Feature number four did the best job by itself, correctly classifying 95.6 percent of the feature vectors in a test set. Feature six was next with 70.8 percent, and so on:

Table 6.1   *Feature Percent of Test Set Correctly Classified Using Only the Given Feature*

4	95.6204379562044
6	70.8029197080292
2	67.8832116788321
3	67.8832116788321
1	48.1751824817518
5	23.3576642335766

Based upon the information in Table 6.1, it looks like a good three-feature set would consist of features 4, 6, and 2 (or 4, 6, and 3). To be sure that these features provide independent information, their "independence" was measured (results below).

The correlation coefficients (denoted by "r") of the six features above are shown in Table 6.2. To find the correlation of two features, say 1 and 6, we look in the row/column with headers 1 and 6, finding r = 0.83. As expected, each feature is perfectly correlated with itself (r = 1).

Some of these "r" values are quite large (close to 1 in absolute value), indicating that there is redundancy between the corresponding features. In particular, features 2 and 3 are perfectly correlated (r = 1.00). There is no reason to use both of these features, since one of them gives all the information available from the other.

Table 6.2   *Correlation Matrix of Features Sorted by Percent Accuracy*

	4	6	2	3	1	5
4	1.00	0.17	0.43	0.43	0.27	−0.03
6		1.00	−0.15	−0.15	0.83	−0.5
2			1.00	1.00	0.10	0.13
3				1.00	0.10	0.13
1					1.00	−0.78
5						1.00

It is desirable to use as few features as possible, since this reduces mining and operational complexity. Now that those features that are strongest individually have been determined and are known to be independent, the focus of the analysis can shift to determine which collection of features is best as a set.

A tool was applied that determines which sets of features give the best performance (high accuracy, ability to recognize all classes, and small size). This measure of quality we dub "efficiency," and show the results for various combinations of features:

Table 6.3

Number of Features	Efficiency	Feature Mask	
1	0.698	010000	(If you can only use 1 feature, use 2)
2	0.555	110000	(If you can only use 2 features, use 1 & 2)

continues

Table 6.3 *(continued)*

Number of Features	Efficiency	Feature Mask	
3	0.370	110100	(If you can only use 3 features, use 1, 2 & 4)
4	0.185	110110	
5	0.111	110111	
6	0.074	111111	

Why was 2 selected as the best single feature to use, rather than 4, which classifies with higher accuracy? It turns out that this population is 95.6 percent "stock stayed the same." Feature 4 got a high score by just answering "stays the same" most of the time. Its "high accuracy" is an artifact of the fact that this population is not balanced by class. Feature 4, the most "accurate" feature, is actually pretty weak.

6.6   Data Preparation

Correction of data problems is necessary and must be accomplished in preparation for data mining activities. Since data that is accurate, consistent, complete, relevant, and is often difficult, if not impossible to acquire, additional data cleansing processes may be necessary. There are many data cleansing tools available as off-the-shelf products, but they typically only solve portions of the transformation problem. For sophisticated enterprises, it is reasonable to expect that considerable effort may be required to identify and correct any but the simplest and most obvious problems. Data cleansing may involve considerable manual effort and require some support from a domain expert. Advanced capabilities for handling data problems such as missing and corrupt data are described in Chapter 12.

6.7   Feature Selection

As discussed in Chapter 3, "features" is the name mathematicians and data miners use for what most Information Technology (IT) professionals call properties, attributes, data elements, or data fields (for those who remember coding forms). Users of spreadsheets, might think an attribute or feature equates to a single cell within a spreadsheet.

Feature selection is driven by several factors

- Availability (measured? retained? timely? accurate?)
- Salience (relevant to the problem?)
- Independence (contribute to the analysis?)
- Cost (inexpensive? manageable?)
- Volatility (stationary?)

Feature selection can be performed in a multitude of ways. Assessing the ability of the resulting feature set to support effective data mining requires answering the four following questions:

1. Do the original attributes themselves contain mineable information? If not, no feature extraction process will produce a mineable feature set. Feature selection *never* creates information; it merely makes information already present more accessible.

2. Does the method chosen to convert the attributes to features preserve the information content of the attributes? Careless conversion can destroy latent information.

3. Can the features produced be used by the mining tool(s) and technique(s) that are applied? It is pointless, for example, to represent attributes as character strings if the available mining tools require numeric input.

4. Can the mining tool(s) handle the complexity and volume of the resulting feature set? It does no good to produce feature vectors with thousands of dimensions or millions of records unless there is compute power available to handle them. An important fact to keep in mind: the "right" number of features is the *smallest* number that gives useful results.

It usually isn't possible to give concise and certain answers to these questions until some analysis has been done. This is one of the reasons that data mining is most naturally done using an iterative prototyping methodology. As feature sets are selected and evaluated, insight is gained that facilitates refinement, leading eventually to a satisfactory feature set, and "mineable" data.

Even when these questions are given affirmative answers, there remains the greatest hurdle of all: making the results of data mining *actionable* within the enterprise. This requires buy-in from process owners, management support, and an integration plan. Data mining insertion almost always crosses organizational boundaries within the enterprise. Carefully planned incremental insertion via limited, well-controlled use cases is often successful. Premature enterprise-wide reliance on emergent processes, whether data mining or otherwise, is always to be avoided.

Features are said to be "salient" when their values are correlated with correct classification outcomes. In general, this correlation is non-intuitive, accounting for the difficulty of effective manual feature selection. Because correlation may be modeled in many ways, "salience" is a relative term. In the ideal situation, salient, independent features are extracted inexpensively from the raw data.

The selection of which features to use for model development is critical to the model's success. Information that is not in the feature set is invisible to methods using that set. The power of modern analytic techniques, as discussed in Chapters 8 through 10, makes possible the identification and exploitation of information present in the data. The issue is whether selected features provide relevant information. The selection of poor features is a mistake that cannot be overcome by data mining tools, no matter how powerful.

6.8   Demographic and Behavioral Customer Data

Since we are largely concerned with "customer-centric" intelligence, it's appropriate to consider the types of customer data we are likely to encounter in our data mining activities. Customers can be described in terms of two different types of data: demographic and behavioral. Demographic data consists of relatively static facts like name, address, customer size, type, and so on. Behavioral data consists of dynamic facts that somehow involve action (change) over time: age of account, number of transactions completed last period, transaction volume, payment timeliness, etc.

"Customer history" is just a sequence of snapshots of behavioral data over time. Since this data is repeated for multiple time periods (e.g., January sales, February sales, etc.), and demographic data is not, behavioral data typically constitutes the bulk of enterprise data used for data mining. Hence, this is one of the reasons why data marts and warehouses can be useful for data mining activities.

Behavioral data has two unique attributes that are very important in data mining applications: temporal depth and temporal resolution. Temporal depth is the length of the time span covered by the data. Temporally shallow data might cover just a few months of an operation, while deep data could cover decades. Temporal resolution is the time between "snapshots." Data with high temporal resolution might consist of weekly snapshots, while low-resolution data might be based on quarters.

Whether the need is for deep data, high-resolution data, or both depends upon the problem. For example, if the objective is to identify seasonal trends in customer behaviors, it would probably be necessary to have data available that is at least two years deep. A single year does not a trend make. Recognizing long-term trends requires depth (typically data covering at least two complete cycles). And, determining the effectiveness of short-term advertising cannot be supported using annual sales data. For such an application, high resolution is needed to enable any sales spikes to be identified that might be reasonably attributed to the ads.

The likelihood of success for a particular data mining application often comes down to what the data will actually support in terms of depth and resolution. For example:

- Type of data available (age, completeness, salience, independence)

- Scale (How much data do you have? How much is really needed?)

- Market (How far ahead can/must you look?)

- Resources (budget, staff, equipment, management support)

6.9   Summary

The fundamental motivation for data mining is the goal of discovering and exploiting patterns in data. Data preparation and representation are essential to enable existing patterns to be detected. Data miners can expect to be confronted with larger and larger repositories of data to mine, whether they are in data warehouses, data marts, in some other form such as multimedia. Actionable patterns are not the result of data volume, but of information content.

7

The Mathematics of Data Mining

Underlying the data mining methods for knowledge discovery and exploitation is a mathematical framework. This framework consists of techniques mostly from linear algebra, probability and statistics, and the calculus of several variables. In this chapter, the basics of representation and analysis of data are presented. Mastery of these ideas is not essential to an understanding of later chapters, but passing familiarity with the general ideas is, so readers who are not interested in theory can skip to section 7.7.

7.1   Introducing Feature Space

Advanced data mining requires data to be expressed in a form that facilitates representation and analysis. Since advanced data mining applications are mathematically intensive, many data mining techniques work exclusively with data in numeric form. Several methods for encoding nominal data in numeric form, along with their implications, are discussed. Once nominal data has been encoded, it can support the mathematics required by data mining. Even more difficult than nominal-to-numeric encoding, is the process of feature extraction: the collection and synthesis of salient, independent features from a broad set of data, as discussed later in this chapter.

Fortunately, mathematicians have provided an ideal framework within which to conduct data mining. It is called "Euclidean space," and the mathematical theory describing it is known as "linear algebra." Euclidean space is named for the Greek mathematician Euclid, who derived many of its properties in his magnum opus, "The Elements." There are infinitely many Euclidean spaces, which is quite beneficial because there are infinitely many data mining problems, and each one needs an appropriate framework. *Every data mining problem using numeric data can be formulated in its own Euclidean space.*

Different Euclidean spaces have many properties in common, but they can be distinguished from one another by their *dimension*. The technical definition of dimension is "cardinality of a minimal spanning set," but what may be an intuitive notion of dimension as "the number of coordinates of a point" is adequate, and is explained further by the following examples.

One-dimensional Euclidean space, denoted R^1, is simply the number line. Plotting data values on a number line represents them as a collection of points in one-dimensional Euclidean space. The set $\{1, 3, -2, 5\}$ is illustrated in Figure 7.1.

Figure 7.1

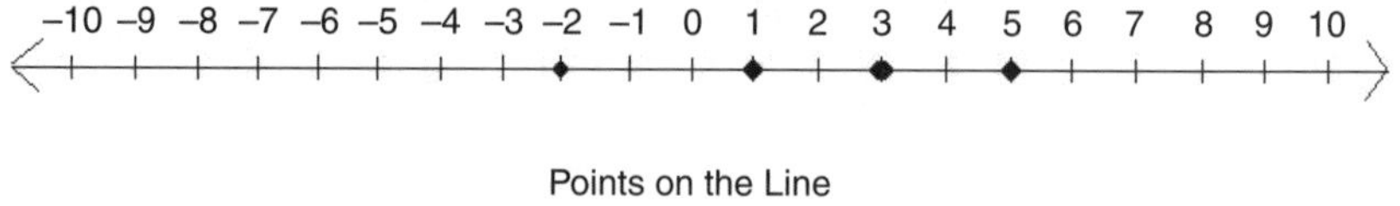

Points on the Line

Two-dimensional Euclidean space, denoted R^2, is simply the coordinate plane. Plotting data values in the plane represents them as a collection of points in two-dimensional Euclidean space. Specifying a point in this space requires that two values, the x-coordinate and the y-coordinate, be specified. The set $\{(2,-2), (-2, 2), (3,1), (-4,0)\}$ is illustrated in Figure 7.2.

The order of the coordinates in two-dimensional space is crucial; if the coordinates are reversed, the location of the point is different, as seen in the case of the first two points in the figure. Because order is significant, the pairs of coordinates denoting points in two-dimensional space are often called *ordered pairs*.

Three-dimensional Euclidean space, denoted R^3, is precisely like the three-dimensional space we all inhabit, where the ordered values represent height, width, and depth. Plotting data values in *3-space* represents them as a collection of points in three-dimensional Euclidean space. Specifying a point in this space requires that three values: the x-coordinate, y-coordinate, and z-coordinate be specified. The set $\{(0,0,3), (0,7,0), (4,0,0)\}$ is illustrated in Figure 7.3.

Figure 7.2

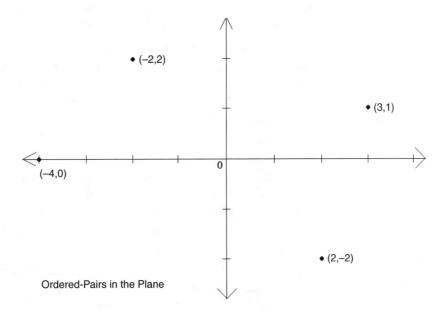

Ordered-Pairs in the Plane

Figure 7.3

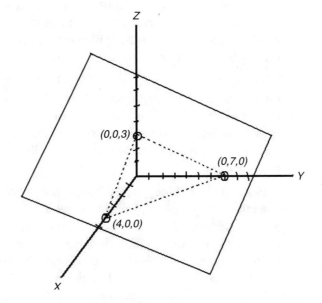

As in the case of two-dimensional Euclidean space, the order of the coordinates in three-dimensional space is crucial. If the coordinates are reordered, the location of the point is different, as seen in the case of the first two points in the figure. Triples of coordinates for points in 3-space are called *ordered triples,* or *3-tuples.*

Although it is very difficult to imagine what a physical space consisting of more than three spatial dimensions might be like, mathematically ordered tuples with more than three numbers in them are the logical extension of the familiar two- and three-dimensional frameworks.

N-dimensional Euclidean space, denoted R^N represents collections of ordered N-tuples of numbers (where N is greater than three). When the tuples have two coordinates, the space is two-dimensional. When they are triples, the space is three-dimensional. And, when the tuples have 47 coordinates, the space is 47-dimensional. Such dimensionality could be considered to be "Euclidean *hyperspace.*"

Essentially all of the mathematical characteristics of two-dimensional space generalize to N-dimensional space. There are angles and distances in hyperspace, just as there are in the plane. This means that the same intuition about geometry in normal physical space applies in "hyperspace." However navigating (e.g., rotating perspectives) in hyperspace can be quite complex, because human intuition has not been developed to this extent.

The majority of the computational effort that is required to carry out standard manipulations (such as rotations, normalization, reflections, rescaling, etc.) of data in N-dimensional space can be efficiently implemented using matrix arithmetic. MATLAB, a product of MathWorks, provides an excellent toolbox for performing such manipulations.

Plotting data values in N-dimensional space represents them as a collection of points in N-dimensional Euclidean space. Specifying a point in this space requires that N values, x_1 , x_2 , x_3 , ..., x_N , be specified. As in the case of "low" dimensional Euclidean spaces, the order of the coordinates in N-dimensional space is crucial. Tuples in N-space are called *ordered N-tuples*. Examples of N-dimensional graphic displays are included in the discussion of visualization, in Chapter 8.

Note that not all dimensional frameworks of greater than three dimensions are Euclidean. The four space and time dimensions of Einstein's General Theory of Relativity are notable examples. However, discussion of modern physics is beyond the scope of this data mining discussion.

7.2   Moderate Statistics Apply

The degree of statistical expertise that is necessary to conduct effective data mining activities can be debated. Certainly a high degree of skill is necessary for those who design and develop data mining tools and techniques. However, modest knowledge of statistics is adequate to enable data mining applications to be applied for significant benefit. The principal danger faced by less sophisticated users of data mining applications is not that they will overlook patterns, but that they will fail to correctly appraise the value of the patterns they find. A discussion of the basic statistical knowledge required to perform effective data mining follows. For further discussion of basic statistics, see Appendix D.

Statistics is vital to successful data mining. While data mining searches for patterns, statistics provides the mathematical formalism for *quantifying* the presence and significance of these patterns. Statistics is used to:

- estimate the complexity of a data mining problem;

- suggest which data mining techniques are most likely to be successful; and

- identify data fields that contain the most "surface information."

Statistics is a mathematical way of approaching patterns among data. Most statisticians and mathematicians agree that statistics is less a branch of mathematics than it is an objective methodology for reasoning about patterns in data. The purely mathematical component of statistics is "probability theory."

The basic goal of statistics is to extend knowledge about a subset of a collection to the entire collection. For example, to determine the average income of families residing in Florida, we could conduct a survey, contacting every family in the state. But this is expensive and time-consuming, and some people would refuse to divulge the information. A more practical approach would be to conduct a poll, querying a manageable number of Florida families. The responses to this smaller set can be used, through the proper application of statistical techniques, to draw conclusions about Florida's families as a whole. This example illustrates some of the fundamental terms used in statistical methods.

Population: the collection of interest whose attributes are to be estimated. In our example, the population is "families residing in the State of Florida."

Parameter: the value of an attribute for a population. The average income of Florida families is the population parameter to be estimated in our example.

Sample: a subset of the population. The sample in our illustration is the small group of families included in our poll.

Statistic: the value of an attribute derived from a sample. The average income of Florida families is the sample statistic to be computed from our sample.

Samples must be selected according to an appropriate methodology (e.g., random sample, judgment sample, etc.). It is important that a sample be:

1.   Large enough to be representative of the population

2.   Small enough to be manageable

3.   Accessible to the sampler

4.   Free of bias

Notice that populations are characterized by their *parameters*, and samples are characterized by their *statistics*. Populations are often big, unknowable, and inaccessible, while samples are smaller and better known, and more available. Statistical inference is a methodology for inferring the *parameters* of a population from the *statistics* of a sample.

The effectiveness of statistical techniques in estimating population parameters from sample statistics depends upon several factors. The most important of these is the size of the sample. When the sample consists of the entire population, no statistical extrapolation is needed; such an exhaustive sample is called a *census*. Large samples are less prone to error arising from random variation in the selection of sample points, so-called *sampling error*.

There are two types of statistical methodologies used in data mining: parametric and non-parametric. Parametric techniques rely on the estimation of population parameters, such as averages. Non-parametric techniques rely on *vigilance parameters*, which are generally independent of the data. Bayesian analysis is an example of a parametric technique, while unsupervised clustering is an example of a non-parametric techniques analysis. (These and other techniques are explained in Chapters 8 through 10.)

Population parameters are of great interest in data mining because they serve as the basis for all descriptions of the population and its subsets. Advanced data mining techniques often use certain basic population parameters for data cleansing, registration, normalization, and segmentation, as explained in Chapter 8. The population parameters of greatest interest for most data mining applications are the simple intuitive ones: minimum, maximum, midrange, mean, variance, median, and mode. These are generally referred to as measures of central tendency.

Histograms provide an intuitive and familiar view of probability distributions. Also called bar-charts, they show the number of occurrences of the various values, or ranges of values, within a population. Figure 7.4 depicts the annual incomes of a certain population of 100 people. Notice, for example, that 36 of these people have incomes in the 15k to 20k range.

Figure 7.4

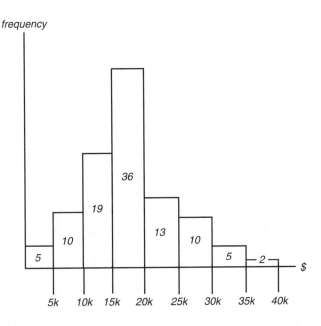

Histogram of Salaries for 100 Persons

For most data mining applications, we are less interested in the *number* of individuals in particular histogram bars than in the *probability* that a random selection from the population will result in a member of a given bar. For this reason, it is natural to replace the histogram with a *relative frequency distribution*, also called a *discrete probability distribution*. This is accomplished by dividing the bar/bin frequencies by the total number of members in the population (see Figure 7.5). Of our sample, 36% have incomes in the 15k to 20k range.

Figure 7.5 ⟶

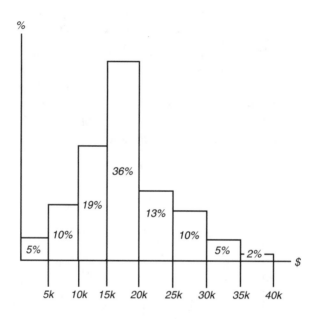

Relative Frequency of Salaries

The fundamental difference between a histogram and a discrete probability distribution is the units used on the vertical axis: Histograms use frequency, and probability distributions use probability. Probabilities can be represented either as percentages, or decimal fractions in the range zero to one (e.g., 0.25 corresponds to 25 percent).

Narrower bars could be used for the histogram, for example, only $1,000.00 wide. This smaller *quantum* would allow more precise representation of information about the population. Estimation error that arises from using large bars is called *quantization error*, but it isn't always negative. It occurs naturally when wide bars are used to ignore irrelevant low-level detail and to provide generalized information about a population. If a quantum of $1.00 was used for our income example, the result would be 40,000 bars, showing bars for incomes at $25,000.00 and $25,001.00, which is of dubious value.

When the horizontal axis represents a continuous variable, such as income, the bars could be imagined to become narrower and narrower without limit. The result would be an infinite number of bars, each having zero width. This kind of limiting distribution is called a *continuous probability distribution*. These theoretical distributions are tremendously important in applications, because they describe many real-world situations. There are many different discrete and continuous probability distributions. These distributions serve as statistical models for describing data of many kids, and can be indispensable in the analysis phase of data mining.

7.3   Probability Distribution

The two most important general probability distributions for data mining applications are the *normal distribution* (also called the *Gaussian distribution* or "bell curve"), and the *uniform distribution* (see Figure 7.6).

Figure 7.6

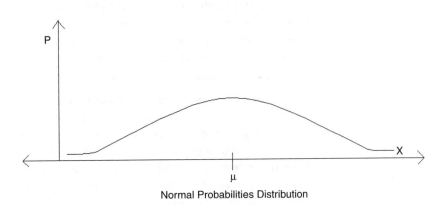

Normal Probabilities Distribution

The normal distribution is symmetric about the mean, which is to say that the mean equals the median. The normal distribution is also unimodal, with mode also being equal to the mean. The shape of the normal distribution indicates that observing values close to the average is more likely than observing values far from the average. A good example of a normal distribution is the distribution of IQs (intelligence quotients) in a major city. The distribution of Stanford-Binet IQ scores, for example, has a mean of 100 and a standard deviation of 16. Lots of information is given by these simple facts:

1. Because the median and mean of a normal distribution are equal, it can be concluded that a randomly selected person is just as likely to be found to have an IQ below 100 as he or she are to have an IQ above 100.

2. Because normal distributions are symmetric about the mean, it can be concluded that the probability of a randomly selected person being found to have an IQ of 80 or less (20 points or more below the mean) is the same as the probability of a randomly selected person being found to have an IQ of 120 or more (20 or more points above the mean).

3. Because normal distributions follow the "68 percent rule" (see section 7.4) the probability that a randomly selected person will be found to have an IQ within 1 standard deviation of the mean (that is, between 84 and 116) is 68 percent.

Many other inferences can be made about populations that are normally distributed. This gets into the theory of *sampling distributions*, which will not be addressed here (sampling distributions express the probability that statistics will be observed to have certain values in a sample drawn from a given population).

The uniform distributions graph is a horizontal line. See Figure 7.7 for an illustration. This indicates that when data is uniformly distributed, the probability of any value being observed is equal to the probability of any other value being observed. A good example of a discrete uniform distribution is the distribution of probabilities for the outcome of the roll of a fair die. The probability that "1" will come up is 1/6, the probability that "2" will come up is 1/6, and so on, for all 6 possible outcomes.

The uniform distribution has no mode. Then mean and median coincide at the middle of the distribution. The uniform distribution describes many real-world situations, particularly those for which probabilities have been forced by design to be "fair."

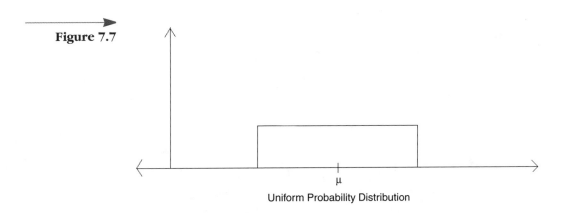

Figure 7.7

μ

Uniform Probability Distribution

7.4   Standard Deviation and Z-score

Standard deviation measures the variability of the data. For example, if the sample values are all equal (no variation), the standard deviation is zero. For data with a normal distribution, about 68 percent of the data are within 1 standard deviation of the mean, 95 percent of the data are within 2 standard deviations of the mean, and 99 percent of the data are within 2.56 standard deviations of the mean. These are referred to as the "68 percent rule," the "95 percent rule," and the "99 percent rule," respectively. The standard deviation is extremely important in data analysis.

In Figure 7.8, the distribution on the left has a mean of 100, and a standard deviation of 20. The distribution on the right has a mean of 180, but a standard deviation of 10. The vertical lines mark the 1-sigma distances above and below the mean. The "rules" apply consistently to normal distributions no matter what their standard deviation is.

The standard deviation is used in three ways during data mining: to describe the data, to sanity-check the data, and to normalize the data. *Z-scores* relate individual data values to the distribution. The *z-score* of a data value is its distance from the mean measured in standard deviations. So, the mean of a population has a z-score of 0. A value that is 1 standard deviation higher than the mean has a z-score of 1. A value that is 2 standard deviations higher than the mean value has a z-score of 2. For values less than the mean, negative z-scores are used: A value that is 2 standard deviations below the mean value

Figure 7.8

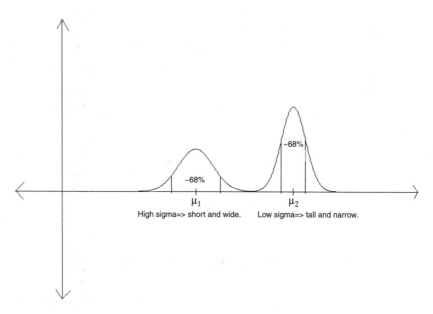

has a z-score of –2, and so on. The z-score for a data value x is computed:

$$z(x) = (x - mean) \div sigma$$

If a population happens to have a standard deviation of 0, this formula would result in an undefined operation (division by zero). But, in that case, the population consists of only a single value equal to the mean, since a standard deviation of zero implies no deviation from the mean. In such a case, z(x) is defined to be 0.

The computation of z-score can be reversed. If the mean and standard deviation of a population are known, the original data value associated with a z-score can be easily recovered:

$$x = mean + (sigma \times z(x))$$

Because z-scores represent data in terms of their distances from the population mean, they provide a natural and consistent way of describing data that takes its distribution into account. The "68 percent rule" can be restated in terms of z-scores: For a normally distributed population, 68 percent of the data have z-scores between –1 and +1. Similarly, 95 percent of the data have z-scores between –2 and +2, while 99 percent of the data have z-scores between –2.56 and +2.56. These rules all hold for any normally distributed population, regardless of how spread out it is, because the z-score compensates for the spread.

Standard deviation is useful for "sanity checking" the data to be used in a data mining exercise. If the mean and standard deviation of valid data are known, z-scores can be calculated for any "suspect" data. z-Score values less than –2.56 or greater than +2.56 are expected in only 1 out of 100 cases. Frequencies much greater than 1 percent suggest that some the high-z data are bad.

Encountering z-scores of 5 or 6 in a data set is significant. The probability of finding a z-score of at least 5 for valid data in a normally distributed population is only 3 in 10,000,000. Large z-scores indicate either that the data is bad, or the population is far from normally distributed. Non-normal distributions are not bad, but it is important to recognize them. Data values that generate large positive or negative z-scores can be detected automatically by software. These data should be manually checked before they are used for mining, since they are likely to be outliers. Once problem data are detected, appropriate replacement values can be inserted, or the data can be removed.

Data come in all sizes and distributions. Display and analysis of data is hindered when the data values cover huge ranges, or are all very large or very small. A natural way to normalize data is to replace each data value with its z-score. This provides three advantages:

1.   After z-scoring, the data will have a mean of zero, so it will be nicely centered at the origin.

2.   After z-scoring, 99 percent of the data will assume values between –2.56 and +2.56, giving a controlled range of values.

3.   After z-scoring, the data will have a standard deviation of 1.

Using the standard deviation to z-score data transforms even very spread-out, ungainly distributions into distributions of essentially fixed width and zero mean. Similarly, z-scoring converts distributions that are so narrow that detail is lost into distributions of essentially fixed width and zero mean. Thus, the z-score is very useful for normalizing data, and reducing it to a standard form well-suited to visualization and other forms of manual analysis.

7.5   Z-score in Feature Space

Euclidean space is important for data mining because it provides a natural and mathematically rich framework for numeric data of the type usually encountered by decision makers. Every decision problem is different, but there is a common thread running through most of them that immediately suggests a Euclidean framework: The objects being analyzed are represented as a list of their attributes.

The objects being analyzed are drawn from a population of interest, for example, retail sales transactions. Such transactions can be described by listing their attributes: item sold, date of sale, time of sale, location of sale, purchase price, and name of salesperson. When these attributes are represented as numbers and placed into an ordered tuple, transactions become points in R^6, 6-dimensional Euclidean space:

Transaction = (ITEMID, DAY-OF-MONTH, HOUR-OF-DAY, OUTLETID, PRICE, SALESID)

Within this framework, the transaction history of a retail business becomes a collection of points in a Euclidean space that can be analyzed mathematically for patterns. An ordered n-tuple of attributes in this scheme is called a *feature vector*, and each attribute a *feature*. The number of features is the dimension of the space; the space itself is referred to as the *feature space*. Anything that can be reliably measured can be used as a feature. The application of data mining techniques to feature spaces having hundreds of dimensions has become commonplace. The true power of the feature space concept is not evident when problems are simple. A range of less sophisticated Business Intelligence tools easily addresses simple problems.

The feature space framework supports the automated correlation of all features simultaneously, without necessarily requiring human hypotheses as starting points. Some of the more challenging questions that can be addressed naturally within the feature space framework are:

1.   Are there certain items that customers often buy together?

2.   Are total sales by outlet cyclical? Are the cycles the same for all outlets?

3.   Do groups of different items have related sales patterns? What are these groups and patterns?

This is more than just theory. Monte goes to a particular fast-food restaurant twice a week: for lunch on Friday, and for breakfast on Saturday. He sees many of the same "Friday-customers" and "Saturday-customers" week after week. He always orders the same thing, as may many of the other "regulars." Does the fast-food restaurant know about these patterns, and does it use them to reduce the turn-around time and latency of its products? According to recent news reports, this particular chain does. And it learned these patterns by mining a feature space populated with hourly sales data.

There are several fundamental computations that are performed in feature space. These serve as the basis for the mathematical analysis underlying advanced data mining. As a simple example, let our population consist of adult males and our features be H = height in feet and W = weight in pounds. Using H and W as coordinates in a two-dimensional feature space, we can produce a plot of our population data (see Figure 7.9).

Figure 7.9

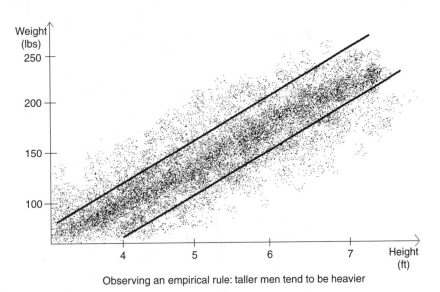

Observing an empirical rule: taller men tend to be heavier

Height is along the horizontal axis, and weight is along the vertical axis. In this representation, taller individuals are farther to the right, and heavier individuals are higher up (points in the upper

right-hand of the plot represent tall, heavy men). Several observations can be made about this population from the distribution of
data in feature space. Taller men tend to be heavier; not all short
men are light; most men fall along a band that extends from lower
left to upper right, etc.

The observation that much of the data lies in a diagonal band suggests that there might be a rule relating weight and height. If this
rule can be specified mathematically, it might be useful for prediction: Having only a man's weight, give a reasonable estimate of his
likely height. Such a mathematical relationship provides a *predictive
model*, allowing the values of some features to be estimated ("predicted") from others. Predictive modeling is discussed in greater
depth in Chapter 10.

It must be emphasized that predictive models based entirely on
observation data are purely empirical: They exploit, without any
true understanding, apparent consistencies among data. Even when
such models "work," they do not *prove* a causal relationship among
data. The relationship might be observed because one set of features
is causal for another, or purely by consequences of a common cause.
It is also possible that observed relationships are nothing more than
associations that occur frequently.

As the Scottish philosopher David Hume pointed out, what we
call "causality" cannot be proven to be anything more than a failure
to detect inconsistency. Great height does not always imply great
weight, and increasing ones weight is unlikely to increase ones
height. *Post hoc ergo propter hoc.* "It exists afterwards, therefore it
is because of" is a logical fallacy to which data miners are particularly vulnerable.

But, it is also true that if relationships exist in the data, they can
be useful whether causality is involved or not. In many Business
Intelligence applications, it really doesn't matter why a model
works, as long it does. Knowing why a model works can help
explain results, and can be used to improve performance; but, even
at its inscrutable worst, a working model is still a working model,
and can provide value.

7.6   Feature Space Computations

The term "coordinate-wise" is used to refer to an operation performed individually on each feature in a feature vector. The basic computations in feature space are described in the following paragraphs.

7.6.1   Multiply (or Divide) a Feature Vector by a Constant

To multiply a feature vector by a constant, multiplication is done coordinate-wise:

If $V_1 = (3, 5, -3)$, then 4 times V_1, denoted $4V_1$, is given by:

$$4 (3, 5, -3) = (4 \times 3, 4 \times 5, 4 \times (- 3)) = (12, 20, -12)$$

Division of a vector by a constant is also done coordinate-wise:

$$(8, 4, -16) \div 4 = (8 \div 4, 4 \div 4, -16 \div 4) = (2, 1, -4)$$

Multiplying or dividing a vector by a non-zero constant changes its length, but not its direction.

7.6.2   Add Feature Vectors

Vectors in Euclidean space are added together coordinate-wise to obtain another vector:

If $V_1 = (3, 5, -3)$ and $V_2 = (3, 1, 1)$, then

$$V_1 + V_2 = (3, 5, -3) + (3, 1, 1) = (3 + 3, 5 + 1, -3 + 1) = (6, 6, -2)$$

Note, now that the vector sum and division by constants have been defined, the average of two vectors can be defined as half their sum, that is, as their coordinate-wise average:

$$\text{The average of } V_1 \text{ and } V_2 \text{ above} = ((3, 5, -3) + (3, 1, 1)) \div 2$$
$$= (3 + 3, 5 + 1, -3 + 1) \div 2$$
$$= (6 \div 2, 6 \div 2, -2 \div 2) = (3, 3, -1)$$

The average of two points in feature space gives the point in feature space that is at the midpoint of the line segment joining the two points:

Figure 7.10

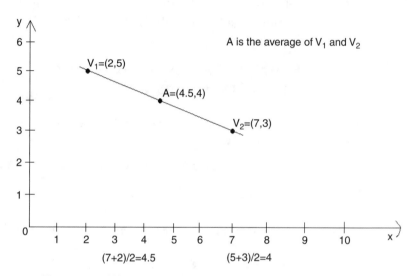

The average of V_1 and V_2 is the mid-point of the segment connecting them.

7.6.3   Difference Feature Vectors

If $V_1 = (3, 5, -3)$ and $V_2 = (3, 1, 1)$, then

$$V_1 - V_2 = (3, 5, -3) - (3, 1, 1) = (3 - 3, 5 - 1, -3 - 1) = (0, 4, -4)$$

Note that two vectors are equal if, and only if, their difference is zero.

7.6.4   Compute the Length of a Feature Vector

The length of a feature vector is computed by summing the squares of its coordinates, then taking the square root (we use the notation SQR(x) to denote the square root of x):

If $V_1 = (0, 4, -3)$ then length of V_1, denoted $|V_1|$, is:

$$|V_1| = |(0, 4, -3)| = SQR(0^2 + 4^2 + (-3)^2) = SQR (0 + 16 + 9) = SQR(25) = 5$$

Note that the length of a vector is a non-negative number.

7.6.5 Compute the Distance Between Two Feature Vectors

This is a tremendously important calculation, because the distance between two feature vectors is the principal measure of how similar the vectors are. Vectors that are close together in feature space are similar, while distant vectors are dissimilar. The application is clear. If the goal is to identify good customers and examples of good customers are available and known, the feature vectors of interest are those that are close to the feature vectors of known good customers. The process is similar when looking for fraud, churn, hot stock picks, and so on.

There are many different ways one can define the distance between two feature vectors. Every Euclidean space is endowed with its own distance function, called the Euclidean distance, which establishes the standard method of computing distances in that space. This metric computes the distance between two vectors V_1 and V_2 as the norm of their difference:

$$d(V_1, V_2) = |V_1 - V_2|$$

For example, if $V_1 = (3, 5, -2)$ and $V_2 = (3, 1, 1)$, then

$$d(V_1, V_2) = |(3, 5, -2) - (3, 1, 1)| = |(3 - 3, 5 - 1, -2 - 1)| = |(0, 4, -3)|$$
$$= SQR(0^2 + 4^2 + (-3)^2) = SQR(0 + 16 + 9) = SQR(25) = 5$$

By definition, the distance between two vectors is never a negative number, and two vectors are equal if, and only if, the distance between them is zero. Distance in hyperspace is computed in exactly the same way; there is a term for each dimension. Distance in hyperspace means the same thing it means in 1, 2, and 3-dimensional spaces: It is the linear separation between two given points, and is computed as the norm of the difference of those points.

7.6.6 Compute the Inner Product (also Called the Dot Product or the Scalar Product) of Two Feature Vectors

The inner product is a kind of multiplication of vectors, but the result it gives is not a vector, but a number. The inner product of two vectors is the sum of their coordinate-wise products:

If $V_1 = (3, 5, 4)$ and $V_2 = (-3, 1 \ 1)$, then

$$V_1 \cdot V_2 = (3, 5, 4) \cdot (-3, 1, 1) = (3 \times (-3)) + (5 \times 1) + (4 \times 1) = -9 + 5 + 4 = 0$$

The dot product contains information about the angle between two vectors. Some important facts are that, for non-zero vectors, the dot product is positive if the angle between the vectors is less than 90 degrees. The dot product is negative if the angle between the vectors is greater than 90 degrees. Two non-zero vectors are perpendicular (form a 90 degree angle) if, and only if, their dot product is zero. So, the feature vectors in the example above form a right angle.

The dot product is tremendously important in data mining work because it can be used to compute a correlation or similarity between two vectors. It serves precisely this function in a type of neural network called a multi-layer perceptron (see Chapter 10). The basis for the similarity measure obtained from the dot product can be derived from a theorem in trigonometry called "The Law of Cosines." Using this theorem, it can be shown that the cosine of the angle between two vectors can be computed by dividing their dot product by the product of their lengths:

Cosine of Angle (in radians) between V_1 and $V_2 = (V_1 \cdot V_2) \div (|V_1| \ |V_1|)$

This theorem is true in all Euclidean spaces of dimension 2 and higher. Consider, for example, the two 4-dimensional vectors $V_1 = (1,2,3,4)$ and $V_2 = (-4,3,-1,1)$. Based on the calculations demonstrated above, we find their lengths to be:

$$|V_1| = |(0, 2, 4, 4)| = SQR(0^2 + 2^2 + 4^2 + 4^2)$$
$$= SQR(0 + 4 + 16 + 16) = SQR(36) = 6$$
$$|V_2| = |(-4, 0, -2, 4)| = SQR((-4)^2 + 0^2 + (-2)^2 + 4^2)$$
$$= SQR(16 + 0 + 4 + 16) = SQR(36) = 6$$

So, Cosine of Angle $= (V_1 \cdot V_2) \div (|V_1| \ |V_1|)$
$$= \{(0 \times (-4)) + (2 \times 0) + (4 \times (-2)) + (4 \times 4)\} \div (6 \times 6)$$
$$= (-8 + 16) \div 36 = 8 \div 36 = 2 \div 9, \text{ which is approximately } 0.22222.$$

Using a calculator, we find that the angle having a cosine of 0.22222 is 77.16 degrees.

7.6.7 Compute the Standard Deviations of Sets of Feature Vectors

The ability of the standard deviation to give information about the distribution of sets of real numbers can be applied to the analysis of multi-dimensional sets of points. By computing the coordinate-wise standard deviations for a set of feature vectors, measures of the extent of the set in each dimension are obtained. If the standard deviations in each dimension are roughly equal, the set will have about the same extent in all dimensions, and be "round" like a ball. If the standard deviations in some dimensions are noticeably different from each other, the set will have greater extent in some dimensions than others, and be ellipsoidal. If the differences in the standard deviations in different dimensions are great enough, the set can appear "thin" in some dimensions and "thick" in others (e.g., like a pancake, which is narrow in one dimension and wide in the other two).

Figure 7.11 shows four sets (A, B, C, and D) of feature vectors in 2-dimensional space (i.e., ordered pairs). The standard deviations in x and y have been computed for each of these sets. The standard deviation of the x-coordinates for the points in set A is equal to the standard deviation of the y-coordinates for the points in set A. Therefore, set A has the same "variability" horizontally and vertically, so it is "round." In contrast to this, the standard deviation of the x-coordinates for the points in set B is about 3 times as large as the standard deviation of the y-coordinates for the points in set B. Therefore, set B has more horizontal "variability," and looks like an ellipse about three times as wide as it is high.

For set C, the standard deviation of the y-coordinates for the points is about 6 times as large as the standard deviation of the x-coordinates for the points, and set B is a narrow vertically oriented ellipse. Set D has a standard deviation along x of zero, and a standard deviation along y of 1; it is a vertical line segment of zero width.

7.7 Clusters

A final fundamental concept within Euclidean space is the *cluster*. It is: a collection of points positioned relative to one another in such a

Figure 7.11

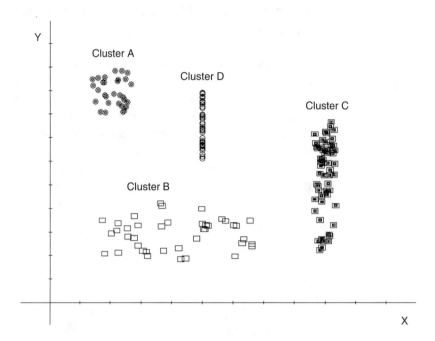

way that they form a group. There is really no better definition than
this intuitive one. Mathematical definitions of the term cluster are
necessarily ad-hoc, rarely satisfactory. The human eye's notion of
when points "go together" and when they don't is too subjective for
a one-size-fits-all definition to work. A particular collection might be
deemed a cluster by one person, and not another. Or, everyone
might agree that a collection of points constitutes a cluster for one
use of the data, but not another. It is helpful to think of clusters as
"coherent aggregations of points," adjusting the definition of coherent to fit the application.

How many clusters do you see in Figure 7.12? In the figure, it
would be easy to justify cluster counts of three, four, five, or more,
depending upon how you draw boundaries. How far apart do two
parts of a cluster have to be before they become two separate clusters? Does shape matter? Size?

In practice, the definition of cluster is usually driven less by mathematical analysis and more by practical business considerations.
Customers that are just one mile apart might be regarded as very distant if, for example, the state line happens to fall between them.
Business sense, along with tax and fee structures, may dictate that

Figure 7.12

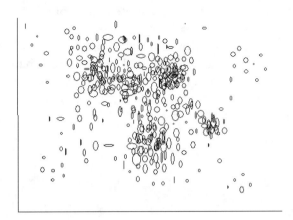

customers in different states be treated differently, even when they are the same in all other respects.

The process of assigning points in a population to clusters is called *clustering* the data. Humans are effective at visually clustering data as long as it is of dimension 3 or less. They don't perform well in high-dimensional spaces, or when clusters start to overlap at the edges.

Data sets often consist of some clusters that are large and diffuse, along with some clusters that are small and tight. This means that the definitions of "far apart" and "big" are different in different parts of the space. An "adaptive" method is needed: one that adjusts its clustering rules to suit the arrangement of data in the part of space in which it's working. It is partially the human's ability to adapt his or her decision-making methods in real time that makes him or her good at visually clustering low-dimensional data.

Since humans, who are terrific adaptive pattern matchers, have a difficult time agreeing on how high-dimensional or complex data should be "clustered," it is not surprising that clustering data automatically with a computer is also difficult. There are two basic techniques (top-down, or centroid methods, and bottom-up, or boundary methods); these are discussed in Chapter 8.

7.8 Making Feature Sets for Data Mining

Recall that *features* are just symbolic or numeric attributes of members of a population. A population of commercial customers will have members whose attributes are things like name, address, phone number, date of last purchase, size of last purchase, number of purchases last month, total revenue from purchases last year, credit score, etc. Features could be prepared that capture the information contained in these attributes, creating in a feature space that can be mined. If these attributes are put into a spreadsheet, they might look like this (see Figure 7.13).

Figure 7.13

NAME	ADDRESS	PHONE#	DOLP	SOLP	#PLM	TRPLY	CSCORE
AAA Inc.	1234 S. Main	000-123-4567	7/20/99	2.2	0	5.1	781
BBB Inc.	2345 N. Fitch	000-123-4568	8/23/00	1.4	3	17	440
CSI Inc.	1235 Evans Road	321-676-2923	8/14/00	7.7	26	82	1000
DDD Inc.	4567 W. Juniper	000-224-4569	8/30/00	8.1	1	0	140
EEE Inc.	2834 Williams Ave.	000-123-4570	7/12/00	5.5	0	23	898
FFF Inc.	23 Down Street	000-224-4571	6/1/00	6	0	62	n/a
GGG Inc.	3382 S. Main	000-123-4572	8/17/00	0.4	14	0	564
HHH Inc.	493 Avenue-A	000-123-4573	5/16/99	3.2	0	3.2	786
III Inc.	1 Mellow Drive	000-224-4574	1/17/97	4.9	0	0	798
JJJ Inc.	33485 Business Park	000-224-4575	11/6/98	0.1	0	0	977
LLL Inc.	2331 Access Air Ln.	000-224-4576	8/28/00	8.1	6	4	n/a
MMM Inc.	23 Sandy Way	000-123-4577	8/21/76	2.4	0	0	534
NNN Inc.	457 Exeter Road	000-224-4578	7/8/98	5.4	0	0	187
OOO Inc.	6 Olivia Run	000-224-4579	8/24/00	6.8	3	51	881
PPP Inc.	20 Ben Circle	000-224-4580	8/24/00	1.9	2	14	453
QQQ Inc.	3426 Queen Street	000-123-4581	7/24/00	2.7	4	71	685
RRR Inc.	16 Katherine Avenue	000-224-4582	8/19/00	7.8	6	12	467
SSS Inc.	414 Bag Street	000-123-4583	8/24/00	2.3	8	16	789
TTT Inc.	43913 Sixth Street	000-123-4584	8/24/00	1	19	2	620

Here, DOLP is data-of-last-purchase (MM/DD/YY), SOLP is size-of-last-purchase (thousands of dollars), PLM is number-of-purchases-last-month, TRPLY is total-revenue-from-purchases-last-year (thousands of dollars), and CSCORE is a credit score reported by a bureau (maximum score = 1000, minimum score = 0, higher score means better rating).

Some of these attributes are nominal: Name, address, and phone number are all basically names of things. Others are numeric.

Phone numbers are "codes" for addresses on a communication network. The codes have meaning, but the numeric values arbitrarily chosen to represent them do not. That's why it doesn't make sense to compute, for example, ratios or averages of phone numbers.

To convert these attributes to features, a method of representing each attribute symbolically or numerically must be formulated. This can be done manually by a domain expert, or automatically using software tools designed for this purpose. In some cases, the original values of the raw attributes can be used "as is." More often, some kind of *normalization* (transformation that controls the size and range of feature values) and *registration* (transformation that establishes a common reference value for the features) is required. For example, it might be desirable to transform the attributes so that the resulting features have a mean of 0 (registration), and don't fall outside, say, the range –5 to +5 (normalization). For these purposes, the z-score, as discussed previously, can be used to convert numeric attributes to numeric features.

In this example, the analyst decides to normalize two of the original attribute values by rescaling them. She divides TRPLY by 10, and CSCORE by 100, in both cases obtaining features roughly in the range 0 – 10. The ADDRESS field is deemed irrelevant for this stage of the analysis, and is removed. It can be restored during a later stage of analysis if desired.

7.8.1 Converting Nominal Data to Numeric: Numeric Coding

Nominal features like phone number (and ZIP code, gender, month-of-year, day-of-week, etc.) can be converted to numeric features by *numeric coding*, the assignment of a meaningful numeric value to a non-numeric symbol.

In Figure 7.14, the three-digit phone number exchanges have been converted from their nominal values in the following way: "123" becomes 1.00, "224" becomes 0.87, and "321" becomes 0.22. This odd looking scheme has been chosen because the analyst knows that customers in the 123 exchange have a relative shipping cost of 1.00, those in exchange 224 a correspondingly lower cost of 0.87, and those in 321 the lowest relative cost of 0.22. In this way, instead of excluding this nominal attribute from numeric analysis, the analyst has converted it to a numeric measure of an important component of business cost. Of course, there is nothing special about shipping cost; any business factor associated with exchange could have been used as the basis for coding.

7.8.2 Converting Numeric Data to Nominal: Symbolic Coding

One form of symbolic coding that has already been discussed is quantization, in which numeric data in ranges are represented by reconstruction values (e.g., "decades" of salary). More sophisticated symbolic encodings of data are possible. These encodings are usually carried out by the applications of heuristics based upon domain expertise.

In this example, the analyst knows that customers that make more than 10, but fewer than 20 purchases in a month, fall into a special cost category. Up until 10 purchases a month, certain fixed costs drive profit. Between 10 and 20 purchases a month, efficiency is maximized and other factors become important. Many customers that make more than 20 purchases in a month are part of a partnering or some other agreement, and yet another cost model applies.

To capture this important information in the most efficient possible way, the analyst assigns the code "A" to customers who made nine or fewer purchases last month, the code "B" to customers who made 10–19 purchases last month, and the code "C" to all others. This captures the useful business content of the PLM attribute in the smallest number of codes (see Figure 7.14).

Figure 7.14

NAME	PHONE#	SOLP	#PLM	TRPLY	CSCORE
AAA Inc.	1	2.2	A	0.51	7.81
BBB Inc.	1	1.4	A	1.7	4.4
CSI Inc.	0.22	7.7	C	8.2	10
DDD Inc.	0.87	8.1	A	0	1.4
EEE Inc.	1	5.5	A	2.3	8.98
FFF Inc.	0.87	6	A	6.2	n/a
GGG Inc.	1	0.4	B	0	5.64
HHH Inc.	1	3.2	A	0.32	7.86
III Inc.	0.87	4.9	A	0	7.98
JJJ Inc.	0.87	0.1	A	0	9.77
LLL Inc.	0.87	8.1	A	0.4	n/a
MMM Inc.	1	2.4	A	0	5.34
NNN Inc.	0.87	5.4	A	0	1.87
OOO Inc.	0.87	6.8	A	5.1	8.81
PPP Inc.	1	1.9	A	1.4	4.53
QQQ Inc.	1	2.7	A	7.1	6.85
RRR Inc.		7.8	A	1.2	4.67
SSS Inc.	1	2.3	A	1.6	7.89
TTT Inc.	1	1	B	0.2	6.2

7.8.3   Creating Ground-Truth

For many data mining problems, the discovery of information is most useful when it supports insight into some other factor: next quarter's revenues, next month's churn, fraud detection, tomorrow's stock market close, etc. In these cases, it is often useful to assign a ground-truth to the generated feature vectors. Ground-truth in this sense amounts to an assessment of the principal significance of this vector for some application. If this assignment of ground-truth is done in a consistent way, it can become the basis of predictive model.

Ground-truth can sometimes be naïvely assigned to members of a population in the obvious way: "this feature vector represents the attributes of a customer who was defrauding me, so ground-truth = fraud." In other cases, the assignment of ground-truth is much more difficult. For the example being discussed, a method of creating a ground-truth assignment directly from the features will now be illustrated. Keep in mind that this is an ad-hoc procedure—the user ultimately determines what is important.

For this example, the user has decided to assign "value" to customers according to the following rules.

If PLM is "A", then "Value" = CSCORE × {3 × TRPLY + (5 × SOLP)}/10000
If PLM is "B", then "Value" = CSCORE × {2 × TRPLY + (3 × SOLP)}/10000
If PLM is "C", then "Value" = CSCORE × {TRPLY + (2 × SOLP)}/10000

Figure 7.15 shows the computed "value" for each customer according to the three-part rule defined by the user. Further, the user has decided to designate customers as "good" if their "value" is greater than 1.0, and "bad" otherwise. These assignments give the ground-truth the user is interested in for this data mining experiment.

It doesn't really matter whether the definitions of "good" and "bad" in this example are meaningful to us, as long as they capture the user's conception of "good" and "bad." The point is that ground-truth for data mining applications can be a multifaceted ad hoc combination of whatever business factors are important to the user.

Figure 7.15

NAME	PHONE#	SOLP	#PLM	TRPLY	CSCORE	"value"	Ground-Truth
AAA Inc.	1	2.2	A	0.51	7.81	0.97859	BAD
BBB Inc.	1	1.4	A	1.7	4.4	0.5324	BAD
CSI Inc.	0.22	7.7	C	8.2	10	2.36	GOOD
DDD Inc.	0.87	8.1	A	0	1.4	0.567	BAD
EEE Inc.	1	5.5	A	2.3	8.98	3.08912	GOOD
FFF Inc.	0.87	6	A	6.2	n/a		BAD
GGG Inc.	1	0.4	B	0	5.64	0.06768	BAD
HHH Inc.	1	3.2	A	0.32	7.86	1.33306	GOOD
III Inc.	0.87	4.9	A	0	7.98	1.9551	GOOD
JJJ Inc.	0.87	0.1	A	0	9.77	0.04885	BAD
LLL Inc.	0.87	8.1	A	0.4	n/a		BAD
MMM Inc.	1	2.4	A	0	5.34	0.6408	BAD
NNN Inc.	0.87	5.4	A	0	1.87	0.5049	BAD
OOO Inc.	0.87	6.8	A	5.1	8.81	4.34333	GOOD
PPP Inc.	1	1.9	A	1.4	4.53	0.62061	BAD
QQQ Inc.	1	2.7	A	7.1	6.85	2.3838	GOOD
RRR Inc.		7.8	A	1.2	4.67	1.98942	GOOD
SSS Inc.	1	2.3	A	1.6	7.89	1.28607	GOOD
TTT Inc.	1	1	B	0.2	6.2	0.2108	BAD

7.9   Synthesis of Features

The term "synthesis of features" can refer to two distinct activities within the context of the development of enterprise models. Both are necessary to knowledge discovery and model development:

1.   The extraction of features from raw data (optimized for combination of salience and independence)

2.   The selection and use of disparate features (using features together in the "right mix")

In many ways, feature extraction is a data compression activity: A complex data set with many components, such as a customer record, is reduced to a smaller, simpler data set (perhaps a single number), in such a way that information necessary to support analysis is preserved. As a data compression activity, feature extraction is distinguished from conventional data compression in that recovery of the original record is not intended. *Feature extraction*, then, may be characterized as very lossy data compression that preserves, at a minimum, the ability to discern the ground-truth of the original.

Viewing feature extraction in this way allows the tools and formalism of information theory to be applied directly. Entropy, correlation, likelihood, and innovation can all be used to optimize the synthesis of feature sets with respect to suitably formulated objective functions. This optimization may be iterative (genetic algorithms), but need not be (e.g., associative feature selection; see below).

7.10 Good Features

Features are said to be "salient" when their values are correlated with ground-truth. In general, this correlation is non-linear and non-intuitive, accounting for the difficulty of effective manual feature selection. Because non-linear correlation may be modeled in many ways, "salience" is a relative term.

Features are said to be "independent" when they are uncorrelated with each other. "Uncorrelated" here is usually taken in a statistical sense, for example, the covariance matrix of the population of feature vectors is (essentially) diagonal.

In the ideal situation, salient, independent features are extracted inexpensively from the raw data. To mitigate the "curse of dimensionality," information-redundant (i.e., highly correlated) features are culled. Generally speaking, a "good" feature set is an inexpensive set of low dimension that supports effective classification.

There are two general approaches to enhancing feature sets. One is to improve the salience of the features themselves; the other is to improve the salience of the features as a group. A carefully selected mix of weak features may outperform a randomly selected mix of strong features, and is often less demanding of collection and processing power. Good feature sets are a "gestalt"—the whole is more than the sum of its parts.

A simple-minded example of the "gestalt" nature of features for data mining is helpful here. Suppose that a manufacturer is offering a free exclusive distributorship for a new product. It is known that there is unlimited demand at $100.00 per unit for this product. Certainly the information given here is essential to potential distributors, but is it enough? Of course not. Return-on-Investment (ROI) cannot be determined solely from revenue data.

Now, suppose instead that it is known only that there is unlimited demand for a new product at some unknown price, and that distributors' costs are known to be less than $50.00 per unit regardless of volume. Once again, this is essential information, but with only the cost side of the equation, ROI cannot be estimated.

In this example, both revenue and cost are essential components of understanding the problem. These features taken singly are weak. But, together, as a set of features, they provide the foundation for a good business decision. Here, as is often the case in building feature sets for data mining, 0% + 0% = 100 percent.

8

Data Mining Techniques: Knowledge Discovery

Data mining has two components: *Discovery*, during which meaningful patterns are detected in data and characterized formally, and *exploitation*, during which meaningful patterns are used to create useful applications (models). In this chapter, and the next, discovery of knowledge from data is addressed. Exploitation is the focus of Chapter 10.

The process of discovering knowledge in data is referred to as *Knowledge Discovery (KD)*. When the data is being worked from a conventional data store (as opposed to a data warehouse, online transaction system, etc.), the acronym KDD is sometimes used *(Knowledge Discovery in Databases)*.

Knowledge discovery can be performed manually (by a human) or automatically (by a machine). This treatment of knowledge discovery will address, at a conceptual level, the elements of both. In-depth treatments of knowledge discovery can be quite technical. One of the greatest intellectual achievements of the age (Godel Incompleteness Theorem, 1931) was made during a formal study of "knowledge." Interested readers are encouraged to consult the literature.

8.1   Knowledge Is Connections

It is difficult to give a universally applicable definition of the term "knowledge." The notion used here is that *knowledge* is a *sequential connection between facts*. For example, stock brokers "know" that when the Federal Reserve Board (Fed) lowers interest rates, the stock market goes up. This "knowledge" is a connection between a prior fact ("Fed lowers rates") and a subsequent fact ("market goes up"). The prior fact is called the *antecedent*, and the subsequent fact, the *consequent*.[1]

No assumption of an underlying cause-and-effect relationship between the antecedent and consequent should be made. Sequential connections of this sort are not statements about "causality." The only assertion being made is that these facts are regularly observed together in this sequence.

Neither is it required that the connections constituting knowledge be categorical. Sometimes the Fed lowers interest rates, and the market falls. Connections can have a probability associated with them, and be partial and tentative. Bayesian analysis and fuzzy logic are two (related) formalisms for using such "uncertain" knowledge. By incorporating a "state variable," these ideas can be further generalized to a universal theory of computing ("Turing Machines"). This extension isn't needed for this treatment.

Given all this, several things are clear.

1.   To have knowledge, there must be facts. Knowledge is impossible without facts.

2.   But, knowledge and facts are not the same thing. Knowledge is a *connection* between antecedent facts and consequent facts. It is not the facts themselves.

3.   Data is not knowledge. (The fictional idea of a computer becoming intelligent because it accumulates a sufficient mass of data is absurd.)[2]

4.   Most importantly, knowledge, as sequential connections between facts, can be stored in a computer. This "machine knowledge" may take the form of "if-then-else-rules" (e.g., in a knowledge-based expert system (KBES)), or it might consist of a complex mathematical transformation (e.g., as a neural network). The *form* of machine knowledge varies according to implementation; the *essence* of machine

---

1.   The term "meta data" is a general term meaning roughly "data about data." Knowledge as defined here is a type of meta data. We have not used this term because in data mining parlance, "meta data" has a restricted meaning, applying to what data is represented within a database, mart, or warehouse, and has nothing to do with "knowledge."

2.   Data isn't a "fact," either, properly speaking. A *fact* is a connection between data: "The temperature is 67" is a fact, connecting the alphanumeric datum "temperature" to the numeric datum "67." But we don't need to go this far into semantics.

knowledge is the creation of sequential connections between facts.

To see what machine knowledge might look like, consider the problem of determining whether a potential credit customer is a "desirable" customer based upon two pieces of data: their total indebtedness, and their average monthly credit card expenditures. The indebtedness will be called X, and the monthly expenditures, Y.

Suppose that analysis of many customers' credit histories shows that "desirable" customers have some debt (indicating a willingness to spend) but not too much (indicating solvency); and they incur regular monthly expenditures (so will probably buy from us), but not too much (indicating stability). This collection of realizations is a piece of knowledge that can be stated like this:

"If a customer's total indebtedness is between two specified values, and his or her average monthly expenditures are between two specified values, then he or she is a 'desirable' customer. Otherwise, he or she is not."

Let X(C) and Y(C) be indebtedness and expenditures of customer C, respectively. Once the low and high indebtedness values are determined (X1 and X2), and the low and high expenditure values are determined (Y1 and Y2), this piece of knowledge can be stated in the following "computer friendly" form (BASIC computer language):

```
IF (X(C)>X1 AND X(C) <X2) AND (Y(C)>Y1 AND Y(C)<Y2) THEN
DESIRABLE=TRUE
ELSE
DESIRABLE=FALSE
END IF
```

This is an "IF-THEN-ELSE" rule. The origin of the term should be clear. In this piece of knowledge, the antecedent facts are "indebtedness and expenditure fall into certain ranges of values," and the consequent facts are "the customer is desirable" and "the customer is not desirable," depending upon whether the antecedents are true or not.

Better still, a picture can be drawn in the feature space that shows the feature vectors selected as "desirable" by this piece of knowledge. The antecedent facts mark out the boundary of the region containing desirable customers. Because of the form of the antecedent, this region will be a rectangle (see Figure 8.1).

Figure 8.1

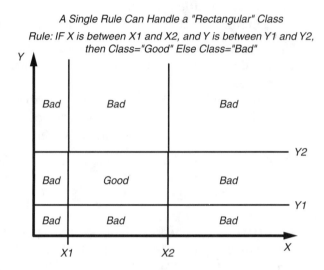

A Single Rule Can Handle a "Rectangular" Class
Rule: IF X is between X1 and X2, and Y is between Y1 and Y2,
then Class="Good" Else Class="Bad"

This is all pretty esoteric, but it has led us to a working definition of knowledge that can be stated in English, can be represented visually, and that makes sense in the context of computer science. Perhaps more importantly, the discovery of this kind of knowledge can be automated, as will be seen later in this chapter.

8.2   Taxonomy of Knowledge Discovery Techniques

A simple taxonomy of KD techniques might look like the following:

Knowledge Discovery Techniques

  —Manual Discovery Techniques

  —OLAP

  — Knowledge Engineering

  —Visualization

  —Automated Discovery Techniques

—Auto-clustering

—Link analysis

—Regression (white box)

—Rule Induction

For reasons of space and pedagogy, the discussion will be limited to four fundamental techniques, in the following order: Auto-clustering, link analysis, visualization, and rule induction. Knowledge discovery using regression is so intimately related to regression modeling that the discussion of regression will be deferred until Chapter 9.

8.3   Cluster Analysis and Auto-Clustering

In order to begin looking for patterns in data, we must have some meaningful definition of what a "pattern" is. Patterns might be defined as regularities in data. But data that is completely regular provides no useful information. It's the variation in data that gives us information that can be applied. When we mine business data, we are looking for patterns that tell us something about behaviors. These behaviors may be our own, they may be those of our customers, or they may be those of our suppliers. Quite frankly, data mining would be a waste of time if data were completely regular. It's the irregularities, the "surprises," that are the jewels.

For numeric data, the most useful and interesting irregularity is the "cluster." In data mining parlance, a cluster is a "coherent aggregation of data points." A good analogy is the small cliques of persons that form at cocktail parties. These "clusters" are groups of people engaged in a common behavior. In enterprise data, clusters are significant because they represent entities with similar characteristics. Customers who buy the same products, suppliers who have similar business cycles, market regularities of various sorts; all of these can show up as clusters in enterprise data.

In textbook examples, clusters are usually depicted as nice, round, normally distributed aggregations of non-overlapping point sets. In the real world, of course, clusters are rarely so. They are long thin strands of data points, or ragged blobs having various shapes and sizes. Often, data sets consist of a mixture of clusters of various sorts. They frequently overlap in complex ways, making it difficult to determine where one cluster ends and another begins.

"Coherence" means that the points within a cluster "hold together" in some intuitive sense that we hope to make precise mathematically. The term "aggregation" is used as a neutral word for the mathematical term "set."

The mathematical methods developed for analyzing these coherent aggregations are referred to under the general term of "cluster analysis." Most modern techniques are extensions of methods developed as part of mathematical statistics, though some have arisen out of data management techniques developed by computer scientists.

Parametric statistics, such as mean and standard deviation, can also be used to describe clusters. Nonparametric statistics use more arcane terms and methods. Nonparametric statistics are particularly useful when the number of data points in the population is small.

For both types of techniques, the analyst builds a model of the data. The model is usually mathematical, and might be represented as a graph, table, or drawing. A model is an explanation of the data. If the model is good, it might be capable of supporting prediction about future data points. Such predictive models are regarded by some as the "Holy Grail" of data mining.

Cluster analysis can provide a foundation for predictive modeling. For example, to develop a model to identify clients likely to commit fraud, common indicators or information patterns among separate fraudulent and honest customer clusters would be sought out. Once these aggregations are located and formally delineated, data on prospective clients can be examined to identify in which cluster they are likely for "membership."

The two mathematical approaches to modeling clusters in data sets are boundary modeling and centroid modeling. In boundary modeling, clusters are distinguished by specifying the boundaries between them. In centroid modeling, clusters are distinguished by specifying their locations and extents. Boundary modeling is sometimes referred to as "bottom-up" modeling, because boundaries are determined by looking at the locations of individual points rather than the population as a whole. Centroid modeling is sometimes referred to as "top-down" modeling, because locations and extents are determined by the distribution of the points as a whole.

Clustering that is performed automatically by computer software is called auto-clustering. Although humans are adept at visually detecting clusters in data, they are at the same time severely limited due to their subjectivity, and lack of ability when data exceeds three dimensions. Auto-clustering algorithms executing on computing machinery have neither of these limitations.

The purpose of auto-clustering is to identify collections of feature vectors that, as a group, have similar properties. These clusters of feature vectors presumably represent sets of similar individuals. If we can identify significant properties of one individual in a cluster, there is a possibility that these properties will hold for other members of the cluster. This is a tantalizing prospect considering that auto-clustering might be used to identify "high interest" subpopulations: high-value customers, customers at risk of churn, instances of fraud, and so on.

Another application of cluster analysis is the evaluation of feature sets themselves. Clusters exist in feature space when the feature data leads to natural grouping of the data. If this natural grouping corresponds to groupings of interest, such as ground-truth classes for a classification problem, then efforts to construct a predictive model will almost certainly meet with success. If however, no natural clustering occurs in feature space, or the clusters that exist do not correspond to subpopulations of interest, the construction of an effective predictive model will be difficult, if not impossible. When the natural clustering of feature vectors in feature space appears unrelated to the ground-truth clusters imposed by the problem to be solved, it may very well be that the features selected do not support the development of the predictive model sought.

The power of a regression technique required to produce an effective predictive model is directly related to how closely the natural clustering of the feature data matches the defined ground-truth. When the natural clustering is a close approximation of the ground-truth clusters, even a weak predictive model can be effective. This rarely happens in real-world situations, and never happens for hard problems, because it's this clustering inconsistency that makes hard problems hard. Problems that have good clustering in feature space can often be solved by a database lookup, or some other elementary technique. Sophisticated predictive modeling is never applied to problems like this; it's overkill.

Even when the natural clustering of the data in feature space is inconsistent with the defined ground-truth classes, it may still be possible to construct an effective predictive model, provided a sufficiently sophisticated technique is used. This is where advanced regression models such as neural networks, adaptive logic networks, radial basis functions, and the like, come in. The worst-case scenario occurs when there is no clustering at all: All the feature vectors reside in a single, uniform, spherical ball, totally nondescript and lacking definition. A set of features giving rise to one of these formless expressions of the problem has provided no information to support model development.

Auto-clustering can be used as a rule induction technique. The boundary values in each dimension for high-interest clusters (fraud, churn, etc.) can be stored, and applied in a rule to data collected in the future to determine whether it contains points in this high-interest cluster.

Auto-clustering is an excellent technique for detecting outliers. Data points that have been corrupted during collection or pre-processing will probably not fall into natural clusters, making suspicious vectors easy to identify. Occasionally, entire clusters of outliers will be discovered, suggesting the existence of systematic error in data collection or pre-processing. These outliers can then either be corrected or removed from the population before continuing the analysis.

Auto-clustering can be a computationally intensive technique, but is not as demanding as many other correlation methods. Therefore, it is a natural first technique to apply to a new data set. The data miner is looking for patterns, and so hopes to see "structuring" in the data. This structuring need not be consistent with the definition of the ground-truth classes initially. It is often possible to apply feature enhancement techniques (selection, registration, normalization, etc.) to make natural clustering more consistent with the defined problem, if there is structure there initially.

Here "consistency" with ground-truth clustering is defined in terms of cluster homogeneity. First, the data is auto-clustered. Then, within each cluster, the class homogeneity is determined: Do most of the points in each auto-cluster aggregation have the same ground-truth? This is an excellent test to use for evaluating a feature set for likely success on a classification problem. Suppose a data set was auto-clustered into four clusters, with the following results:

Cluster 1:   21 vectors with ground-truth class 1

2 vectors with ground-truth class 2

0 vectors with ground-truth class 3

Cluster 2:   4 vectors with ground-truth class 1

6 vectors with ground-truth class 2

50 vectors with ground-truth class 3

Cluster 3:   4 vectors with ground-truth class 1

2 vectors with ground-truth class 2

3 vectors with ground-truth class 3

Cluster 4:   4 vectors with ground-truth class 1

71 vectors with ground-truth class 2

5 vectors with ground-truth class 3

The majority class (class with the most members) in cluster 1 is class 1, with 21 vectors. Class 1 has a total of 23 vectors, so its *homogeneity*, the size of the majority population divided by the total population, is $21 \div 23 = 91.3$ percent.

The majority class in cluster 2 is class 3, with 50 vectors. Class 2 has a total of 60 vectors, so its homogeneity is $50 \div 60 = 83.3$ percent.

The majority class in cluster 3 is class 1; cluster 3 has a homogeneity of $4 \div 9 = 44.4$ percent.

The majority class in cluster 4 is class 2; cluster 4 has a homogeneity of $71 \div 80 = 88.8$ percent.

An overall score, which we call the *disambiguity*, can be assigned to this clustering of the data by computing the geometric mean of the cluster homogeneities (the geometric mean of N values is the nth root of their product):

$$(0.913 \times 0.833 \times 0.444 \times 0.888)^{1/4} = 0.740 = 74 \text{ percent}$$

Notice that the disambiguity will be 1 if, and only if, the auto-clustering gives clusters that are "pure." They contain vectors of only a single ground-truth class. As long as none of the clusters are empty, the disambiguity will be greater than zero. Modeling problems with disambiguity close to one are easy; those with disambiguity close to zero are hard.

A useful side-effect of auto-clustering is that it often tells us not only how hard a classification problem might be, but which feature vectors constitute that hard part. In the example above, the auto-clustering did well everywhere except cluster 3, which had a homogeneity of only 44 percent. It is the feature vectors that are close to those in cluster 3 that will be difficult to classify.

Finally, auto-clustering can be used to build classifiers. If auto-clustering produces a clustering of the data with a relatively high disambiguity, future data points can be classified by determining which cluster they fall into, and assigning them the ground-truth of that cluster's majority class. The homogeneity of the cluster can be used as the "confidence factor" for this classification.

8.4   Link Analysis

Link analysis is a powerful and important technique for discovering information in large, complex data sets. *Link analysis* is a data mining strategy for identifying "events" which occur together. An "event" in this sense can be any outcome the analyst might care to define: customer attrition, commission of fraud, occurrence of a certain kind of sale/purchase, a critical price reaching a threshold value, etc. The goal of link analysis is usually to find common indicators of an event so that the corresponding opportunity can be exploited.

There are many algorithms for performing link analysis; the technique of choice depends upon the type of data being mined, and the intended goal. There are three general types of link analysis that arise frequently in CRM applications:

- *Associations* are groups of "events" that regularly occur together. For example, if the goal is to determine ways to enhance sales of product A, it might be important to discover that buyers of product A are usually homeowners. Associations are the simplest link relationships, and the easiest to discover. They are often used to suggest hypotheses for data mining: "Which demographic types of customers are most likely to return products?"

- *Sequential Patterns* are associations that vary in consistent ways. The change might be over time, and it might not (e.g., buyers of product A who also bought product B will often buy product C). Sequential patterns that occur reliably can be used to formulate heuristics (rules of thumb): "We should pitch product C to customers who buy both products A and B."

- *Sequential Time Patterns* are sequential patterns whose elements occur in a regular time order. For example, a sequential time pattern exists when the occurrence of certain events regularly precedes another in time: "Buyers who file two complaints in a quarter have a 75 percent chance of closing their account within the next year." Sequential time patterns can be used to build predictive models: "Given the outstanding bids and current market, what is the likelihood that next quarter's revenues will fall below or exceed $3 million?"

8.4.1 Link Analysis Algorithms

The simplest form of link analysis is called stratification (in marketing talk, "segmentation"). Stratification divides the population into "strata" for some analytic purpose, in this case, to answer a question.

Stratification can be used to perform link analysis by retrieving records from the data store *using the hypothesized links as the retrieval keys*. For example, suppose that an analyst suspects that high-income clients are more likely than low-income clients to buy a certain product. This hypothesis may be tested by retrieving from the data store four lists:

1. High-income clients who bought the product

2. All high-income clients, whether they bought the product or not

3. Low-income clients who bought the product

4. Low-income clients, whether they bought the product or not

The number of clients in list 1 divided by the number of clients in list 2 is an empirical prior probability that a high-income client will buy the product. The number of clients in list 3 divided by the number of clients in list 4 is an empirical prior probability that a low-income client will buy the product. Comparison of these two probabilities gives insight into the relative likelihood of sale vis-a-vis income level.

This technique has the obvious disadvantages of requiring what might be an expensive retrieval, and requiring the analyst to suspect the presence of the link.[3]

A more sophisticated form of link analysis can be applied when the data are numeric. The correlation coefficient of all possible pairs of data items can be computed (assuming that sufficient compute power is available) and placed into a matrix for manual or automatic analysis. If the values of two factors are highly correlated, an exploitable association may exist. This technique has the advantage that it *quantifies* the strength of the association (correlation coefficients close to zero show weak association), and does not require the analyst to guess which data items might be linked. The computation of the correlation coefficient is straightforward, and can be found in any elementary statistics text. The amount of computation required is proportional to the square of the number of data fields. This could be prohibitive if the data are high-dimensional, or consist of many records. Applying this technique to triples, 4-tuples, etc., is problematic, due to the amount of computation required. Most folks stop with pairs of factors.

A correlation coefficient for non-numeric data, the Spearman Rank Correlation Coefficient, is sometimes useful for detecting the existence of links between data items. For the computation of this statistic, it is required that the data be ranked in some kind of order, a procedure that is often (though not always) meaningful for nominal data. Once again, most elementary statistics texts will illustrate the procedure.

More advanced techniques for performing link analysis usually involve dividing the feature space into "bins," and counting the number of feature vectors that end up in each bin. Vectors that end up in the same bin possess *de facto* links: When feature 1 was "high-income," feature 2 was "bought product C." The definition of the bin amounts to a description of the link among the feature vectors it contains. This amounts to an "all-ways stratification" of the population, and can be very time-consuming.

Probably the most frequently sought links are sequential time links. The reason is obvious. If it is discovered that events A, B, and C

---

3.   This example is somewhat simple-minded. There could be other factors at work. Perhaps the product was offered more frequently to low-income clients than high-income clients. Caution must always be used in interpreting unstandardized empirical probabilities.

are happening in order, it almost guarantees that event D will happen next. A predictive rule for the occurrence of D has been found. Many predictive models of this sort exist, and a multitude of applications. The underlying formalisms for these models use a variety of techniques, including conventional regression, Kalman filtering, stochastic models, and neural networks. See Chapter 22 for an example of a time-series model that predicts the demand for electrical power.

8.5   Visualization

Data visualization is far more than depiction of data in interesting plots. The goal of visualization is to help the analyst gain intuition about the data being observed. Therefore, visualization applications frequently assist the analyst in selecting display formats, viewer perspectives, and data representation schemas that foster deep intuitive understanding.

Several conventional techniques for visualization of information include: scatter-plots of features by pairs, histograms, relationship trees, bar charts, pie charts, tables, and other familiar techniques for depicting relationships among data. Modern visualization tools do much more. They might appear to be the conventional representations at first glance, but often support such advanced features as:

- Drill-down

- Hyper-links to related data sources

- Multiple simultaneous data views

- Roam/pan/zoom

- Select/count/analyze objects in display

- Dynamic/active views (e.g., Java applets)

- Using animation to depict a sequence or process

- Creative use of color

- Morphing

- Use of glyphs (icons indicating additional information about displayed objects)

Plenty more could be said about visualization applications currently in use; rather than go into an extended survey of visualization forms, though, we turn our attention to how visualization is used as a manual knowledge discovery technique. For this we only need look at a couple of visualization techniques, since the concepts underlying visual knowledge discovery are largely independent of the visualization modality.

8.5.1 Applications of Visualization for Data Mining

The most effective pattern recognition equipment known to man is "grayware"—the stuff between your ears. Manual knowledge discovery is facilitated when domain data are presented in a form that allows the human mind to interact with them at an intuitive level. Visual data presentation provides a high-bandwidth, naturally intuitive gate to the human mind.

Visualization offers capabilities unique among data mining techniques. It also has unique weaknesses, which are in many ways complementary to its strengths. As with other data mining techniques, visualization can give deep insight and it can mislead.

A distinction is made here between two kinds of visualization, for which we coin the terms "Conventional Visualization," and "Spatial Visualization." Each has its place in the data mining tool box. Both of these techniques have been around for a long time, but conventional visualization longer, so it is better developed. Business decision makers rarely use spatial visualization of multi-dimensional data, but data mining analysts do.

By *Conventional Visualization* we mean graphs and charts that depict information *about* a population, not population data itself. For example, a pie chart showing the relative proportions of sub-populations is a visual depiction of a population statistic, not a depiction of the population. Conventional visualization is really a visual depiction of certain types of meta data, not the data itself. Conventional visualization, therefore, involves computation of descriptive statistics such as counts, frequencies, ranges, proportions, moments, and so on, which are the values actually displayed.

By *Spatial Visualization* we mean plots that depict actual members of the population in their feature space. For example, a graph of employees as income-age pairs in the plane is a visual depiction of the income and age data itself. There is no computation of descriptive statistics. This depiction preserves the geometric relationships among the data (orientation, extent, density, clustering, etc.), which are the "spatial" characteristics of the population or sample being visualized. Spatial visualization leaves reduction of the data entirely up to the viewer.

Both categories of visualization are important and useful. Each serves a different purpose. Conventional visualization provides a summary description of a population in visual form. Spatial visualization provides an uninterpreted geometric depiction of a population in visual form. Knowledge discovery is facilitated by both.

8.5.2 Strengths of Visualization

1. Visualization allows the analyst to develop "intuition" about a population. When an analyst is able to see data, she develops an intuitive understanding of it that can be obtained in no other way.

2. Visualization can lead to the direct discovery of "rules." When the closing value of the stock market is plotted on one axis, and the meeting calendar of the Federal Reserve Board on another, rules relating these two sequences of events are easily seen and extracted.

3. Visualization is the quickest way to tell whether a classification problem is "easy" or "hard." For example, in some feature space, plot high-value accounts as red dots, and low-value accounts as blue dots. If clearly separated "clusters" of red and blue dots are seen, the problem of building a system to tell high-value accounts from low-value will be easy. If, on the other hand, the plot is a swirl of red and blue dots jumbled together, the classification problem in this feature space will be hard. In this way, visualization can be used to assess the salience of features, either individually, or in groups.

4. Visualization is an effective way to scan large amounts of data for "significant differences" between classes. If the red and blue dots above are well separated along some axis, this will be visually apparent. The feature represented by that axis, then, accounts for some of the difference between the two classes.

5. Visualization is a good technique for detecting poorly conditioned data. When data is plotted, errors in data preparation often show up as unexpected irregularities in the visual pattern of the data.

6. Visualization is a good technique for selecting a data model. For example, data that is normally distributed will have a characteristic shape. Visual analysis lets the analyst "see" which of several models might be most reasonable for a population being studied.

7. Visualization is a good technique for spotting outliers and missing data. When data is visualized, outliers (data not conforming to the general pattern of the population) are usually easy to pick out. Missing records may show up as "holes" in a pattern, and missing fields within a record often break patterns in easily detectable ways.

8. Visualization is a good technique for detecting quantization/coding error. Data that has been incorrectly quantized or coded often breaks visual patterns in the data.

These strengths of visualization are generally present no matter what visualization method is used. The power of visualization to tell the analyst that something "isn't quite right" makes visualization particularly useful during the early stages of a data mining project, where data is usually not well understood, and data cleansing is not complete.

8.5.3 Limitations of Visualization for Data Mining

Most visualization techniques support display of only a few dimensions at a time. This is a serious shortcoming for data mining applications, which regularly deal with hundreds or thousands of dimensions.

N-dimensional visualization allows analysts to display geometrically faithful depictions of data in more than 3 dimensions on a single plot. This modality has the advantage that it preserves intuitive spatial relationships among the data.

Figure 8.2 is a depiction of an 8-dimensional population of data for a customer "churn" problem. Each point is a single customer, represented by 8-feature values. The thick, dark lines are coordinate axes. (Five are visible, the other three are roughly along the viewers line of sight, and cannot be seen.)

In Figure 8.2, there is obvious "structuring" of the data. Far from being random, it can be immediately seen that there are patterns of various scales. In gross terms, the population from this vantage point shows two parts: a "lower" part, which is roughly confined to a single "sheet"; and an "upper" part having many threadlike subpopulations, and trailing off to the upper right of the display.

Figure 8.2

The planar and threadlike patterns seen in the visualization suggest that there are linear relationships among some of the eight features, a phenomenon called multicollinearity. The presence of these patterns indicates that special conditioning of the data may be required if "explanatory models" like logistic regression are used for data analysis.

The even spacing seen between the threads suggests the presence of quantization, which occurs when a feature(s) assumes discrete values rather than a continuous range of values. Quantization patterns are usually not significant, because they arise from the way the data has been represented, rather than from relationships among the data.

When the data points are tagged by color to indicate their ground-truth class, much can be learned from a spatial visualization. If the "lower" part of the data consists mostly of a single class, it will appear as a collection of points having the same color; a rule has been discovered: "Customers in the "lower" part are in class so-and-so."

The figure here is black and white; on the display screen, tagging the points with color shows that the different classes of customers ("churn" vs. "non-churn") are well mingled. Said differently, "churners" look a lot like "non-churners" in this feature space. This is a strong indication that building a churn-predictor using the 8-features from which this display was constructed will be difficult.

Another powerful visualization method for high-dimensional populations was invented in the 1970s by Alfred Inselberg. Inselberg's *parallel coordinate* plot allows the display of data in any (finite) number of dimensions. While Inselberg plots are not as intuitive as conventional spatial methods, they provide a powerful way of comparing subpopulations in high-dimensional space.

To see how parallel coordinate plots represent data, consider Figure 8.3 below. In this figure is plotted the same 8-dimensional population shown in the N-dimensional display of the previous figure. The figure below contains two Inselberg plots: The top one depicts "stable" customers, and the bottom "likely-to-churn" customers:

Figure 8.3

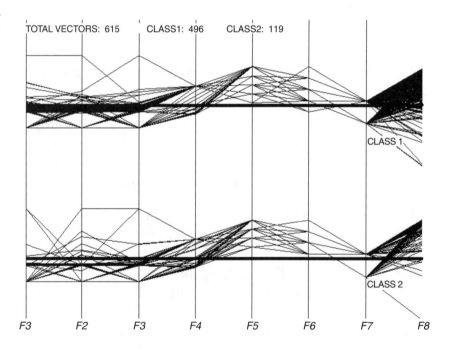

TOTAL VECTORS: 615   CLASS1: 496   CLASS2: 119

CLASS 1

CLASS 2

F3   F2   F3   F4   F5   F6   F7   F8

The Inselberg plot is called a "parallel coordinate" plot because the components of the vector are plotted on a set of parallel vertical axes. To plot an ordered 8-tuple, each feature value is plotted on its corresponding vertical axis; these points are then connected from left to right to form a path.

For example, to plot the feature vector (4,3,1,-2,0,4,2), the feature 1 value ("4") is plotted on the F1 axis, the feature 2 value ("3") is plotted on the F2 axis, and so on. These plotted feature values are then connected to form a piecewise-linear trace across the display. In this way, a point in a high-dimensional space is represented on a single display as a "zig-zag" path.

Quantization can be seen in the regular spacing of values apparent in several of the features, notably F5, F6, and F7. Multicollinearity is difficult to see on an Inselberg plot.

Intuition for interpreting Inselberg plots comes with practice. Little intuition, though, is needed to use these plots to compare one population with another. Even the inexperienced eye can see some differences between the "non-churners" (top plot) and the "churners" (bottom plot) as two groups of "squigglies." For example, stable customers have more variability in features 1, 2, and 3, than churners, as indicated by the thicker dark band in these features. Notice also that churners assume only 4 different values in feature F5, while stable customers assume 5. A similar difference exists for F6.

The principal strength of visualization is in quickly providing intuitive insight into the difficulty of a problem and the quality of the selected features.

Selecting the proper vantage point from which to view data can be difficult. This is not a problem for conventional visualization, which produces basically flat depiction intended to be viewed from a single vantage point. Spatial visualization, however, particularly in many dimensions, requires that a vantage point be chosen. The vantage point determines which "view" of the data will be presented. Perspective views have the additional problem of selecting a scale for the plot. Consider Figure 8.4.

How many differently shaped objects are depicted in Figure 8.4?

Figure 8.4

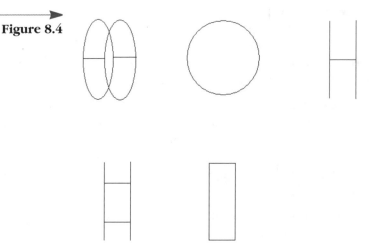

Just one. The upper left-hand object consists of a wire frame that is two circles of the same size connected at opposite edges by two straight segments. By viewing this object from various vantage points, it can appear as any of the shapes in the figure.

Now, suppose that in feature space, your data has the shape of this object. As the manager of Data Analytics, you receive reports from three data mining initiatives, A, B, and C, which are looking at this data. The analyst from initiative A comes to you and tells you that "visualization has shown that the data form a circle." The analyst from initiative B comes to you and tells you that "visualization has shown that the data form an oblong rectangle." And, initiative C reports that "visualization has shown that the data form the letter "H." Each analyst supports his conclusion with an appropriate screen dump. They are all right—and all wrong. No great imagination is required to appreciate the complexities that arise when this limitation is pushed from 3 dimensions to 300. Let the visualizer beware!

As seen above, inferred visual patterns can be misleading. But the facts are worse than might be supposed. One way that high-dimensional data are often visualized is as a collection of pairs of two-dimensional "thumbnail" plots. A 10-dimensional space, for example, gives rise to 45 pair-wise plots, each showing a different pair of dimensions plotted against each other. It is a fact well-known to statisticians that data can be correlated in pairs of dimensions, and not correlated in all dimensions. In other words, depictions of high-dimensional data as collections of pair-wise plots can show "patterns" that don't really exist, and completely miss patterns that do. Let the visualizer beware!

Visualization tools are typically very compute-intensive. Graphics computing is still both I/O (input/output) and compute bound.

The strengths and weaknesses described above give ample reason to use visualization for manual data mining—with caution. As a fast, general technique that provides lots of insight, it is hard to beat. Its limitations, however, relegate it largely to the early stages of analysis, as a general, "jump-start" method for assessing data in gross, general terms.

9

Data Mining Techniques: More Knowledge Discovery

One of the hallmarks of data mining technology is the automated discovery of knowledge from data. Chapter 8 addressed "clustering" methods used for this purpose. These methods have been around for over 30 years. In this chapter, we move into the present with a discussion of the underlying concepts of modern rule-induction methods for automated knowledge discovery.

9.1   Rule Induction and Decision Trees

In what follows, much of the mystery of *rule induction* ("creating rules directly from data without human assistance") will be removed. When you see the nature of the approach, you'll probably think, "Of course! It's obvious!" With a little imagination, you might even create some rule-induction strategies of your own.

There was a time when computers were *only* programmed. A human being that understood how to solve a particular problem would create a step-by-step procedure *(program)* for solving it. When this procedure was slavishly followed by a piece of electronic circuitry, the same solution was produced—as long as nothing unexpected was encountered. This sort of "procedural cognition" has offloaded a lot of work once done by humans, but tends to be very narrow. It isn't really what anyone would want to call "intelligence."

This approach worked well until there arose the need to automate solutions to problems that no human being understood, or that couldn't be reduced to hard-coded sequences of rote operations.

Suppose, though, that certain instances of the very problem of *learning* itself could be automated. Were this the case, perhaps machines could be programmed to *learn* solutions to problems no human being understands or can program.

There probably isn't any better way to gain an understanding of rule-induction than to see it happen, step-by-step, before your very eyes. In this section, a simple example of machine learning will be worked through in detail. The simplicity of the example is maintained for the purposes of illustration only; the machine learning technique employed is directly applicable to demanding "big data" problems in high-dimensional space. Using this understanding as a starting point, it will be possible later (Chapter 10) to provide a concise treatment of neural networks, expert systems, and other cognitive applications.

The reader should be warned that this section of the book, and the later discussion of predictive modeling in Chapter 10, are immensely provocative. They are so because they present the essence of the two crowning practical achievements of 60 years of cognitive research: *automatic knowledge discovery* and *automatic knowledge application.*

Monte has a clear recollection of the moment that this essence was revealed to him (oddly enough, it occurred as part of a few passing remarks from a technical conversation that he overheard while otherwise engaged). He was thunderstruck; it literally changed his life. Of course, most people don't have such a reaction. But many are intrigued, and most pleasantly surprised.

Such has been a recurring experience along these lines, as one who often gives technical briefings on machine intelligence. The seminal instance occurred in England about 15 years ago. After completing a briefing on certain aspects of the theory and application of computer intelligence; the audience had mostly gone, and as he was collecting his materials, Monte was approached by a lingering attendee. He explained that he had fully understood the presentation, but wanted to know "what was really going on" when intelligent programs were in operation, independent of human control.

"So, you want to know the secret?" Monte said, almost in a whisper. The attendee leaned forward and said, "Yes!"

With narrowed eyes, Monte laid bare the truth. "This is it. If you take the most astounding application in artificial intelligence in the world today, and open the lid of the computer, what you'll see is zeros and ones."

There isn't any magic, and the basic ideas are straightforward. Not much software is needed, not much memory, disc space, or computer power. Most machine learning techniques, from low-end to world-class are, at least conceptually, variations on a few simple themes.

But the fact that machine learning is *comprehensible* does not mean that it is easy. Performing optimized rule induction in big data sets can be very hard, and take a lot of time. There are usually some false starts as patterns begin to be revealed and evaluated, and then some frustration after the "low hanging fruit" is exhausted. The law of diminishing returns applies, and should be considered in any estimate of the Return-on-Investment (ROI) for a data mining project.

9.1.1 Some Rule-Induction Examples

The goal of rule induction is the generation of rules directly from data without human assistance. Rules express spatial patterns in feature space as *symbolic patterns* that humans and machines can use. Useful rules will be meaningful for some specified purpose. For this example, rules will be induced that classify data into one of two groups, one type will be represented by boxes, the other by circles (Figure 9.1).

The best way to gain an understanding of rule induction is through a simple, detailed example. The simplicity of the example is maintained for the purposes of illustration only; the machine learning technique employed is directly applicable to demanding problems with loads of data in high-dimensional space. The understanding gained through this example will serve as a starting point for later concise treatments of neural approaches.

The following extended discussion addresses rule induction in several different populations. The first refers to an artificial population **P**, created for the purposes of illustration.

Each member of **P** has three attributes. The first, which we'll call the "class," unambiguously assumes one of two values. For example, class might be gender, assuming one of the two values "male/female." Problems for which exactly one of two mutually exclusive outcomes will occur are called *binary decision problems*.

The second and third attributes are continuous, bounded numeric values. For example, these two attributes might be "age in years" and "income in dollars."

Considering all three attributes, the data being mined could, for example, be related to the question of buying or selling (class) publicly traded stocks based upon their current bid price (attribute 1) and current asking price (attribute 2). Or, determining whether a client will churn or not (class) given the amount of a price increase (attribute 1) and their sales volume (attribute 2).

An important transition is about to be made, and it shouldn't be missed. The formalism of feature space is about to be used to represent our binary decision problem in two numeric factors as a collection of points in the plane. In the terms of material presented in Chapter 7, the problem is being put into feature space.

Rather than pick specific classes and attributes (which choices might cloud the discussion), the two classes will just be represented as abstract shapes: Members in class one are "squares," and members in class two are "circles." Further, the two numeric attributes will just be called "X" and "Y," respectively. These will be normalized so that they range in value from zero to one, inclusive. These "X Y pairs" can be regarded as coordinates in the plane, $\mathbf{R}^2$.

This yields a population $\mathbf{P}$ consisting of data represented by circles and squares distributed in a 2-dimensional grid. Figure 9.1 depicts the population $\mathbf{P}$ in exactly this way. All of the extraneous factors have been removed; the problem of determining the precise relationship between members of the population has been reduced to pure geometry.

Figure 9.1

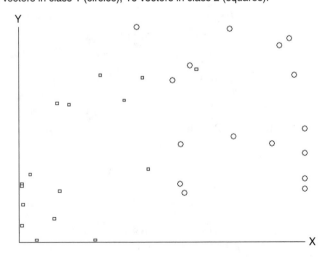

16 vectors in class 1 (circles), 16 vectors in class 2 (squares).

The population **P** consists of 32 members, evenly divided among circles and squares. Consideration of the plot indicates that in general, squares tend to have smaller X values, and smaller Y values than circles. But this is not strictly true; there are squares with larger X and Y values than some circles. Notice that P is *unambiguous*: There are no points in feature space occupied vectors of different classes. In real-world applications, ambiguity is often a problem.

9.1.2   A Rule-Induction Algorithm

Rule-induction algorithms function by determining decision surfaces of a specified type that correctly classify as much of the given data as possible. Most rule-induction algorithms use decision surfaces that are combinations of points, lines, planes, and hyper-planes. The algorithm described here, which we call **M**, uses lines during a first pass, then, during a second pass, converts these to boxes. The boxes are then expressed as familiar "IF-THEN" rules.

The algorithm proceeds by cycling through a sequence of steps. During each pass through the cycle, a portion of the population is "understood" by the inducer, and removed from further consideration. This process is repeated until every feature vector has been "understood," and no feature vectors remain. If the original population is finite, the procedure is guaranteed to terminate in a finite number of cycles, yielding two rules: one that perfectly classifies squares, and one that perfectly classifies boxes. (Of course, if **P** were ambiguous, this would not be possible.)

M is a particularly simple rule-induction algorithm. It is similar in concept to the algorithms used by high-end inducers, but avoids the mathematics involved (entropy computations, etc.). **M** produces pretty decent, but not optimal results. In all general ways it is like the best of its class, and ideal for pedagogical purposes.

M is a two-stage algorithm. During the first stage, it uses a "splitting" technique to detect "clusters" of feature vectors having the same class. During the second stage, it uses these clusters to create rules describing the classes.

Most rule-induction algorithms are based upon such a "splitting" technique. These splits amount to the creation of decision surfaces that can be expressed as predicates in rules. **M** performs its splits by placing a "crosshair" at the average of the class centroids. Other rule-induction techniques use other splitting methods (e.g., "two-ing," "GINI").

The splits applied by **M** divide the remaining data into four parts, each of which is then split into four subparts during the next cycle, and so on. Eventually, the feature space will be divided up into "cells" small enough that each contains only feature vectors of the same class. The process will become clear as we apply it to **P** below.

The "crosshair splits" generated by **M** divide regions of feature space into quarters, called *quadrants*. The standard scheme for labeling quadrants assigns them the numbers 1 through 4, starting from the upper right and going counterclockwise (see Figure 9.2).

Figure 9.2

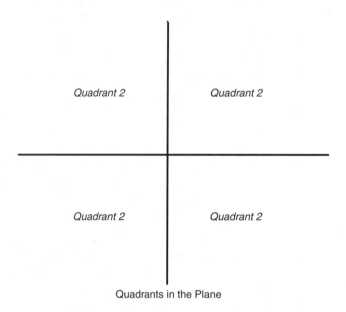

Quadrants in the Plane

There are four steps in each stage–1 cycle of **M**:

1. For the remaining feature vectors, compute the centroid (i.e., average) of class 1, C_1, and the centroid of class 2, C_2.

2. Compute the midpoint of the line connecting C_1 to C_2 = $(C_1 + C_2) \div 2 = (X_d, Y_d)$.

3. Split the remaining feature vectors into four groups, using the "crosshair" centered at (X_d, Y_d):

- Quadrant 1 (12 o'clock to 3 o'clock): feature vectors with $x \geq X_d$, and $y \geq Y_d$

- Quadrant 2 (9 o'clock to 12 o'clock): feature vectors with $x < X_d$, and $y \geq Y_d$

- Quadrant 3 (6 o'clock to 9 o'clock): feature vectors with $x < X_d$, and $y < Y_d$

- Quadrant 4 (3 o'clock to 6 o'clock): feature vectors with $x \geq X_d$, and $y < Y_d$

4. Check each quadrant for homogeneity by class. If a quadrant contains only vectors of a single class, remove these vectors. As a pure, 1-class subset, from the population. They're done!

We now proceed to apply **M** to **P**, and illustrate the results of each step with a figure.

9.1.3   Stage 1: Performing the Splits

9.1.3.1   Cycle 1:

1. For the remaining feature vectors, compute the centroid of class 1, C_1, and the centroid of class 2, C_2.

    The larger icon of three nested circles is the centroid of the remaining squares, C_1. The x-coordinate of C_1 is the average of the x-coordinates of the remaining circles; its y-coordinate is the average of the y-coordinates of the remaining circles.

    The larger icon of three nested boxes is the centroid of the remaining boxes, C_2. The x-coordinate of C_2 is the average of the x-coordinates of the remaining boxes; its y-coordinate is the average of the y-coordinates of the remaining boxes (see Figure 9.3).

2. Compute the midpoint of the line connecting C_1 to C_2 = $(C_1 + C_2) \div 2 = (X_d, Y_d)$.

    Average C_1 and C_2 to obtain the point (X_d, Y_d) halfway between C_1 and C_2. Place a "crosshair" at this point, splitting feature space into four quadrants.

3. Split the remaining feature vectors into four groups, using the "crosshair" centered at (X_d, Y_d).

Figure 9.3

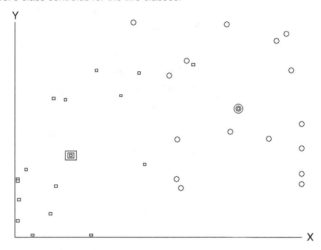

The level 0 class centroids for the two classes.

The crosshair has been drawn, dividing the plane into four quadrants, and **P** into four subsets.

4.   Check each quadrant for homogeneity by class. If a quadrant contains only vectors of a single class, remove these vectors from the population and they're done!

The feature vectors in quadrant 3 (lower left) are all squares; this quadrant is homogeneous, so these feature vectors may be removed from consideration. Likewise, the feature vectors in quadrant 4 (lower right) are all circles; this quadrant is homogeneous, so these feature vectors may be removed from consideration (see Figure 9.4).

9.1.3.2   *Cycle 2:*

The process of splitting is now repeated within each of the four quadrants produced during the previous cycle. Feature vectors removed from consideration because they were in homogeneous quadrants have been iconized to points.

1.   For the remaining feature vectors, compute the centroid of class 1, C_1, and the centroid of class 2, C_2.

The centroids have been computed using only the feature vectors in quadrant 1, the upper left-hand region created during the previous cycle (see Figure 9.5).

Figure 9.4

This shows this quadrant's split lines, giving 4 subquadrants.

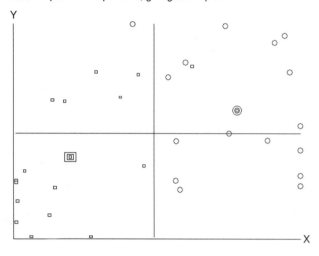

Figure 9.5

The level 1 class centroids for quadrant 1.

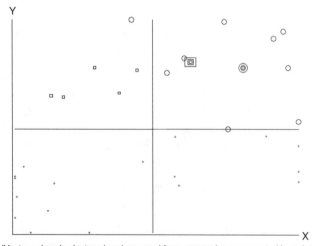

(Vectors already clustered and removed from processing represented by points)

2. Compute the midpoint of the line connecting C_1 to C_2 = $(C_1 + C_2) \div 2 = (X_d, Y_d)$.

The new C_1 and C_2 have been averaged to obtain a new (X_d, Y_d) for quadrant 1, and a "crosshair" placed at this point, splitting quadrant 1 into four subquadrants (see Figure 9.6).

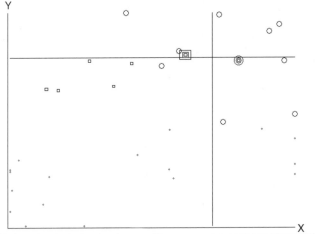

Figure 9.6

This shows this quadrant's split lines, giving 4 subquadrants

(Vectors already clustered and removed from processing represented by points)

3.   Split the remaining feature vectors into four groups, using the "crosshair" centered at (X_d, Y_d).

4.   Check each quadrant for homogeneity by class. If a quadrant contains only vectors of a single class, remove these vectors from the population and they're done!

The feature vectors in quadrant 1 (upper right) are all circles, and the feature vectors in quadrant 4 (lower right) are all circles; these quadrants are "homogeneous," so these feature vectors may be removed from consideration. Quadrants 2 and 3 are heterogeneous. Proceed to split quadrant 2 (see Figure 9.7).

Only quadrant four (lower right) is heterogeneous, so its centroids are computed (see Figure 9.8).

The midpoint of the centroids is used to split, leaving only the upper-right quadrant still heterogeneous (one square, and one circle (see Figure 9.9).

The final centroids coincide with the only two remaining feature vectors (see Figure 9.10).

Figure 9.7

This shows this quadrant's split lines, giving 4 subquadrants

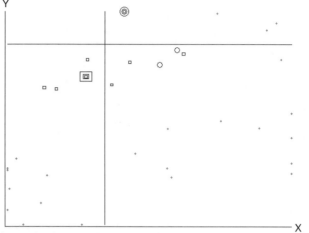

(Vectors already clustered and removed from processing represented by points)

Figure 9.8

The level 2 class centroids for quadrant 4

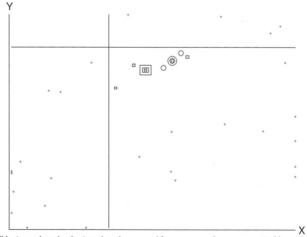

(Vectors already clustered and removed from processing represented by points)

The final split puts the last remaining circle in the upper left, and the last remaining square in the lower right (see Figure 9.11). This completes the split processing.

Figure 9.9

This shows this quadrant's split lines, giving 4 subquadrants.

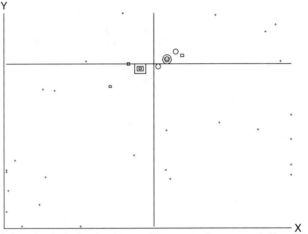

(Vectors already clustered and removed from processing represented by points)

Figure 9.10

The level 3 class centroids for quadrant 1

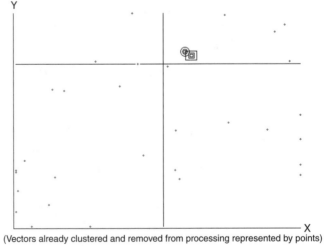

(Vectors already clustered and removed from processing represented by points)

→
Figure 9.11

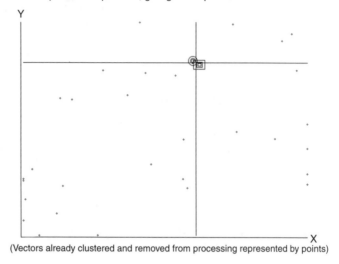

This shows this quadrant's split lines, giving 4 subquadrants.

(Vectors already clustered and removed from processing represented by points)

9.1.4   Stage 2: Formatting the Induced Rules

As the splits were performed, **M** removed collections of feature vectors, known to all to be of the same class. That is the purpose of the splits: to identify grouping of vectors in feature space that are of the same class. **M** recorded the locations of the "detected clusters" as they are removed, so they can be used during Stage 2 to construct rules representing these clusters.

Formatting the rules is easy once homogeneous sets of feature vectors have been formed. For example, in Figure 9.6, three circles were discovered in the upper right-hand quadrant of a split: They are removed together, since they form a homogeneous "cluster" of class 1 points at (0.73, 0.90), (0.95, 0.86) (0.93, 0.82).

Using the minimum and maximum X and Y coordinates of these points, we can construct an enclosing rectangle: a rectangle with lower left-hand corner at (0.73, 0.82) and upper right-hand corner (0.95, 0.90) will enclose these points (some will be on the boundary). Because of the way **M** found these points, it is *guaranteed* that this rectangle *will contain only circles.*Another way of saying this is that **M** has *discovered* the following rule:

> *"**IF** a feature vector has an X coordinate between 0.73 and 0.95, **AND** a Y coordinate between 0.82 and 0.90, **THEN** that feature vector is a circle."*

All of the enclosing rectangles discovered by **M** are depicted in the following figure. These rectangles are not the most "efficient" possible rectangular decompositions of **P,** because **M** is not an optimal rule inducer. With a little post-processing, some of these rectangles could be combined (see Figure 9.12). Also, the maximum and minimum values have been extended slightly to actually get all the feature vectors *inside* the enclosures instead of on the boundaries.

Figure 9.12

Induced 11 rules from data. They form 'boxes' in feature space.
Note that all the vectors in a box are of the same class.

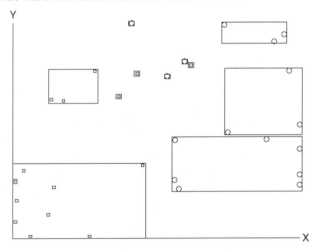

Using the max/min definitions for the discovered rectangles, the following pair of rules is induced. This pair perfectly classifies **P** (see Figure 9.13).

9.1.5   Top-Down vs. Bottom-Up: Another Algorithm

The rule-induction algorithm discussed in the previous section begins with the entire population as a single group, and creates

Figure 9.13

The rule induced to determine class 1 vectors is:

```
IF
        .5510676<X<1.01 and .1912003<Y<.4215393
    OR  .7261172<X<.9555729 and .8191677<Y<.9085373
    OR  .5858796<X<.6058796 and .7323225<Y<.7523225
    OR  .7386578<X<1.01 and .4311243<Y<.7134077
    OR  .3984099<X<.4184099 and .89622<Y<.91622
    OR  .524993<X<.544993 and .6700973<Y<.6900973

THEN the vector (X,Y) is in class 1 .
```

The rule induced to determine class 2 vectors is:

```
IF
        .4184421<X<.4384421 and .6818136<Y<.7018136
    OR  -.01<X<.4585865 and -.01<Y<.3112606
    OR  .3550725<X<.3750725 and .5850624<Y<.6050624
    OR  .6077269<X<.6277269 and .7171721<Y<.7371721
    OR  .1177064<X<.2902214 and .5672873<Y<.7119557

THEN the vector (X,Y) is in class 2 .
```

rules by splitting this group into subsets until "pure" aggregations are obtained and removed from the process. In this sense, it is a "top-down" method. In this section, we discuss a "bottom-up" rule-induction method. The technique chosen is called *region-growing*. Small subsets of the population are combined with other "nearby" subsets to obtain larger aggregations from which rules can be constructed. This is similar to the technique that was used to catch the cheating college kids in Chapter 3.

Techniques that might be put into the "top-down" category are those relying primarily on the gross distribution of the data: CART, CHAID, k-means, some kinds of neural networks, and many parametric statistical classifiers (e.g., Bayesian classifiers). These methods build clusters by determining their "*centers and extents*," often at the expense of accuracy at the boundaries.

Techniques that might be put into the "bottom-up" category are those relying primarily on decision surfaces that are adjusted to accommodate individual data points: region-growing techniques, most black-box regression techniques, and some non-parametric classifiers. These methods build clusters by determining their *boundaries.*

This organization of induction techniques into top-down and bottom-up is not perfect; some techniques are hard to place in either category. For example, logistic regression, a conventional explanatory modeling technique, could be called a bottom-up technique because it is fundamentally a boundary-oriented method. However, its decision surface is conditioned mostly by data distribution rather than adjudication of minor "boundary disputes," so it could be regarded as top-down.

Since top-down and bottom-up methods do not operate in the same way, they often give results that are quite different. They have different strengths and weaknesses and are appropriate for different kinds of problems.

Top-down methods tend to be easier to implement, less consumptive of memory, learn more quickly, and have a very natural termination condition (quit when all the aggregations are homogeneous). Top-down methods often produce relatively small sets of rules, readily understandable to human experts. These advantages are mostly side effects of the fact that top-down methods are managing data by aggregations, rather than looking at individual points. Top-down methods are ideal for linearly separable problems, and other problems for which the clusters naturally occurring in the population have normal distributions.

Bottom-up methods tend to be harder to implement, more consumptive of memory, learn more slowly, and have no natural termination condition (when should no more clusters be merged?). They tend to produce relatively large sets of what appear to be ad-hoc rules. These disadvantages are mostly side effects of the fact that bottom-up methods devote much effort to controlling large numbers of individual data points at cluster boundaries, rather than focusing on sets of points.

All other things being equal, one wonders why bottom-up techniques would ever be selected. The answer is that many hard problems are hard precisely because the natural clusters of different classes overlap at the cluster boundaries. Since bottom-up methods focus on the boundaries, they are generally better suited to the construction of predictive models for non-linearly separable problems, and other problems for which the ground-truth classes are ragged and irregular in feature space.[1]

---

1.   Many classical statisticians would take issue with the previous paragraph. This is because classical statistics has historically taken the view that *good models* must be *explanatory*. The decision rules they implement must be statistically valid, and based upon independent factors having appropriate distributions. For this reason, some data mining tools offer extensive support for explanatory statistical modeling (e.g., managing multicollinearity), but comparatively little support for relatively few black-box regression techniques.

At some level, though, the distinction between these top-down and bottom-up techniques does vanish. If a top-down technique subdivides the feature space so finely that it develops many subsets consisting of a few points each, (e.g., RBFs), it becomes localized, and essentially bottom-up. And, if a bottom-up technique is able to discard all but one or two cluster boundaries, it becomes globalized, and essentially top-down.

Because region-growing makes progress by merging subsets that are "close to each other," it is able to discover clusters that are not "round." Region-growing can follow long filaments of data points as they wind their complex ways through high-dimensional space. Cluster-centric top-down techniques, on the other hand, do a terrible job of handling raggedly intertwined aggregations of data, because this kind of data cannot be separated by a few hyper-planes, or a few ellipsoids drawn around cluster centroids.

There are three prices that must be paid for solving hard classification problems using bottom-up methods, because these methods amount to "micro-management" of class boundaries:

1.   The classifier will probably have many parameters (tens of thousands is not uncommon).

2.   The classifier will be inscrutable (induced rules appear ad-hoc).

3.   The classifier might not generalize (complex "patterns" at the boundaries might just be "noise").

Special care must be taken with these models to ensure their validity. Blind-testing, and its generalization, n-fold cross validation (Chapter 11), are essential.

Using region-growing to induce rules is conceptually similar to using splits. The feature space is divided into regions, which are then described by rules. The primary difference is that in splitting, homogeneity by class is the primary driver, whereas in region-growing, distance between points is the primary driver. Since points close together in feature space can be in different ground-truth classes, region-growing can't use homogeneity by class as a termination condition. In region-growing, clusters are built by proximity, and will often be a mixture of classes.

We now describe a region-growing rule-induction algorithm, which we call **G**. Like **M**, it produces pretty decent, but not optimal results. Unlike **M**, it is a one-stage algorithm. It uses a "combining" technique to create clusters of feature vectors that are close together in feature space. (This is where the term "region-growing" comes from.) These clusters are immediately converted into descriptive rules.

Recall that an "aggregation" is merely a collection of feature vectors from the population. **G** begins by defining every single feature vector as a separate, one-point aggregation. This means that at the beginning of the induction process, **G** will have created a distinct ad-hoc rule for each vector in the training set. This large collection of rules will correctly classify all the training vectors, but won't capture any generalizable facts about the classification problem. The goal of **G** is to reduce the number of rules by combining aggregations, so that a relatively small number of salient, general rules are finally obtained.

There are four steps in each cycle of **G**. These steps determine which two aggregations to combine during the current cycle, merge the selected aggregations, and generate the reduced rule set. Cycling continues until some termination condition is satisfied. The algorithm described here will just continue until the number of aggregations has been reduced to a user-specified target value.

9.1.5.1   *Steps in a Cycle of G*

1. Compute the distances between all pairs of existing aggregations, A_k. The distance between two aggregations A_1 and A_2 is the intuitive one: the smallest distance between any pair of vectors (V_1, V_2), where V_1 is in A_1 and V_2 is in A_2.

2. Scan the list of distances produced in Step 1 to determine which two aggregations are closest together. These are the aggregations that will be merged, forming a new, larger "region."

3. Combine the two nearest aggregations found in Step 2 to obtain a single aggregation consisting of all the vectors from both of the two original nearest aggregations.

4. Remove the two bounding boxes (and the two rules) that described the merged aggregations before they were combined. Take "maxima" and "minima" to create a single bounding box (hence, a rule) for the new, merged aggregation.

Notice that step four is identical to Stage 2 processing from the "splitting" induction method described previously.

It is important to note that, unlike algorithm **M**, algorithm **G** *ignores* the ground-truth class of the vectors during the induction process. It relies entirely on the natural "clustering" of the data. This means that the final enclosing boxes produced by **G** are virtually certain to contain a mixture of feature vectors from multiple ground-truth classes. During rule formatting in Step 4, **G** must compute for each rule the probability that a vector of each class will be in the defining box for that rule. This is done by computing the observed probability of each class in the box for the training set. For example, if a box for a rule ends up with three class 1 vectors and two class 2 vectors, the rule will report that any vector found in the box during classification should be assigned a probability of 60 percent of being in class 1 (3 out of 5), and a probability of 40 percent of being in class 2 (2 out of 5). These "empirical probabilities" can be combined to determine a classification decision when the rules are applied in operation.

The fact that **G** does not use ground-truth makes its performance very sensitive to the number of cycles. As will be seen in the example below, **G** will work well for a while, but will fail suddenly when it is allowed to cycle too many times. In practice, the correct number of cycling operations is usually determined by trial and error on a calibration set, and then this termination condition is used for training.

9.1.6   Example 1: An Easy Problem

The following sequence of figures shows the progress of **G** during cycling against two classification problems: an easy problem, and a hard problem. In both problems, the population consists of 100 feature vectors, 25 in each of 4 ground-truth classes. Icons are used to make the classes visually distinguishable: X's, dots, circles with + signs, and circles with dots.[2]

The first sequence of figures shows region-growing rule-induction applied to the easy problem, a problem that is, in fact, linearly

---

2.   The reader might notice that the boxes selected by G don't appear to be for the closest pairs of points. This is because the distance measure used by this routine ("weighted L1") is designed to give special consideration to regions that are parallel to the axes. This is a characteristic of many real-world problems.

separable. In the first figure, no cycling has occurred; the display notes that the algorithm is about to perform "pass 1," and there are 100 clusters, one for each member of the population (see Figure 9.14).

Figure 9.14

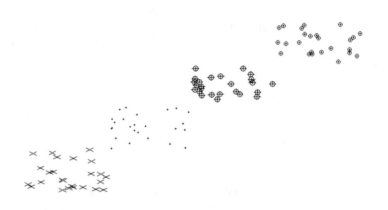

PASS: 1   CLUSTERS: 100
THE WINNER-TAKE-ALL POWER OF THIS RULE SET IS 100 % .

After 19 cycles have been performed, a number of boxed aggregations can be seen. Most aggregations still consist of a single data point (see Figure 9.15).

After 60 cycles have been performed, many boxed aggregations are apparent, and the general "four cluster" character of the overall population begins to stand out (see Figure 9.16).

After 85 cycles have been performed, most aggregations a human would intuitively select have been detected. The classification is still 100-percent accurate, since no merging across the four ground-truth classes has yet occurred (see Figure 9.17).

Figure 9.15   PASS: 20   CLUSTERS: 81
THE WINNER-TAKE-ALL POWER OF THIS RULE SET IS 100 % .

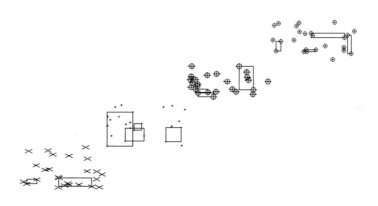

Figure 9.16   PASS: 61   CLUSTERS: 40
THE WINNER-TAKE-ALL POWER OF THIS RULE SET IS 100 % .

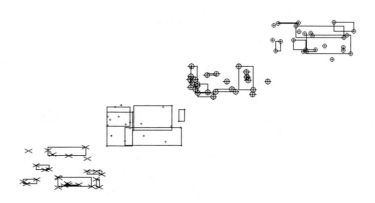

Figure 9.17   PASS: 86   CLUSTERS: 15
THE WINNER-TAKE-ALL POWER OF THIS RULE SET IS 100 % .

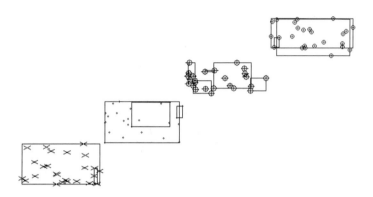

After 92 cycles have been performed, some misaggregation has occurred: A box has been drawn which spans some circle with dots and circles with +'s. Classification accuracy has dropped to 98 percent. From this point on, continued cycling will cause the performance of the rule set to increasingly confuse classes; training has gone "too far" (see Figure 9.18).

At 97 cycles, accuracy has dropped to 77 percent, as more and more vectors of different types are aggregated erroneously (see Figure 9.19).

At 99 cycles, accuracy has dropped to 50 percent. Four ground-truth classes have been squeezed into two aggregations, resulting in misclassification of half the feature vectors. As stated above, the rules produced by **G** will be poor if over-training occurs (see Figure 9.20).

The following are the rules induced by **G** after 85 cycles. Each rule is an IF-THEN construct telling how much belief should be assigned to each possible classification of a vector falling within the box defining that rule. Keep in mind that these rules were constructed automatically by the induction algorithm, and written to a file in the form they appear here.

Figure 9.18   PASS: 93   CLUSTERS: 8
THE WINNER-TAKE-ALL POWER OF THIS RULE SET IS 98 %.

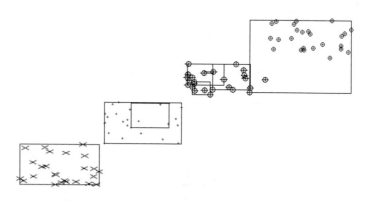

Figure 9.19   PASS: 97   CLUSTERS: 4
THE WINNER-TAKE-ALL POWER OF THIS RULE SET IS 77 %.

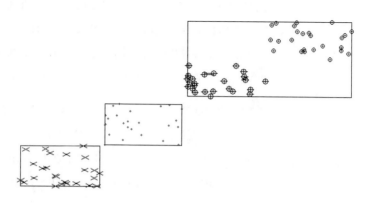

Figure 9.20   PASS: 99   CLUSTERS: 2
THE WINNER-TAKE-ALL POWER OF THIS RULE SET IS 50 %.

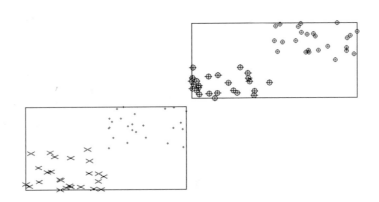

9.2   Ten Rules Created from the Data Files

9.2.1   This Set of Rules Correctly Classified 100 Percent of the Training Vectors

RULE 1 CONTROLS 22 PERCENT OF THE POPULATION:

IF A FEATURE VECTOR IS IN BOX 1, THEN:

100 PERCENT IS THE PROB. THAT IT'S IN CLASS 1.

0 PERCENT IS THE PROB. THAT IT'S IN ANY OTHER CLASS.

RULE 2 CONTROLS 3 PERCENT OF THE POPULATION:

IF A FEATURE VECTOR IS IN BOX 2, THEN:

100 PERCENT IS THE PROB. THAT IT'S IN CLASS 1.

0 PERCENT IS THE PROB. THAT IT'S IN ANY OTHER CLASS.

RULE 3 CONTROLS 5 PERCENT OF THE POPULATION:

IF A FEATURE VECTOR IS IN BOX 3, THEN:

  100 PERCENT IS THE PROB. THAT IT'S IN CLASS 2.

  0 PERCENT IS THE PROB. THAT IT'S IN ANY OTHER CLASS.

RULE 4 CONTROLS 20 PERCENT OF THE POPULATION:

IF A FEATURE VECTOR IS IN BOX 4, THEN:

  100 PERCENT IS THE PROB. THAT IT'S IN CLASS 2.

  0 PERCENT IS THE PROB. THAT IT'S IN ANY OTHER CLASS.

RULE 5 CONTROLS 5 PERCENT OF THE POPULATION:

IF A FEATURE VECTOR IS IN BOX 5, THEN:

  100 PERCENT IS THE PROB. THAT IT'S IN CLASS 3.

  0 PERCENT IS THE PROB. THAT IT'S IN ANY OTHER CLASS.

RULE 6 CONTROLS 8 PERCENT OF THE POPULATION:

IF A FEATURE VECTOR IS IN BOX 6, THEN:

  100 PERCENT IS THE PROB. THAT IT'S IN CLASS 3.

  0 PERCENT IS THE PROB. THAT IT'S IN ANY OTHER CLASS.

RULE 7 CONTROLS 2 PERCENT OF THE POPULATION:

IF A FEATURE VECTOR IS IN BOX 7, THEN:

  100 PERCENT IS THE PROB. THAT IT'S IN CLASS 3.

  0 PERCENT IS THE PROB. THAT IT'S IN ANY OTHER CLASS.

RULE 8 CONTROLS 2 PERCENT OF THE POPULATION:

IF A FEATURE VECTOR IS IN BOX 8, THEN:

  100 PERCENT IS THE PROB. THAT IT'S IN CLASS 3.

  0 PERCENT IS THE PROB. THAT IT'S IN ANY OTHER CLASS.

RULE 9 CONTROLS 8 PERCENT OF THE POPULATION:

IF A FEATURE VECTOR IS IN BOX 9, THEN:

100 PERCENT IS THE PROB. THAT IT'S IN CLASS 3.

0 PERCENT IS THE PROB. THAT IT'S IN ANY OTHER CLASS.

RULE 10 CONTROLS 25 PERCENT OF THE POPULATION:

IF A FEATURE VECTOR IS IN BOX 10, THEN:

100 PERCENT IS THE PROB. THAT IT'S IN CLASS 4.

0 PERCENT IS THE PROB. THAT IT'S IN ANY OTHER CLASS.

9.2.2 Example 2: A Hard Problem

Now, a second sequence of figures is presented that shows **G** applied to the hard problem, a problem that is non-linearly separable. In the first figure, no cycling has occurred; the display notes that the algorithm is about to perform "pass 1," and there are 100 clusters, one for each member of the population (see Figure 9.21). Three of the classes overlap.

Figure 9.21   PASS: 1   CLUSTERS: 100
THE WINNER-TAKE-ALL POWER OF THIS RULE SET IS 100 %.

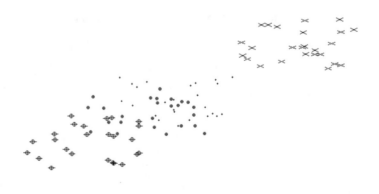

After 19 cycles have been performed, a number of boxed aggregations can be seen. Most aggregations still consist of a single data point. The boxes generated for this data set are smaller at this stage than those of the easy problem, owing to the closer proximity of the feature vectors (see Figure 9.22).

Figure 9.22   PASS: 21   CLUSTERS: 80
THE WINNER-TAKE-ALL POWER OF THIS RULE SET IS 95 %.

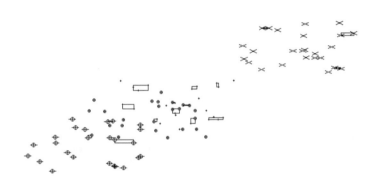

After 50 cycles have been performed, many boxed aggregations are apparent, but no general character of the overall population is seen. Classification performance stands at 86 percent (see Figure 9.23).

After 90 cycles have been performed, the population is seen to fall into two broad aggregations. The classification is only 80 percent accurate. Over-training is beginning to occur (see Figure 9.24).

After 95 cycles have been performed, classification accuracy has dropped to 77 percent (see Figure 9.25).

At 99 cycles, accuracy has dropped to 50 percent. Four ground-truth classes have been squeezed into two aggregations, resulting in misclassification of half the feature vectors. This is the same result obtained at this level on the "easy" problem (see Figure 9.26).

Figure 9.23   PASS: 51   CLUSTERS: 50
THE WINNER-TAKE-ALL POWER OF THIS RULE SET IS 86 %.

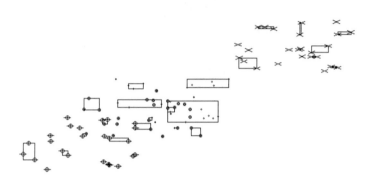

Figure 9.24   PASS: 91   CLUSTERS: 10
THE WINNER-TAKE-ALL POWER OF THIS RULE SET IS 80 %.

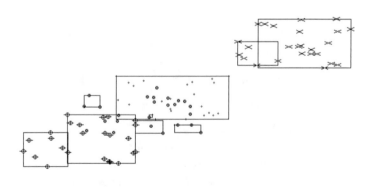

Figure 9.25 PASS: 96   CLUSTERS: 5
                 THE WINNER-TAKE-ALL POWER OF THIS RULE SET IS 77 %.

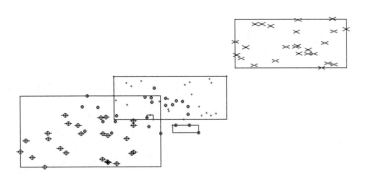

Figure 9.26 PASS: 99   CLUSTERS: 2
                 THE WINNER-TAKE-ALL POWER OF THIS RULE SET IS 50 %.

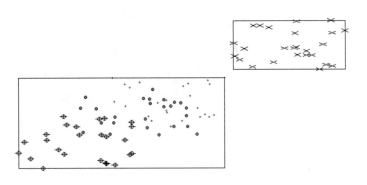

The following are the rules induced by **G** after 90 cycles. Each rule is an IF-THEN construct telling how much belief should be assigned to each possible classification of a vector falling within the box defining that rule. Keep in mind that these rules were constructed automatically by the induction algorithm, and written to a file in the form they appear here.

9.3   Rules Created from Data File

9.3.1   This Set of Rules Correctly Classifies 80 Percent of the Vectors

RULE 1 CONTROLS 6 PERCENT OF THE POPULATION:

IF A FEATURE VECTOR IS IN BOX 1, THEN:

100 PERCENT IS THE PROB. THAT IT'S IN CLASS 1.

0 PERCENT IS THE PROB. THAT IT'S IN ANY OTHER CLASS.

RULE 2 CONTROLS 19 PERCENT OF THE POPULATION:

IF A FEATURE VECTOR IS IN BOX 2, THEN:

100 PERCENT IS THE PROB. THAT IT'S IN CLASS 1.

0 PERCENT IS THE PROB. THAT IT'S IN ANY OTHER CLASS.

RULE 3 CONTROLS 1 PERCENT OF THE POPULATION:

IF A FEATURE VECTOR IS IN BOX 3, THEN:

100 PERCENT IS THE PROB. THAT IT'S IN CLASS 2.

0 PERCENT IS THE PROB. THAT IT'S IN ANY OTHER CLASS.

RULE 4 CONTROLS 33 PERCENT OF THE POPULATION:

IF A FEATURE VECTOR IS IN BOX 4, THEN:

66.66667 PERCENT IS THE PROB. THAT IT'S IN CLASS 2.

33.33333 PERCENT IS THE PROB. THAT IT'S IN CLASS 4.

0 PERCENT IS THE PROB. THAT IT'S IN ANY OTHER CLASS.

RULE 5 CONTROLS 20 PERCENT OF THE POPULATION:

IF A FEATURE VECTOR IS IN BOX 5, THEN:

75 PERCENT IS THE PROB. THAT IT'S IN CLASS 3.

25 PERCENT IS THE PROB. THAT IT'S IN CLASS 4.

0 PERCENT IS THE PROB. THAT IT'S IN ANY OTHER CLASS.

RULE 6 CONTROLS 8 PERCENT OF THE POPULATION:

IF A FEATURE VECTOR IS IN BOX 6, THEN:

100 PERCENT IS THE PROB. THAT IT'S IN CLASS 3.

0 PERCENT IS THE PROB. THAT IT'S IN ANY OTHER CLASS.

RULE 7 CONTROLS 4 PERCENT OF THE POPULATION:

IF A FEATURE VECTOR IS IN BOX 7, THEN:

50 PERCENT IS THE PROB. THAT IT'S IN CLASS 3.

50 PERCENT IS THE PROB. THAT IT'S IN CLASS 4.

0 PERCENT IS THE PROB. THAT IT'S IN ANY OTHER CLASS.

RULE 8 CONTROLS 4 PERCENT OF THE POPULATION:

IF A FEATURE VECTOR IS IN BOX 8, THEN:

25 PERCENT IS THE PROB. THAT IT'S IN CLASS 2.

75 PERCENT IS THE PROB. THAT IT'S IN CLASS 4.

0 PERCENT IS THE PROB. THAT IT'S IN ANY OTHER CLASS.

RULE 9 CONTROLS 2 PERCENT OF THE POPULATION:

IF A FEATURE VECTOR IS IN BOX 9, THEN:

50 PERCENT IS THE PROB. THAT IT'S IN CLASS 2.

50 PERCENT IS THE PROB. THAT IT'S IN CLASS 4.

0 PERCENT IS THE PROB. THAT IT'S IN ANY OTHER CLASS.

RULE 10 CONTROLS 3 PERCENT OF THE POPULATION:

IF A FEATURE VECTOR IS IN BOX 10, THEN:

100 PERCENT IS THE PROB. THAT IT'S IN CLASS 4.

0 PERCENT IS THE PROB. THAT IT'S IN ANY OTHER CLASS.

The following are the rules induced by **G** after 99 cycles. At this level, substantial over-training has occurred, and the two rules that survive have little power to discriminate between the four classes. As before, these rules were constructed automatically by the induction algorithm, and written to a file in the form they appear here.

9.4   Rules Created from Data File

9.4.1   This Set of Rules Correctly Classifies 50 Percent of the Training Vectors

RULE 1 CONTROLS 25 PERCENT OF THE POPULATION:

IF A FEATURE VECTOR IS IN BOX 1, THEN:

100 PERCENT IS THE PROB. THAT IT'S IN CLASS 1.

0 PERCENT IS THE PROB. THAT IT'S IN ANY OTHER CLASS.

RULE 2 CONTROLS 75 PERCENT OF THE POPULATION:

IF A FEATURE VECTOR IS IN BOX 2, THEN:

33.33333 PERCENT IS THE PROB. THAT IT'S IN CLASS 2.

33.33333 PERCENT IS THE PROB. THAT IT'S IN CLASS 3.

33.33333 PERCENT IS THE PROB. THAT IT'S IN CLASS 4.

0 PERCENT IS THE PROB. THAT IT'S IN ANY OTHER CLASS.

10

Data Mining Techniques: Predictive Models

It has been said that "knowledge is power." Business knowledge produces power by enabling its possessor to take the right action at the right time. It is knowledge made *actionable* that wields power.

Knowledge that is not applied might as well not be known. Once knowledge has been obtained from a human expert or extracted through discovery techniques, it must be put to work to provide value.

Recall that data mining has two components: *discovery*, during which meaningful patterns are detected and characterized in data; and *exploitation*, during which meaningful patterns are used to create useful applications (models).

Data mining models typically classify or predict, so are called *predictive models*. The term "predictive" does not suggest that there is any prognostication involved. Predictive models are basically "pattern classifiers." Applications that estimate credit worthiness based upon a credit report, or that sift through thousands of transactions and identify instances of fraud, or predict tomorrow's closing S&P500 index, are all examples of predictive models.

The process of building predictive models using data mining methods and tools is referred to as *predictive modeling*.

One of the most attractive facets of data mining is the development of insight into the business process that makes possible the development of predictive models. In competitive markets, niche selection, product release timing, and marketing focus all stand to benefit from the use of predictive models.

Predictive models can be based upon conventional methods (control charts, Gantt charts, spreadsheets, etc.), but these are largely manual. Emerging applications for advanced "cognitive engines" for predictive modeling are becoming available to commercial users.

The treatment of predictive modeling here is intended not to be exhaustive, but suggestive. Several fundamental predictive modeling techniques are discussed, with tutorial examples. Some real-world examples are described in case studies in later chapters.

10.1 Surveying Predictive Modeling Techniques

Predictive models can be constructed in many ways, because there are many ways to approach the problem of exploiting patterns in data. This chapter summarizes some of the capabilities and applications of predictive models that are based upon pattern processing using polynomial regression, KBES, and neural networks. There are many others that could be discussed, but a review of these constitutes a fairly good general survey of the techniques in current use. None of the treatments is very deep, and the focus is on functionality rather than internal operation.

The science underlying predictive modeling is a mixture of mathematics, computer science, and domain expertise. A purely formal mathematical approach unaided by business knowledge runs the risk of discovering useless facts, while a purely business-savvy approach runs the risk of overlooking subtle information spread thinly across many factors. Computer science and technology enable reasonably efficient implementations of data mining applications using large enterprise data repositories.

Some aspects of data mining technology are very technical. This book is not intended to prepare technicians to create new data mining technologies, but rather to provide insight for business people with real problems on ways data mining technology can help them. Since the reader may be new to data mining, jargon and complex mathematical notation is avoided as much as possible. (A glossary is included as Appendix A).

In the few years that data mining technology has been generally available, a technical vocabulary has rapidly developed. While such a vocabulary facilitates research, it tends to put off practitioners. Those investigating data mining for the first time encounter a pretty scary "semantic edifice." Those who desire additional information should refer to the bibliography in Appendix B.

While many of the concepts are logical and therefore basically intuitive, readers are encouraged to reflect on the subtleties in order to refine their appreciation of data mining techniques. Fortunately, many of the fundamental concepts in data mining can be represented pictorially. Such representations are favored over equations within this chapter. Those readers having substantial mathematical backgrounds should be able to infer the underlying formalism from the intuitive descriptions given, or may refer to the technical references.

It must be pointed out that analysts engaged in predictive modeling face some dangerous technical "land mines." The danger is not so much that certain techniques will fail to work, but that they will *appear* to work while giving false information. We sometimes call these "pitchforks," and describe them further in Chapter 11. Avoiding these requires at least a minimal understanding of how data mining techniques actually operate.

10.2   Current Techniques Have the Power

Some predictive modeling problems are easy, and some are hard. The problem of determining a person's gender given the number of "Y" chromosomes he or she has in each cell is an easy problem. It can be solved by a simple, one-rule model: Females have none, males have one. The problem of determining a person's gender given his or her age and height is harder, requiring a more sophisticated decision technique, and even then can only be solved approximately.

The mathematical methods used in modern data mining applications are very powerful. "Power" in this sense refers to the method's ability to model complex systems. For example, a *linear* model can handle the computation of payroll FICA for most workers, but doesn't have the "power" to model the growth of a certificate of deposit (a *non-linear* problem). Using inadequate modeling methods can place important discoveries and applications out of reach.

Fortunately, there is a formal demonstration that current predictive modeling technologies have "sufficient" power. In 1957, the Russian Mathematician Andrei Kolmogorov proved a theorem that showed that current predictive modeling techniques are theoretically adequate to handle hard problems. Now referred to as the *Kolmogorov Mapping Neural Network Existence Theorem*, this theorem basically states that modern methods have the "power" to support adequate models of any well-posed problem. *Well-posed problems* in this sense are those for which there is a single correct answer.

But the Kolmogorov Theorem's affirmation of technical power is not the whole story. In applications, there is the matter of practicality, as well. The Kolmogorov Theorem asserts the *existence* of effective models using modern architectures, but doesn't tell us *how to find them*. It has been proven that the construction of advanced regression models is computationally very difficult (refer to the literature for information regarding NP-hard problems[1]). Even worse, a model that is built to be effective on a training sample of data might not generalize to data the model hasn't seen. Certain key data items might be missing or the available data may not support the application at all. In nightmare cases, predictive models have been developed that required tens-of-gigabytes of data and hundreds of machine-hours in prototyping, but provided negligible improvement over existing methods.

Currently available advanced data mining methods have the theoretical power to handle any unambiguous modeling problem whose answer exists in historical data; but the implementation of these models may or may not be practical under real-world constraints of cost and schedule. Data mining is like every other enterprise activity: The business case has to be made, because there are no guarantees of success.

This should all be expected, since data mining is the search for hidden value—value that is there to a greater or lesser degree, in types and amounts unknown. Data mining is producing very good results in a growing number of applications in various industries. With the emergence of a variety of "off-the-shelf" data mining tools, the case for funding data mining initiatives is becoming easier to make.

There is a theoretical formalism for assessing the representational power of classification algorithms, called the theory of PAC Learning. (PAC is an acronym for "probably approximately correct.") This formalism begins with a definition of complexity for classification problems using a concept called the "VC Dimension" (Vapnik-Chervonenkis Dimension). Many of the results of this work are still

1.   The reference to NP-hard problems is included for the benefit of experts; those unfamiliar with this term need not concern themselves.

"on the drawing board"; within a few years, more of this theory will move into the laboratory to become "technology." From there, it will finally move out into the marketplace. The treatment here takes a layman's approach, defining the "power" of a technique in terms of its mathematical pedigree, and the complexity of the problems to which common implementations are suited. Techniques that able to solve problems that are intuitively more complex are regarded as having more power.

The diagram below is an ordering of predictive modeling techniques by our intuitive conception of their "power." This order is not necessarily the same as the theoretical power of the techniques, but shows the relative power of common implementations. More powerful techniques are near the bottom of the list[2].

10.2.1 An Ordering of Predictive Modeling Techniques by Power

10.2.1.1 Low Power

N-Way Decision Rule

("IF number of 'Y's' is zero, THEN female, ELSE male" is a 2-way decision rule.)

The defining characteristic of this technique is that discrete decision values serve to divide the population into the desired classes. The decision value for the chromosome example could be one-half: females ("Y's" = 0) are on one side, males ("Y's" = 1) are on the other. These are easy to implement and use, and offer insight into the problem.

Simple Linear Regression

("IF $3x - 7y + 5z - 8w - 6u < 12$, THEN female, ELSE male.")

---

2. Practitioners of predictive modeling all have their favored techniques; statisticians, for example, will not agree with the placement of logistic regression among low power techniques. If the goal of a predictive modeling project is to *explain* the data while maintaining the statistical integrity of the features, they will be right: logistic regression is a very "powerful" technique. But if the goal is to solve a hard, non-linearly separable classification problem, it must be allowed that logistic regression, which uses a linear decision surface, will not be competitive *as a classifier* with techniques at the bottom of the list.

The defining characteristic of this technique is that the population is split into classes by a linear decision surface (line, plane, hyper-plane). These are fairly easy to implement and use, and offer some insight into the problem.

Logistic Regression

("IF L(3x – 7y + 5z – 8w – 6u) < decision value, THEN female, ELSE male.")

The defining characteristic of this technique is that the "direction" and "distance" from a linear decision surface are computed and used to assign a numeric measure of confidence that the input is in a particular class. The confidence is computed by a logistic function, L, a mathematical transform having a particular form.

These are fairly easy to implement and use, and offer deep insight into the problem.

Logistic regression models are *explanatory models*. The values of the model parameters give information about the importance of each feature used. Most other regression techniques do not have this useful property. However, logistic regression can give misleading interpretations of the data if there are linear relationships among the features (multicollinearity).

10.2.1.2   Moderate Power

Model-Based Regression (Polynomial, Power Series, etc.)

("gender = $3x^3 - 7 x^2y^3 + 5 x^4z - 8yzw - 6uz$.")

The defining characteristic of this technique is that a mathematical model with many parameters (in the example, 3, –7, 5, 8, and –6), produce the classification directly as an output of the model. The regression takes the features as inputs and "transforms" them directly to a final answer.

These models are somewhat difficult to build, are subject to numerical instability and over-fitting, and generally give little insight into the problem. They are subject to *uncontrolled regression*: They make wild guesses when given input data they haven't seen before.

Statistical Regression (Bayes' Theorem)

("IF prob (x,y,z,w,u) female > prob (x,y,z,w,u) male, THEN female, ELSE male.")

The defining characteristic of this technique is its assumption that certain probabilities are known, and its subsequent use of classical probability (typically, Bayes' Theorem) to compute the probability that a feature vector is in a particular class.

The difficulty of building these models depends upon how many classes there are and how well the assumptions hold up. When they work, they give some insight into the problem.

Knowledge-Based Expert System (KBES)

The defining characteristic of this technique is its codification of human expertise in the form of rules, which are executed in an order determined by a formalized inference methodology.

These models are difficult to build, require the support of domain experts, and give very deep insight into the problem.

10.2.1.3   High Power

Decision Trees (Traverse Tree, Report Type of Terminal Node)

The defining characteristic of this technique is the application of a "splitting rule" to the data, subdividing the population into smaller and smaller subsets to obtain a collection of single-class subsets. The hierarchy is then arranged in a tree structure that can be used as a classifier.

These models are fairly easy to build. Properly interpreting their output can give deep insight into the problem.

Black Box Regression Models (NN, ALN, RBF, Support Vectors)

- NN: neural network (usually a synonym for "multi-layer perception," or MLP)

- ALN: adaptive logic network, a self-constructing piecewise linear regression function

- RBF: radial basis function, a kernel-based classifier

- Support Vectors: a boundary-modeling regression function

The defining characteristic of these techniques is that they are "trained," rather than programmed. They adaptively create complex non-linear decision surfaces between classes in feature space.

These models are generally difficult to build. They usually give little insight into the problem.

Because these models are trained rather than programmed, and their internal use of their many parameters is inscrutable, these models can be difficult to test. They may be subject to uncontrolled regression.

With this brief taxonomy of predictive modeling techniques establishing a rough survey of the technology, more detail can be developed in the following section.

10.3 Mathematical Basics

Predictive modeling can be viewed as a "regression problem." In regression, a model is constructed that accepts specified inputs, and through some kind of mathematical transformation, produces a desired output. The inputs are features, and the output is the answer: a credit score, a fraud decision, a stock market prediction. The transform that computes the desired output from the inputs is called the *regression function*. The problem of determining this function and its parameters using data mining techniques is called the *regression problem*.[3]

Determining the parameters for a linear model (e.g., slopes and intercepts) is called *linear regression*. Determining parameters for a statistical model (e.g., means and variances) is called *statistical regression*. The corresponding models are called *regression models*.

The construction of effective predictive models is an important goal of modern data mining technology. Humans rely on their experience to make predictions. Answering the question, "What's going to happen tomorrow?" begins with a look at the question, "What happened yesterday?" This is true both for humans and machines. If we want to know what our customers are going to do tomorrow, we can begin by looking at what they did yesterday. If what happened yesterday is no longer relevant to tomorrow, then data mining will not help. Data mining involves looking for information in enterprise history that is relevant to enterprise future.

---

3.   This use of the term regression is different from that made by statisticians. Statisticians use the term regression to refer to the process of determining population parameters (e.g., mean, variance), typically from sample data.

When the output of a regression model is discrete (e.g., "A," "B," or "C"), the prediction is a "classification," and the input feature vectors have been assigned by the regression to one of the discrete classes. When the outputs of regression are continuous data, the regression is often called "estimation."

In most real-world problems, models fit the data only approximately. This is principally a result of the fact that all real-world measurements are subject to error, and this error is carried into model development. But even if we have "perfect" data to use in building a model, data the model later processes will be subject to error, and the model must be able to accommodate this. For example, the data used by a predictive model to estimate a credit score might contain gaps, requiring data cleansing before processing.

10.4 Polynomial Regression Models

Polynomial regression refers to the use of a polynomial as a model for a given data set.

Polynomials are functions whose output variable is a sum of multiples of products of powers of the input variables. This moderately precise definition being incomprehensible, some examples are provided. All of the following functions are polynomials:

$$y = 3$$
$$y = 3 + 5x - 2x^2$$
$$x = 2 - 5y - y^{19}$$
$$z = 7 - x + 3y + 5x^2y - 2x^4y^2$$

None of the following functions is a polynomial:

$$y = 1/x$$
$$x = \cos(y)$$
$$y = e^x$$

A "polynomial in x" is any function that can be written in the form:

$$P(x) = a_0 + a_1x + a_2x^2 + \ldots + a_nx^n$$

The a_i are real numbers, called *coefficients*, and can be positive, negative, or zero. The powers to which the independent variable x are raised are all non-negative integers. The largest such exponent, "n," is called the *degree* of the polynomial.

Given a collection of (x,y) pairs in the plane, polynomial regression can be used to find an expression that relates a given x value to its corresponding y value. Regression in this sense is equivalent to "curve fitting." As a predictive modeling problem, the x value is the input feature vector, and the y value is the corresponding ground-truth.

Polynomial regression is being discussed here not because it is a frequently used predictive modeling technique; it is not. But, polynomials are familiar and simple, and the relationship between their power and the number of parameters they use is easy to demonstrate, making them perfect for this discussion.

Some models are more powerful than others, in that they can, by proper selection of parameters, represent a wider range of data. The linear equation y=mx+b can be used to model any linear relationship that might exist between two real variables x and y. Linear relationships can exist among collections of three or more variables, giving rise to models in 3-space whose graphs are planes, and models in n-space whose graphs are hyper-planes.

A linear model is inadequate to represent a quadratic relationship. A linear model can approximately represent part of this more complex relationship, but clearly won't do a good job "in the large."

The general quadratic model for two real variables is given by $y = ax^2 + bx + c$. It can handle the linear relationship depicted in Figure 10.1 below, as well as the situation in Figure 10.3.

Because the quadratic model can do anything the linear model can do, and more, we regard it as a more powerful model. Notice that this extra power comes at a price: We must now determine three model parameters instead of two.

These ideas generalize in the obvious way. Polynomial models of any order can be selected, and their parameters computed directly from sample data. The theory of polynomial regression was pretty well fleshed-out in the late 17th century by Isaac Newton, Joseph Louis Lagrange, and their contemporaries.

Polynomials of higher degree have more representational power. It is even possible to build polynomials of "infinite degree," the so-called "power series." These models are very useful in physics and mathematics, but haven't seen much application in business-oriented data mining.

In Figure 10.1, a scatter-plot of about 100 data points is depicted. A method called least squares has been used to determine the best linear model for this data set. This line is shown on the plot, and its parameters, –0.00499 and 0.113, are shown (in exponential notation) below the plot. This means that the best line, in the least squares sense, for this data is $Y = -0.00499 + 0.113X$.

Figure 10.1

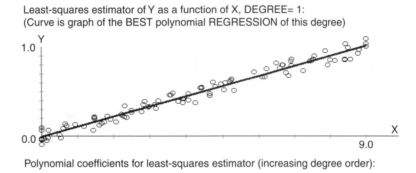

Least-squares estimator of Y as a function of X, DEGREE= 1:
(Curve is graph of the BEST polynomial REGRESSION of this degree)

Polynomial coefficients for least-squares estimator (increasing degree order):
–4.99E–03   +1.13E–01

A line does a pretty good job of fitting the data in the figure, because a linear model has the representational power needed for this regression problem. Suppose, though, that the data to be modeled does not lie along a line. This situation is depicted in Figure 10.2. Once again the best least-squares line is shown; clearly, a linear model does not have sufficient representational power for this data set.

Stepping up to a *quadratic model* (a model based upon a polynomial of degree 2) provides adequate power for this data set. By including a "second degree" term, the graph of the modeling function can bend to better fit the data. This is seen in Figure 10.3, where the best quadratic model is graphed over the data:

$$Y = 0.275 + 0.253X - 0.0274X^2$$

Figure 10.2

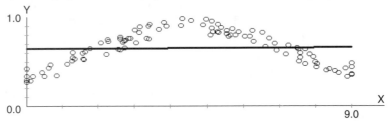

Least-squares estimator of Y as a function of X, DEGREE= 1:
(Curve is graph of the BEST polynomial REGRESSION of this degree)

Polynomial coefficients for least-squares estimator (increasing degree order):

+6.44E–01   +1.78E–03

Figure 10.3

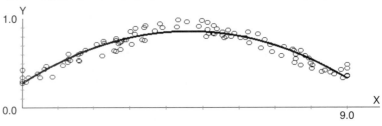

Least-squares estimator of Y as a function of X, DEGREE = 2:
(Curve is graph of the BEST polynomial REGRESSION of this degree)

Polynomial coefficients for least-squares estimator (increasing degree order):

+2.75E–01   +2.53E–01   –2.74E–02

An even more difficult data set is seen in Figure 10-4. A linear model is obviously inadequate for this "step function" data. Overlaid on this plot is the best quadratic model. It, too, is inadequate:

$$Y = -0.171 + 0.0922X + 0.00671X^2$$

Stepping up to a more powerful quintic (degree 5) model, a better fit is obtained:

$$Y = -0.0752 + 0.591X - 0.590X^2 + 0.192X^3 - 0.0235X^4 + 0.000978X^5$$

Notice that as the number of terms in the model is increased, the representational power of the model increases. This shows both the profit and the cost of more powerful models. More powerful models give better fits, but they require that more parameters be computed and stored.

Figure 10.4

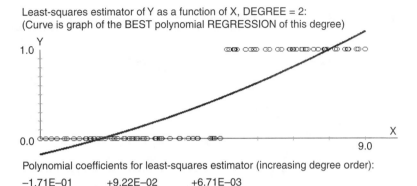

Least-squares estimator of Y as a function of X, DEGREE = 2:
(Curve is graph of the BEST polynomial REGRESSION of this degree)

Polynomial coefficients for least-squares estimator (increasing degree order):

−1.71E−01   +9.22E−02   +6.71E−03

Figure 10.5

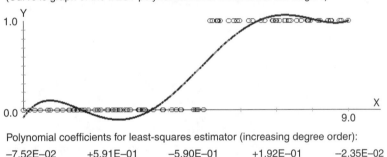

Least-squares estimator of Y as a function of X, DEGREE = 5:
(Curve is graph of the BEST polynomial REGRESSION of this degree)

Polynomial coefficients for least-squares estimator (increasing degree order):

−7.52E−02   +5.91E−01   −5.90E−01   +1.92E−01   −2.35E−02
+9.78E−04

By using high-degree models, the subtle nuances of complicated data sets can be modeled. For example, the data set modeled *adequately* by the quadratic polynomial can be modeled *exquisitely* by a polynomial of degree 9. In the plot shown in Figure 10.6, the slight bends in the data set are captured by the high-degree model.

Not surprisingly, even this ninth-degree model fails when applied to an extremely complicated data set. To handle this set, a much more powerful model would be needed (see Figure 10.7).

This look at polynomial models has shown the relationship between the complexity of a modeling problem, and the power of the model needed to solve it. Powerful models can capture subtle details of a data set. Building a powerful model typically requires the computation and storage of more model parameters than does building a simple model.

Figure 10.6

Least-squares estimator of Y as a function of X, DEGREE = 9:
(Curve is graph of the BEST polynomial REGRESSION of this degree)

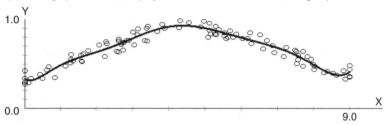

Polynomial coefficients for least-squares estimator (increasing degree order):

+3.33E–01	–2.30E–01	+9.90E–01	–9.84E–01	+4.97E–01
–1.42E–01	+2.36E–02	–2.27E–03	+1.17E–04	–2.47E–06

Figure 10.7

Least-squares estimator of Y as a function of X, DEGREE = 9:
(Curve is graph of the BEST polynomial REGRESSION of this degree)

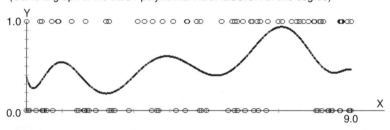

Polynomial coefficients for least-squares estimator (increasing degree order):

+3.77E–01	–1.51E+00	+5.64E+00	–6.94E+00	+4.06E+00
–1.30E+00	+2.42E–01	–2.61E–02	+1.50E–03	–3.60E–05

While polynomial regression models provide a nice pedagogical example for discussions like this one, no one uses polynomial models for data mining. There are mathematical reasons (mostly related to stability and over-fitting), but the real reason is that almost all real-world modeling problems involving numeric data seem to fall into the following two categories:

1.   The data are related by a linear equation, or conform well to a known probability model (e.g., normal distribution).

2.   The data are highly complex, even chaotic.

Said differently, data modeling in the real world is usually either very easy, or very hard.

Knowledge-based expert systems (KBES) will be discussed in the following section. These are mentioned first because they are usually constructed "by hand" rather than trained using adaptive techniques.

10.4.1 Knowledge-Based Expert Systems (KBES)

KBES as they exist today were invented by Dr. Edward Feigenbaum of Cornell University in the 1960s. The use of "heuristics," however, has been around as long as the IF statement. KBES capture expert level human knowledge in executable "rules." The rules are strictly segregated from other code, and codify the expert's intuitive approach to the domain problem. KBES are the most mature "intelligent" paradigm in common use.

The fundamental unit of knowledge in KBES is the "rule," which usually has the form of a structured construct, such as an IF-THEN-ELSE statement. KBES Predictive models can be built which use rules obtained from human domain experts to codify expert knowledge for incorporation into predictive models.

KBES predictive models capture rare, perishable human expertise in executable form, so that it can be retained, copied, and enhanced by successive generations of human experts. This "brain power in a box" will work in any location (or *every* location), can run 24 hours a day, and never asks for a raise. If built with the ability to explain its decisions, such a system can also be used as a training tool.

Some designers of predictive models have forgotten about KBES, probably because the data mining tools currently in vogue generally provide no support for them. But KBES have two things going for them that most other predictive modeling paradigms do not:

1.   KBES explicitly provide a mechanism for using domain knowledge already possessed by human experts.

2.   KBES can be built with the ability to explain their conclusions.

The authors have found that, while KBES do not offer the greatest *predictive* power, they do offer the greatest *explanatory* power, and this can mean the difference between success and failure for a knowledge-intensive predictive modeling project. The highly reliable (but inexplicable) output of a complex black-box model like a neural network is often viewed with suspicion, especially when the stakes for a "bad prediction" are high. Applications such as medical image classification, stock market prediction, and military target identification involve critical decisions. A little insight into how a predictive model came up with its recommendations can really help.

For this reason, it is recommended that predictive models for high-risk applications be built as hybrids of black-and-white–box components. *Hybrid systems*, those having both a black-box part (e.g., neural network) and a white-box part (e.g., KBES), can realize the benefits of both. The black-box is there to exploit complex data patterns for which rules are not available, and the KBES is there to explain how the evidence was used.

This method of combining two or more predictive modeling techniques in a single predictive modeling architecture is called *bagging*. Hybrid predictive models using bagging apply each model to the input feature vector, and combine the outputs to obtain an adjudicated result. This combination process is sometimes called *aggregation*, and the process' algorithm an *aggregation rule*.

Essentially, bagging uses a "committee" of models that separately process the feature vectors, and then vote. Some models may be given more "votes," depending upon the conditions of the problem. KBES are good models to have on such a committee, because they can provide Conclusion Justification Reports (CJR).

Preparing such a report can be done automatically. One easy way to do this is just to include a statement inside each rule that adds appropriate lines to the CJR anytime, should the rule be executed by the inference engine. The following 3-rule KBES produces credit risk scores for people given three features, and produces a CJR as a side-effect of its decision process. Initially, the RISK is set to 50 percent.

10.4.1.1 A Sample Rule Set for Credit Risk

Pre-Process:

RISK=50 percent

"The 3-rule KBES was used to compute a risk score for xxx on DATE."

"Available data was used in the following way to compute the risk score:"

Rule 1:

IF person has a savings account, THEN

RISK = 50 percent × RISK

ADD TO CJR: "Risk *reduced* 50 percent: This person has a savings account."

ELSE

RISK = 120 percent × RISK

ADD TO CJR: "Risk *increased* 20 percent: This person has NO savings account."

END IF

Rule 2:

IF person has been with same employer for more than 1 year, THEN

RISK = 85 percent × RISK

ADD TO CJR: "Risk *reduced* 15 percent: This person has stable employment."

ELSE

RISK = 105 percent × RISK

ADD TO CJR: "Risk *increased* 5 percent: This person DOES NOT HAVE stable employment."

stop IF

Rule 3:

IF person has a credit history from credit bureau, THEN

RISK = (BUREAU RISK + RISK)/2

ADD TO CJR: "Credit bureau rating for this person is *BUREAU RATING*"

ELSE

RISK = 150 percent × RISK

ADD TO CJR: "Risk greatly *increased* because this person has NO credit history."

END IF

Post-Process:

"Based upon these considerations, the credit risk for xxx is RISK percent"

Suppose now that Person A has a savings account, has been with the same employer for 3 years, and has a credit bureau risk of 10 percent. Running the 3-rule credit advisor above on Person A will give the following CJR:

"The 3-rule KBES was used to compute a risk score for Person A on 04/02/2000."

"Available data was used in the following way to compute the risk score:"

"Risk *reduced* 50 percent: This person has a savings account."

"Risk *reduced* 15 percent: This person has stable employment."

"Credit bureau rating for this person is *10 percent*."

"Based upon these considerations, the credit risk for Person A is **16 percent**."

Similarly, Person B has no savings account, is unemployed, and has no credit rating. Running the same 3-rule advisor on Person B will give the following CJR:

"The 3-rule KBES was used to compute a risk score for Person B on 04/02/2000."

"Available data was used in the following way to compute the risk score:"

"Risk *increased* 20 percent: This person has NO savings account."

"Risk *increased* 5 percent: This person HASN'T stable employment."

"Risk greatly *increased* because this person has NO credit history."

"Based upon these considerations, the credit risk for Person B is **95 percent**."

Keep in mind that this intuitive, self-explanatory report is formulated entirely by the KBES. The machine applies its knowledge, draws its conclusions, and explains its reasoning.

The 3-rule system here has some obvious drawbacks; for example, it will produce risks in excess of 100 percent. Through the use of appropriate aggregation rules, these shortcomings can be remedied to build an effective risk advisor that can explain how it knows what it knows. It is easy to imagine adding additional rules that interpret and incorporate the decisions of neural networks, regression functions, and other members of the predictive modeling "credit committee" that could be running in parallel.

As seen in the section on rule induction, usable rules can be induced directly from data that has been annotated with ground-truth. The rules extracted in that discussion could obviously be applied to new data to classify it as circle or square. A collection of rules (from whatever source) can be applied to build classifiers and predictors in the obvious way. Feature vectors are prepared from available data, and the rules are applied.

The application of rules in a KBES is generally done under the direction of an "inference engine," which determines the proper sequence for applying rules. There are several inference methodologies in common use, the two most popular being forward chaining and backward chaining. Advanced techniques for combining the contributions of the rules in a KBES have been developed; the interested reader should refer to the literature.

10.5 Machine Learning and Predictive Models

Humans learn different things in different ways. Humans often learn to solve classification tasks by looking at examples. A child is told by his father that the object in his hand is an apple. The child (subconsciously) notes the attributes of this thing called "apple." This "learning event" can be described as a predictive modeling process: The child performs feature extraction (shape = round, smell = fruity, color = red), and creates the association:

(round, fruity, red) $\rightarrow$ apple

If this association is reinforced by additional experience with other apples over time (a "training sequence" is applied), it may become a "paradigm" for "apple," and move into long-term memory. The training sequence has "converged."

Tomorrow, though, the child may encounter the feature vector (round, fruity, red) in connection with a cherry. A *collision* has occurred in feature space: a representational ambiguity arising when vectors of different ground-truth classes have identical features. This ambiguity may be resolved by creating a new ground-truth class (cherries), and incorporating discriminating features (e.g., size).

(round, fruity, red, *big*) → apple

(round, fruity, red, *small*) → cherry

This process continues as the child encounters green apples, rotten apples, caramel apples, cooked apples in pies, apple juice, drawings of apples, etc. Eventually the child can recognize apples in practically all of their many forms, because she has formulated a robust "apple paradigm."

This type of learning can be described as a feedback control process. The learner has some internal mechanism for storing learned associations, but its contents are initially random (Locke's *tabula rasa*: "The mind is a blank slate upon which experience writes.") During a training pass, the learner is given an example *(exemplar)* of an item to be classified. If the learner gives a correct classification response, the corresponding stored association is strengthened. If the learner gives an incorrect response, the corresponding stored association is weakened.

After a sufficient number of training passes *(epochs)* the learner is able to correctly state the ground-truth for every item in the training set. The classifier has been "trained." This learning algorithm is called *reinforcement learning*.

The learning method described here is an example of *supervised learning*: Ground-truth is made available to the learner. In *unsupervised learning*, ground-truth is not made available to the learner, so artificial classes must be created and populated by similarity matching. (This explains the necessity for colorful colloquialisms like "doohickey" and "widget." Such abstract temporary appellations serve as essential intermediate stages in human association learning.)

Reinforcement learning (as well as many other types of learning) can be automated in software, giving rise to *machine learning algorithms*. The strengthening and weakening of associations performed by such algorithms involve the mathematical adjustment of model parameters. If the model is a simple linear regression, the parameters are slopes and intercepts. If the model is a polynomial regression, the parameters are polynomial coefficients. If the model is a KBES, the parameters may be weights assigned to the rules, and so on.

The feedback process is shown in the following figure. On the left is a training set of feature vectors having ground-truth values T_i. Each vector is fed to the classifier (Inference Methodology), which tries to assign ground-truth using the current set of decision parameters. The machines classification answer is forwarded to the training algorithm, where it is compared with ground-truth; based upon this comparison, the decision parameters P_k are adjusted, and the cycle repeats (see Figure 10.8).

Figure 10.8

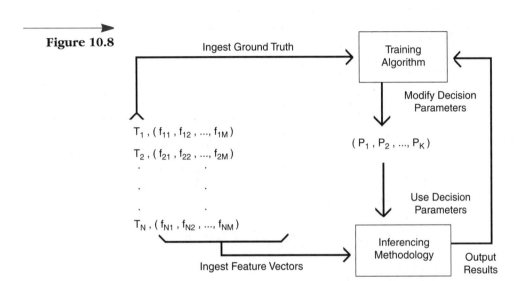

The hard part in all of this is the construction of the training algorithm. Many such algorithms have been created. Most are extensions or applications of numerical methods created long ago. Others are recent innovations. Most "conventional" learning techniques are based upon computational schemes for directly computing or estimating model parameters (e.g., the method of least squares, mentioned above, was invented by Carl F. Gauss, the greatest mathematician of all time, in 1801).

Advanced predictive modeling applications often make use of machine learning algorithms. This is because advanced models are generally attacking problems for which no human can write an explicit closed-form solution, but for which training data is available (e.g., fraud, churn).

The processes by which most modern predictive models are developed are *adaptive*, using numerical methods that adjust model parameters based upon analysis of data and model performance. Reinforcement learning is an example. The machine learning process generates a predictive model through mechanical analysis of data and introspection; model parameters are determined without human involvement. Such a process can rightly be called "learning."

In the following section, the effects of applying the "Delta Rule," one of the simplest machine learning algorithms, are studied.

10.6 Neural Networks (NNs)

Neural Networks (NNs, also called "artificial neural networks," ANNs) as the basis for a computing paradigm have actually been around since the work of McCulloch and Pitts (1943), and perhaps longer. The neural approach has had a colorful history, and is today an effective predictive modeling technique for hard DM problems.

Animal brains have tremendous processing capability. If this capability has a physiological basis, it might be possible to build artificial analogs of these brains that exhibit some of their processing characteristics. The human brain appears to consist of many billions of small processing elements (living neurons) that are organized into cortices, lobes, and hemispheres, and highly interconnected to form a massively parallel device.

The basic idea behind artificial neural networks is to mimic certain gross aspects of brain architecture. As a result, neural network implementations are often highly interconnected networks of simple artificial processing elements (called "neurons") that have been organized in such a way that their stimulus/response patterns solve predictive modeling problems.

10.7 Decision Values and Decision Surfaces

Before a detailed discussion of neural network modeling can be undertaken, some background must be laid. This will be done using population **P**, which was defined in Chapter 9, and is plotted again below.

Values of a feature that split data into subsets by class are called *decision values*. For example, we define a decision value when we say that "any job with a profit under 10 percent is bad, but all others are good." This establishes a rule ("less than 10 percent = BAD, else GOOD") that splits the population of jobs into classes based upon their relationship to the stated decision value (10 percent).

It is clear from the plot below of population **P** introduced in Chapter 9 that there is no vertical line that has all the circles on one side, and all the boxes on the other. Therefore, there is no one X value that separates the two classes. Neither is there any horizontal line with all one class above and the other below; so no single Y value splits the classes. That is, there is no perfect decision value in X, nor is there a perfect decision value in Y for this classification problem. If there were such a value, we could induce a single simple (one predicate) rule that would perfectly classify the given data (see Figure 10.9).

Figure 10.9

16 vectors in class 1 (circles), 16 vectors in class 2 (squares).

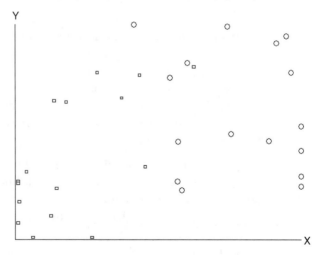

The concept of the decision value can be generalized. A decision value in $\mathbf{R}^1$ is a point, because a point splits this space into two non-intersecting parts. But a point doesn't split $\mathbf{R}^2$, the plane, in this way; a more powerful "divider" is needed: for example, a line. In $\mathbf{R}^3$, a plane might be used; in $\mathbf{R}^4$, a hyper-plane (3-dimensional analog of a plane). In general, the forms that constitute the boundaries between classes are called *decision surfaces*. All classifiers operate by creating, directly or indirectly, decision surfaces between classes.

Additional analysis of our population **P** leads to the conclusion that there is no line of any sort, vertical, horizontal, or oblique, that splits **P** perfectly into the given classes. This is easy to verify by just trying to lay a straightedge on the figure (a pencil will do) in such a way that all the circles are on one side, and all the squares on the other. Classification problems that cannot be solved by any linear decision surface are called *non-linearly separable*. Classifying **P** into circles and squares is a non-linearly separable problem.

The distinction between linearly separable and linearly non-separable problems is an important one, because there is a well-known solution to any linearly separable problem. This solution can be implemented by using a one-layer perceptron and an algorithm called the Delta Rule. This algorithm is guaranteed to produce a perfect decision surface in a finite number of steps, assuming reasonable default values are used in setting up the problem. No such general result exists for non-linearly separable problems. The point is that linearly separable problems are in some sense "easier" than non-linearly separable problems.

This provides a crude but intuitive means of measuring the "difficulty" of a classification problem: If a linear decision surface does a reasonable job on a problem, then it's "easy." If no linear decision surface does a reasonable job on a problem, then it's "hard." (Precise treatment of these notions requires the theory of PAC Learning and VC Dimension, research-level topics requiring specialized knowledge; refer to the references.)

The classification problem for **P** is almost linearly separable: It is possible (in numerous ways) to draw a line through the figure that has all but one of the squares to its left, and all the circles (and the other square) on its right. Such a decision surface correctly classifies 31 of the 32 data feature vectors, and so has an accuracy of (31/32) × 100 percent = 96.9 percent. The classification problem for **P** is very easy.

10.8 Multi-Layer Perceptrons (MLPs)

When the term "neural network" is used, what is most commonly meant is one particular type of neural network, the multi-layer perceptron (MLP). In 1957, Frank Rosenblatt devised a mathematical model of an animal neuron with the ability to both learn and classify patterns. Rosenblatt and his assistant, Charles Wightman, built a working electronic model of this artificial neuron, which they called a "perceptron." This was the first neuro-computer to carry out a useful function. Called the Mark I, it was able to recognize shapes and letters whose images were shown to its 20×20 input array of Cadmium Sulfide photoconductors.

Researchers in this new field of "intelligent machines" began to make some pretty provocative claims for their work. Hype abounded. In response to this, several influential researchers began (c. 1967) to challenge some of these claims. As part of this challenge, Marvin Minsky and Seymour Papert published in 1969 a critique of neural technology as it existed at the time in a book called *Perceptrons*.

In their book, Minsky and Papert showed that neural networks consisting of just a single neuron could not solve certain kinds of problems. They did not substantially address the potential of MLPs, for which no machine learning algorithms had yet been developed.

The resulting collapse of the hype-bubble surrounding "all things neural" caused a general loss of interest in neural networks until about 1983, when new research that addressed the limitations cited by Minsky and Papert began to be widely known. By the mid-1980s, neural network research had again become a credible, mainstream pursuit.[4]

The figure below is an example of a *feed-forward network*, in which feature vectors enter the network through one set of artificial neurons (the *input neurons*), move "forward" through other neurons (the *processing neurons*), and appear as outputs at another set of neurons (the *output neurons*). The figure shows a drawing of the

---

4.   The seminal work was done by Paul Werbos, Stephen Grossberg, Tuevo Kohonen, John Hopfield, David Rumelhart, James Anderson, Shun-ichi Amari, Harry Klopf, David Willshaw, Kunihiko Fukushima, James McClelland, and others. Notable among these brave souls is Ira Skurnick, a program manager in the Defense Science Office of DARPA, who had the guts to begin funding neural network research in 1983. With DARPA's name in the mix, other PM's followed suit.

architecture of such a feed-forward network. The feature vector components are the nodes across the bottom, in the layer titled "F." The input neurons are in the next layer up, L1; the processing neurons are in layers L2 and L3; and the output neurons are in the top layer, L4. Because there are four layers, this is called a four-layer perceptron. Layers 2 and 3, having no direct contact with the outside world, and are called *hidden layers*, and their neurons, *hidden-layer neurons* (see Figure 10.10).

Figure 10.10

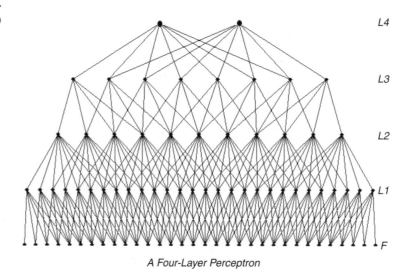

A Four-Layer Perceptron

10.9 Training a Simple Neural Network

Neural networks are black-box regression models that can solve very complex classification problems using parameters "learned" during a training sequence. This fact suggests numerous provocative possibilities for applying these machines to problems that overwhelm conventional techniques, and which even human experts find intractable. Analyzing the training of a multi-layer perceptron is quite complicated. Instead, in this section a typical training sequence is carried out to train a one-neuron machine to solve a classification problem. The "architecture" of this machine is depicted in Figure 10.11. This figure depicts a neuron having five inputs.

Figure 10.11

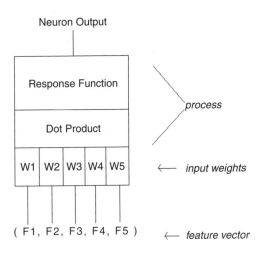

One Neuron Machine

In the case of population P, there are only two dimensions, so the neuron will have only two inputs. For problem P, the neuron has three parameters: The leftmost, W1, is multiplied by feature 1 ("**X**"), and the rightmost, W2, is multiplied by feature 2 ("**Y**"). Both of these products are added to a third parameter, W0, to obtain the sum D = W0 + W1 X + W2 Y. If D is less than 0, the input vector (**X, Y**) will be classified as being in class 1; if D is greater than zero, the input vector (**X, Y**) will be classified as being in class 2. The problem, of course, is how to determine W0, W1, and W2 so that the values assumed by D correctly classify the training data.

In this section, the values of the neural parameters W1, W2, the *synaptic weights*, and the neuron *offset*, W0, will be determined for a non-trivial classification problem. The population for this problem consists of 100 feature vectors, in two classes: 50 circles, and 50 squares. Keep in mind that "circles" could represent "good clients" and squares "bad clients," etc. The figure below shows the population that will be used (see Figure 10.12).

A one-neuron classifier uses a line as a decision surface. The problem of training the classifier is to determine how to position the line so that, to the extent possible, vectors of one class are on one side of the line, and vectors of the other class on the other. Of course, if the

Figure 10.12   PASS: 1

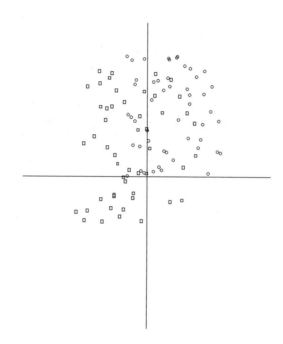

original problem is non-linearly separable, it will not be possible to do this with 100 percent accuracy.

The linear decision surface given by the one-neuron classifier could be positioned manually: A human could use trial and error, and visual judgment to attempt to position the line. Such a "hand-built" classifier can be constructed for easy problems in low-dimensional spaces; but manual techniques cannot be readily applied to complicated non-linearly separable problems in a high-dimensional space. For these problems, a training algorithm to optimize the decision surface is needed.[5]

A method called the Delta Rule provides an effective training algorithm for one-neuron machines (give reference). The Delta Rule begins with a linear decision surface drawn in a randomly chosen way through feature space (for example, in $\mathbf{R}^2$, a line).

The initial configuration for our example might look like the figure below. The diagram has been annotated with an "S" to indicate

---

5.   Experts will note that classifiers based upon one-neuron machines are fundamentally equivalent to conventional logistic regression.

that the half-plane to the "left" of the decision surface is the "square" region, and with a "C" to indicate that the half-plane to the "right" of the decision surface is the "circle" region. In this initial configuration, 78 percent of the circles are in the circle region, for a "circles correct" accuracy of 78 percent, while only 30 percent of the squares are in the square region, for a "squares correct" accuracy of 30 percent. The overall accuracy of the initial, random classifier is 54 percent, since 54 percent of the feature vectors are in "their" region.

As a visual aid in interpreting the figures, correctly classified circles and squares are doubled in size, while incorrectly classified icons remain small (see Figure 10.13).

Figure 10.13

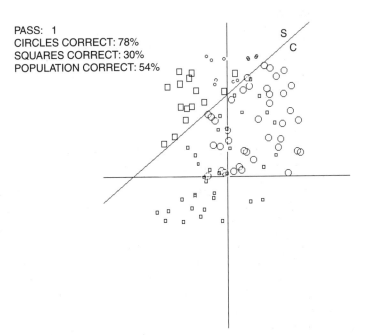

PASS: 1
CIRCLES CORRECT: 78%
SQUARES CORRECT: 30%
POPULATION CORRECT: 54%

Based upon the arrangement of feature vectors of different ground-truth classes, the Delta Rule moves the decision surface slightly in such a way that its ability to discriminate between the classes is likely to be improved. This process is repeated until no further change in the position of the line occurs. There is an important theorem that guarantees that, for linearly separable problems, a proper implementation of the Delta Rule will produce a classifier that gives 100 percent correct classification on the training vectors in a finite number of iterations. For problems that are not linearly separable, the Delta Rule gives results that are near optimal for a linear decision surface.

After 100 iterations of the Delta Rule, the decision surface has been moved to the location indicated. The classification performance on circles has improved to 90 percent, while performance on squares has dropped slightly to 26 percent. The overall accuracy has increased to 56 percent (see Figure 10.14).

Figure 10.14

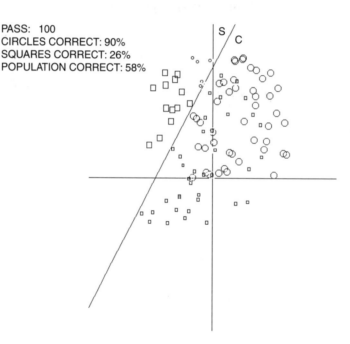

PASS: 100
CIRCLES CORRECT: 90%
SQUARES CORRECT: 26%
POPULATION CORRECT: 58%

After 200 iterations of the Delta Rule, the decision surface has been moved to the location indicated. The classification performance on both circles and squares, as well as the overall accuracy, have continued to improve (see Figure 10.15).

After 500 iterations, overall performance has reached 76 percent. Notice that the decision surface is not moving as rapidly as it was during the first few iterations of the Delta Rule. This is typical; the Delta Rule generally makes rapid improvement early, then slows to a crawl as it approaches a solution (see Figure 10.16).

Figure 10.15

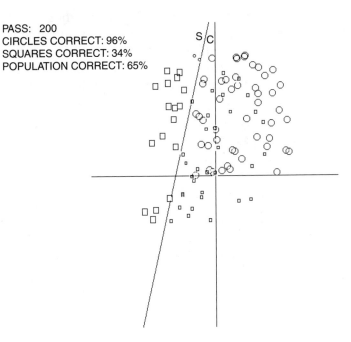

PASS: 200
CIRCLES CORRECT: 96%
SQUARES CORRECT: 34%
POPULATION CORRECT: 65%

Figure 10.16

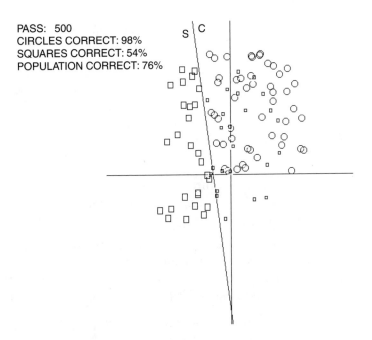

PASS: 500
CIRCLES CORRECT: 98%
SQUARES CORRECT: 54%
POPULATION CORRECT: 76%

At 800 iterations, overall performance has reached 80 percent. This is about as good as a one-neuron classifier can do this non-linearly separable problem. On subsequent passes, the overall accuracy of the classifier can (and in this example, will) drop, because the Delta Rule is not optimizing for classification accuracy. It is optimizing a more general "objective" function (see Figure 10.17).

Figure 10.17

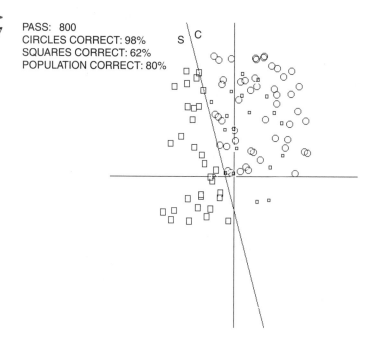

PASS: 800
CIRCLES CORRECT: 98%
SQUARES CORRECT: 62%
POPULATION CORRECT: 80%

Figures 10.18 through 10.20 show the final stages in the convergence of the training sequence. Notice that there is almost no change between the 10,000 iteration model, and the 20,000 model.

In Figure 10.20, the training software has displayed the parameters that give the decision surface, so that it may be applied to classify other feature vectors. These figures tell us that the decision surface found using the Delta Rule has the equation:

$$0.3692936 - 2.057876X - 1.153504Y = 0$$

Figure 10.18

PASS: 2000
CIRCLES CORRECT: 88%
SQUARES CORRECT: 64%
POPULATION CORRECT: 76%

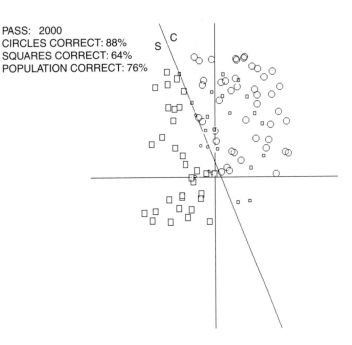

Figure 10.19

PASS: 10000
CIRCLES CORRECT: 76%
SQUARES CORRECT: 76%
POPULATION CORRECT: 76%

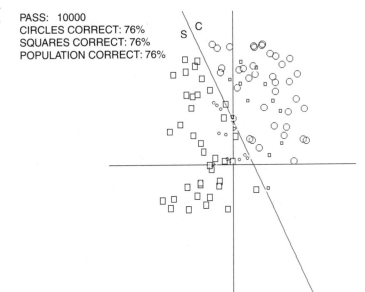

Figure 10.20

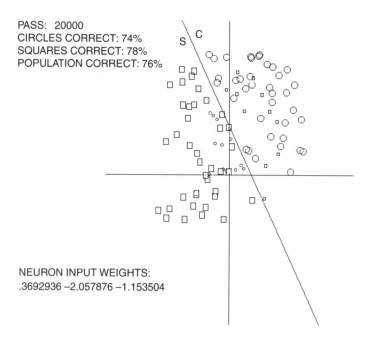

PASS: 20000
CIRCLES CORRECT: 74%
SQUARES CORRECT: 78%
POPULATION CORRECT: 76%

NEURON INPUT WEIGHTS:
.3692936 −2.057876 −1.153504

The question naturally arises, "Is this decision surface unique? If we had initialized the original line in a different way, would we get the same final result?" The answer is "not necessarily." It is a well-known fact that there may be multiple solutions to a given MLP training problem. A discussion of the technical details (i.e., multiple local and global minima of the objective function) would take us far afield. The interested reader should consult the literature.

As illustrated in this example, the Delta Rule provides an iterative algorithm that allows a neural network to "learn" to classify data without human assistance. As black-box models, these classifiers do not provide explanatory information, but they can give excellent predictive models.

10.10 More Complex Decision Surfaces

An obvious weakness of the one-neuron machine just discussed is that its decision surface is a straight line; this machine will never be able to solve a non-linearly separable problem with 100 percent accuracy, no matter how it is trained. This machine just does not have the power to handle such problems.

As is the case with polynomials, a power increase for MLPs comes at the cost of increasing the number of parameters. In the MLP case, this shows up in the form of additional layers in the perceptron. The specifics of the Kolmogorov Theorem include the statement that for any given well-posed classification problem, there exists a three layer MLP with sufficient power to solve it.

As an example of a more complex decision surface, we classify the population P using a radial basis function classifier. The decision surface is overlaid on the population in the figure below. The indentation at "A" was introduced by the RBF just to catch the square there, and the indentation at "C" was introduced to corral the three circles. It is difficult to see in the diagram, but the RBF has actually drawn a tiny ring around the circle at "B," marking it as part of the "circle" class.

Figure 10.21

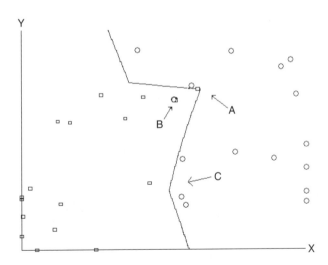

Here it is seen that more powerful models can create very complex decision surfaces with multiple pieces. This opens these models to the real possibility of *over-training*, a situation in which a high-power model is forced to memorize details of a training set that do not generalize to the whole population. For example, if the data

at "A" and "B" are just outliers that happened to make it into the training set, a high-power classifier will create a decision surface with
"bends" that shouldn't be there; this could damage its performance
on blind data.

It is possible to detect over-training during model construction
by applying the partially trained model to a test set not in the training data every so often. As long as performance on the non-training
test set continues to increase, generalized learning is occurring.
When performance on the test set stops improving, training should
be halted.

Part III

Data Mining Management

- Avoiding Pitfalls
- Overcoming Obstacles
- Managing Projects to Success

11

Common Reasons Data Mining Projects Fail

Data mining initiatives sometimes fail. As with any system development project, there are many factors that can contribute to failure. Some of these factors are beyond the control of the data mining analysts (budget cuts for example), but most are the result of mistakes in methodology or technique.

The term "failure" itself requires definition. For most development projects, "failure" means that the effort did not lead to the creation of a system that met the specification. This definition doesn't really fit data mining projects, which tend to be more "exploratory" than constructive. "Failure" for a data mining project usually means one of the following two outcomes:

1. Not finding relevant patterns that are actually present in the data and could be generalized

2. Finding (and exploiting) patterns that do not generalize, are not relevant, or are not actually present in the data

Both of these failures are bad, but the second is generally worse. It could initiate the implementation of a system that, as will be discovered after much time and expense, can't possibly work.

The circumstances leading to data mining failure are ubiquitous. Some are inherent to data mining itself, so there are no simple tricks or data mining tools that will completely insulate a careless analyst from them. The application of a sound data mining process in conjunction with a set of robust data mining tools increases the likelihood of success. But the best ally in avoiding catastrophic data mining failure is vigilance coupled with an awareness of the possible pitfalls. In this chapter, the primary reasons for the failure of data mining projects are described, along with some suggestions for mitigating their effects.

11.1 Data Mining's Seven Deadly Sins

There are classic data mining errors that even experienced analysts make. These errors are fundamentally different from the errors that befall conventional development efforts, and can lead to spectacular, and very embarrassing, failures. Several examples follow.

Table 11.1

Data Mining Error	Analyst Response
Making "discoveries" that later turn out to be false	"It seems our best customers are extra-terrestrials"
Failing to discover things that later turn out to be true	"Really? Profit is related to revenue?"
Building models that don't work in the real world	"It works GREAT on the two examples we chose!"
Ruining data by mishandling it	"Yeah, we just rounded everything off to the nearest $1,000,000"

The most horrific data mining errors arise more often from the way in which the data are prepared, than from the way the subsequent analysis is done.[1]

Given the power of modern data mining tools, if the data are handled correctly, the mining process usually goes mostly right. Conversely, if the data are handled incorrectly, the mining process usually goes mostly wrong. Listed below (in no particular order) are the worst of the lot: the "Seven Deadly Sins" of data mining. Any enterprise that engages in data mining work for any length of time will have opportunities to learn every one of them the hard way. When they do, it's often after the expenditure of much labor from multiple people crossing organizational boundaries. It is best to develop a habit of regularly asking whether your current data mining initiative could be committing one of the sins below.

---

1. The seminal work is Dorian Pyle's book *Data Preparation for Data Mining*.

11.1.1 Failure to Properly Condition the Data

Mining data that has been poisoned by careless handling can produce spurious results. Data that is improperly conditioned can mislead the analyst in two ways: by destroying existing patterns, and by introducing spurious patterns. There are many kinds of data conditioning errors. It isn't possible to provide a comprehensive list here, but it's imperative for the data mining analyst to understand that such errors have a common effect. All conditioning errors produce data that *misrepresent the domain* in some way, making the valid information it contains less accessible. Examples of such misrepresentation include the following.

- Improper rounding of data values can destroy information through loss of precision.

- Clumsy quantization of data can hide relationships.

- Miscoding of data can create relationships where none actually exist.

- Failure to correctly handle missing values in data can corrupt it. For example, replacing missing values with zero, when zero is itself a valid value, leads later to the unfortunate question, "Uh, is this a *real* zero, or a *missing* zero?"

- Creating analysis sets without taking precautions against sampling error is a common conditioning error.

In the final example, it is not the individual feature values themselves that are misrepresented, but the *distribution* information (e.g., statistics) that will be derived from these values. Pity the poor researcher who creates an analysis set by just grabbing the first 10,000 records from a non-randomized data store. This analyst can look forward to discovering many amazing facts about customers... all of whom live in Alabama, Alaska, or Arizona.

11.1.1.1 Dealing with Sin 1

Visualization and reporting tools, when applied by an analyst who is familiar with the data, are generally effective in detecting information damage. The effects of improper conditioning are often apparent when the data are visualized, or subjected to statistical analysis.

"Sanity checking" by a domain expert can also be effective in defending against improper data conditioning. Checking to see that obvious well-known patterns are still present in the data after it has been conditioned is helpful.[2]

11.1.2 Failure to Validate the Model

It's tempting to say "Eureka!" the minute something provocative is found in the data. But the excitement that accompanies the discovery of unsuspected patterns in a data set must be held in abeyance until the presence of these patterns is confirmed in data that were not used to make the discovery. It is always possible that discovered patterns are coincidental. They may result from sampling error when the analysis set was constructed. They may not reflect facts that generalize to the population as a whole.

There is a well-known "validation" horror story about a pattern recognition project to develop an automated system that could detect military vehicles (tanks) in natural terrain directly from aerial photographs. Two sets of photographs were compiled of the terrain: one set with tanks present, and one with tanks absent. After weeks of data mining work, the development team had created a predictive model that could identify aerial photographs as either "tank(s) present" or "tanks absent."

This supposedly "validated" system was later applied to a collection of aerial photographs, some with tanks present, and some not. The system produced what appeared to be random classification results. In reviewing these results, a sharp-eyed analyst noticed that the system always said that tanks were present when the photographs were taken during overcast conditions. A review of the training set revealed that the training data with "tanks present" were all created on a cloudy day. The system hadn't learned to identify tanks at all; it had learned how to spot lousy weather.

11.1.2.1 Dealing with Sin 2

The results of a data-mining project must always be properly validated. For a discovery effort, this is done by showing that the principles gleaned during a discovery activity are still valid when applied to a substantial, representative data set that was not used in the dis-

---

2.   This is similar to regression testing for software, in which modified software is applied to test data to show that it still gives the same results as the old version: No damage has been done. In the same way, it is helpful to demonstrate that the conditioned data still carry the information that was present in the unconditioned set: No damage has been done.

covery process. For a predictive modeling effort, this is done using blind testing and/or cross-validation as described below under "model validation."

Further, if the use of discovered knowledge or a predictive model could have significant enterprise impact should the work later be found to be invalid, it is wise to perform an independent audit of the development process. This can be done by an impartial analyst familiar with the process, techniques, and tools employed.

Finally, demonstrating that a discovery or predictive model applies to multiple data sets sampled from the population (repeatability) is the gold standard of empirical validation methods.

11.1.2.2 *Model Validation*

Validation is the term applied to the process of verifying that a model is functioning "properly." For conventional systems, this process is called system testing, and has grown into an entire engineering discipline. "Proper functioning" for conventional information systems, means that the functional and performance specifications have been met. As was seen in Chapter 4, however, predictive models developed under a rapid prototyping methodology generally are not built "to spec." How, then, are they to be validated?

In practice, data mining models are usually validated by "audition." They are applied to test sets, and their results are compared to known correct answers. While this sounds simple, it can be problematic. There are two cases.

Case 1: Lots of test data for which the correct outcomes are known are readily available.

In this case, the validation method of choice is *blind-testing*. In blind-testing, a representative sample of data of the type to be processed, and which was not used in the creation of the model, is processed by the model, and the results are checked for accuracy.

It is important that the blind-test data be representative of the problem domain. That is, it should include examples of each type of datum that occurs in the population, in the same relative proportions that these types naturally occur. The sample should consist entirely of records not used to build the model (hence the term "blind" testing), to avoid simple memorization, and to test for overtraining.

It is not enough just to report an overall accuracy score (e.g., percent of samples correctly processed), since the population might be unbalanced, and some errors might be more costly than others. A better reporting mechanism is the confusion matrix seen previously. This gives information on the relative frequency of each type of error made.

Case 2: Data with known outcomes are in short supply.

In this case, there might not be enough data available to build a working model while holding back a portion of the data for blind testing. The method of choice then is *n-fold cross validation*.

In n-fold cross-validation, the data are divided into n random samples. One of these samples is held out; the others are pooled and used to build a model. This model is then used to process the hold-out sample (#1), and its performance is documented. This process is repeated n-times, each time holding out a different one of the samples. The resulting accuracy figures for the n-trials are then averaged, and reported as the aggregated performance of the model that is built from all the samples together.

In practice, a typical value for n is 10. It might be noted that the blind testing of Case 1 above is basically the case n = 2.

Other considerations may be applied in validation. For example, if a model is a white-box model (such as an expert system), it is possible to determine whether the right results have been obtained for the *right reasons*. This is accomplished by allowing a human expert to review the inference path taken by the KBES to verify that it is appropriate.

In general, predictive models are verified empirically, under conditions similar to those they will encounter operationally. This gives model validation an experimental flavor, and naturally leads to a statistical scheme for reporting model performance (e.g., "the model is 80 percent correct on 95 percent of the test samples").

11.1.3 GIGOO: Garbage In, Gold Out

Data mining hype has left many would-be miners with the impression that powerful tools can pull extremely valuable information out of any data set. This misconception is equivalent to believing that a big enough shovel will find gold in your backyard. Data mining tools can't create information any more than a big shovel can create gold.

Data mining analysts must always be prepared to redirect their search if it becomes clear that the current ground is barren.

Take careful note: Data mining efforts that do not "find anything" in a data set are often *not* failures. The motivation for undertaking data mining in the first place was the *suspicion* that latent information was present in the data, but not immediately accessible. If carefully executed data mining efforts find no such information, it makes much more sense to fault the suspicion than the effort.

Of course, data owners are likely to take a negative result as a suggestion that their data set is a load of fool's gold, and will insist that the miners have failed. Wise managers will resist the temptation to fault either the data or the miners, since neither necessarily deserves any "blame."

One person's gold is another's garbage. Most enterprise data are collected to support well-defined business activities like accounts receivable, tax preparation, conventional market research, etc. Data mining was not considered when such application systems were specified. This means that data mining analysts rarely receive data that is ideally suited to their purpose. When such a repository is used for a data mining application, it is always possible that the data do not contain information that supports the data mining objectives.

Data mining projects can fail as a result of inadequate or improperly used tools. Data mining tools that cannot handle the mass of data available, don't support the desired application, or are misapplied, don't produce good results.

Many incipient technologies are shipwrecked on their own hype. Data mining projects may produce good incremental results ("10 percent reduction of churn!"), but be deemed "failures" because they didn't live up to unrealistic initial expectations ("Total elimination of churn!"). When this happens, not only are immediate potential benefits lost, but the willingness of the enterprise to engage in future innovation is diminished.

There is value in knowing that a particular data set contains no information about a particular question. This knowledge helps managers focus their decision-making process.

Monte worked on a data mining application several years ago for which the end user wanted to predict the length of a patient's hospital stay based upon diagnostic and demographic information. Sophisticated data mining techniques were applied according to sound data mining methodology: statistical analysis, high-end visualization, feature coding, adaptive clustering techniques, and so on, all in proper context. Although the data didn't offer much initial promise, the data mining team proceeded with the construction of a predictive model to see what the results would be.

A model was developed using a sophisticated regression paradigm of tremendous predictive power—to no avail. It was able to predict broad population trends, but not the length of hospital stay on a patient-by-patient basis. It was just a fancy actuarial table. In this case, the outcome was not attributable to weakness in the regression method, nor was it the result of a haphazard feature extraction process. The data available just did not support the proposed application. This situation is not at all unusual.

11.1.3.1   Dealing with Sin 3

If there is reasonable doubt concerning the information content of the data, it's usually best to conduct a limited experiment in advance of an extended longer-term development. Monte refers to these prototyping experiments as "gauntlets." The problem is thrown on the table, the challenge is taken, an attack is made, and the victor is determined by the results. With the outcome of a limited "attack" known, an intelligent ROI estimate can be made which provides the basis for a "go/no-go" decision.

The "gauntlet" approach to data mining and the construction of predictive models is well suited to a rapid prototyping methodology. A rapid prototyping approach limits risk, while giving insight into the problem. As seen in the hospital-stay example above, data problems are often the culprits when data mining projects yield a null result.

11.1.4 Ignoring Population Imbalance

Real-world populations are always lopsided mixtures of high- and low-interest members. For example, the proportion of telecom customers involved in fraud is fairly small, yet, it is precisely this tiny segment of users that are of most interest in many telecom data mining efforts. This imbalance in the relative proportions of ground-truth classes must be considered in planning, executing, and evaluating data mining activities.

Consider the case of a population consisting of 100 members, 99 in ground-truth class 1, and 1 in ground-truth class 2. By doing *nothing*, and calling every member a class 1, a classification "algorithm" having an accuracy of 99 percent is obtained. But this can hardly be called a successful data mining effort. The construction of predictive models in the presence of population imbalance is particularly troublesome, because adaptive algorithms (e.g., neural network trainers, rule inducers, regression models) are frequently driven by an "accuracy" score. This makes them very susceptible to the "99 vs. 1" problem.

Another difficulty associated with population imbalance is that there may be very few examples of the target behavior available for analysis. Having few examples makes the reliable determination of complex patterns very difficult. Model validation can be compromised when populations are unbalanced. Having few examples of a particular class also makes it more difficult to hold back examples for blind-testing.

11.1.4.1 Dealing with Sin 4

Populations to be used for mining activities can be balanced using techniques such as replication and decimation. The "99 vs. 1" problem can be addressed in predictive models by using a scoring mechanism that takes population imbalance into consideration (e.g., computing a multi-factor score from the confusion matrix).

Sampling, segmentation, coding, quantization, and statistical normalization may also be used to address imbalance. Imbalance can be a difficult problem whose solution may require special expertise.

11.1.5 "Trojan-Horsing" Ground-Truth

This is your worst predictive modeling nightmare.

When user organizations provide data to analysts, they typically turn over large extracts from the enterprise data store consist of many fields and many records. This data is often accompanied by a schema or data dictionary that describes the fields by type, and sometimes, meaning.

What usually isn't communicated to analysts are relationships that exist in the data that are "obvious"—obvious to the data owner, not the data mining analyst. People who have worked with the same data set for a long time lose the ability to distinguish between what is truly obvious, and what is obvious only to them.

This sets the Trojan-Horse trap for data miners, and particularly builders of predictive models. Everyone who has done real-world data mining for any length of time has been caught. The Trojan-Horse trap occurs when one of the features present in the data set is essentially just a recoding of the ground-truth variable.

Trojan-Horsing would occur, for example, if the ground-truth variable is average monthly revenue in dollars, and there is another field in the data set (usually given some helpful name like "XZ_47") that is the average daily revenue in deutsche marks. Our "silver bullet feature," XZ_47, is just the ground-truth multiplied by the currency exchange rate and divided by 30. This amounts to using the revenue to analyze/predict itself.

Trojan-horsing can occur in so many guises that it is impossible even to begin describing them all. The most common instance arises when a data mining analyst somehow makes use of the ground-truth in conditioning feature data. For example, "We'll extract features from class 1 data in one way, and extract features from class 2 data in another."

This sounds like a mistake that no one would make. But this mistake is easy to make if, for example, at some point in the analysis, class 1 and class 2 data are separated, even for an instant. Are you absolutely *certain* that it is *impossible* that something could have happened to one set and not the other while they were apart? Are you absolutely *certain* that merging them again affected them in *identical* ways? If you are, then *why did you separate them in the first place?*

11.1.5.1   Dealing with Sin 5

Trojan-Horsing can often be detected by computing the correlation coefficient of each feature with the ground-truth. If any have absolute value very close to 1, they could be ground-truth masquerading as usable features, and should be checked by a data owner as possible Trojan-Horses. If they are not, you've just found some "silver bullet" features.

Once the data have been extracted from the operational data store for analysis, do not separate data of different classes. Use only tools that allow the analyst to process data without having to create files containing only some of the classes.

Never use the ground-truth class as part of the feature conditioning process! Aside from the fact that this easily results in Trojan-Horsing, there is the other obvious question: If ground-truth is part of the data conditioning process, how will you condition the future operational data that your model is supposed to classify?

11.1.6 Overlooking Temporal Feasibility

When analysts look at a data set to be mined, they typically see many rows of multi-column data, organized into years, quarters, and months. In this kind of cleansed environment, it is easy to get the idea that all the January data arrived simultaneously in January, all the February data arrived simultaneously in February, and so on. But, the reality is that the January data probably arrived in dribs and drabs, some perhaps being entered weeks or months after the record date. Different data fields probably made their way into the data along completely different data paths, went through different processes, and are of different levels of accuracy and completeness.

The analyst building models from a "frozen" enterprise history locked in a cleansed data store is likely to be quite unaware of its asynchronous accretion. He or she is likely to assume that at the moment a user will want to apply the model being developed (say, on the 15th of each month), all of the required data will be there, "pressed, dressed, and ready to go."

In fact, some will be there on the 10th, but require correction as a result of data that arrives on the 20th. Some will arrive via company mail on the 1st, but not be entered into the data store until the 30th. And some won't show up until next year. What looks like a perfectly good business model, under the assumption that everything that eventually ends up in the data store is known at runtime, ends up being a theoretical toy. The model is temporally infeasible.

11.1.6.1   Dealing with Sin 6

Avoiding temporal infeasibility is best accomplished by having a data owner fully conversant with the business process review candidate feature sets for consistency with the business cycle. It can also be helpful to compare corresponding historic data sets (e.g., from, say, a year ago) with those from last month. Such a comparison should clearly identify any temporal problems with the data.

11.1.7 Planless Tinkering

This is a failure of *process*. Specifically, failure to *have* a process.

Data mining projects sometimes languish due to lack of management support. This fosters a "catch-as-catch-can" approach to data mining work that is unlikely to produce useful results. Data mining takes time and commitment of the enterprise. Effective data mining is difficult and complex, and requires the involvement of valuable enterprise experts, technical people, equipment, tools, and time. This all costs money. While it can be attempted on a shoestring, "economy class" data mining usually produces disappointing results. If cost is a concern, it is best to narrow the scope of the initial effort, and fully fund a limited, highly focused data mining initiative on a high-payback problem where a little success will go a long way.

And, of course, data mining "boys" (and women) love their analytic "toys." Undirected analysts can spend infinite time unsystematically pounding on data sets with powerful data mining tools. Lost deep in the hunt, they are unlikely to raise questions about return-on-investment. The jargonization of data mining can also be a problem. The "progress" presented to a bewildered manager in a barrage of big words and neat visuals might just be expensive gibberish.

11.1.7.1 Dealing with Sin 7

Someone who understands the data mining process must establish a plan: There needs to be a "Moses." There also needs to be a "Promised Land." Someone familiar with the needs of the enterprise must establish general goals for the data mining activity. Establishing goals and formulating a good plan are difficult, since data mining is a dynamic, iterative discovery process. Having a data mining expert review the problem, set up a reasonable sequence of experiments, and establish time budgets for each iteration of the spiral will minimize profitless wandering through some high-dimensional wasteland.

To get past jargon, trusted, "disinterested" experts should be involved in project reviews. Keep asking basic questions about business value. Insist that the project plan explicitly show connection to business goals.

11.2 Summary

As illustrated by the "seven deadly sins," successful data mining requires careful adherence to proven methods, and a healthy degree of skepticism. Although a source data set may not fulfill the mission for a particular data-mining project, the project should still be considered successful if it accurately reflects the absence of relevant patterns.

The failures that must be avoided are:

- Not finding relevant patterns that are actually present in the data and could be generalized

- Finding (and exploiting) patterns that do not generalize, are not relevant, or are not actually present in the data

The best mitigation for risk of such failures is the application of a sound data mining methodology (process) in conjunction with a set of capable data mining techniques and tools.

12

Overcoming Obstacles

The previous chapter discussed mistakes that data mining analysts may make during the course of a project. But even if avoiding such mistakes is possible, there may still remain many significant obstacles that must be overcome. This chapter focuses on techniques for overcoming certain specific obstacles to effective data mining. While some such obstacles are common to all application development efforts involving complex data, others are peculiar to data mining. The focus of this chapter is the latter group.

12.1   Correlated/Irrelevant Features

Fortunately, there are data mining tools that can bring some objectivity to determining the significance of apparent patterns in abstract data. For the selection of features that will be used in data mining and predictive modeling, the correlation coefficient, described below, is especially useful.

For efficient data mining, analysis should proceed using the smallest number of features that supports pattern discovery and modeling. This is because "fewer features" means a feature space of lower dimensionality, and therefore less demanding storage and processing requirements. For example, sales data might be mined for relationships among the various components of a general ledger. It clearly makes no sense to use "monthly sales in dollars" as a feature, and also use "monthly sales in hundreds of dollars," because these two features carry exactly the same information about sales, expressed in different units. Nothing is gained by using both; in fact, if both are used, a real (and completely useless) linear pattern is forced into the feature set. Such an artificial pattern can disrupt mining activities.

This example is extreme, but it suggests a way to reduce the number of features used for data mining with minimal risk of losing information. Features that are largely just "different ways of saying the same thing" can be targeted for removal. One mathematical measure of this "informational redundancy" is the correlation coefficient. The correlation coefficient, denoted r, is a number between –1 and +1 that expresses the relative independence of two features.

When features have a correlation coefficient of –1 or +1, they are said to be *perfectly correlated*. When two features are perfectly correlated, the value of one can be exactly computed from the other by simple rescaling and centering. In particular, when one of the features, say f1, changes by a fixed amount d1, the other feature, say f_2, will change by a certain fixed amount d_2. When r is greater than zero, the features are said to exhibit *positive correlation*, and when r is less than zero, the features are said to exhibit *negative correlation*.

Positively correlated features have the property that when one increases, the other does too (on average). And when one feature of a positively correlated pair decreases, so does the other (on average). Negatively correlated features have the property that when one increases, the other decreases (on average). And when one feature of a negatively correlated pair decreases, the other increases (on average).

Usually, correlation between features is not perfect. In such cases, the correlation coefficient will have a value somewhere strictly between –1 and +1. An important special case occurs when r = 0. When the correlation coefficient of two features is zero (or close to zero), they are said to be *uncorrelated*. It is important to keep in mind that the correlation coefficient only measures linear correlation. Features that have r = 0 may very well be related by some more complex, non-linear relationship.

The correlation coefficient can be used during feature selection to reduce the size and enhance the speed of predictive models. In general, only one of a group of highly correlated features needs to be included in the feature set to support a particular model. There are valid exceptions, as when some higher-order correlation is lost when linear correlation is removed. Sometimes, features are even included for psychological reasons, apart from their true utility (e.g., "the end user swears by this feature, so it better be in there"). All other things being equal, less is more when selecting a feature set. The safest way to achieve this is the elimination of weaker, highly correlated features.

12.2 Diluted Information

If the purpose of data mining is to detect and harvest information from data, then in some sense, it is a search problem. The basic data mining assumption is that the data being examined somehow "contain" valuable information that can be detected and extracted by the proper application of appropriate tools and techniques. So where, exactly, is the information that data "contain," and how can it be located?

12.3 Syntax and Semantics

Answering these questions requires the definition of two kinds of information: syntactic, and semantic. The following intuitive discussion skirts the technical prerequisites, which are severe. It sounds a little mystical, but is firmly grounded in semiotics, a part of information theory. The understanding gained here will help explain "where" information is, how to get at it, and how data mining differs from conventional data analysis.

Syntactic information is purely symbolic. It comes into existence when a pattern of symbols is assigned to something. The act of naming this book created syntactic information. The string "X + Y = Z" is syntactic information. Lewis Carrol's, "Twas' brillig and the slithy toves did gyre and gimble in the wabe" is syntactic information. Any symbolic expression of a connection like "x IS y" gives syntactic information. When the string "$100.00" is placed into a spreadsheet in the "sales" column for a transaction, for example, such a connection has been specified: "Sale for this transaction is $100.00."

Note that syntactic information is not just a string of symbols. No syntactic information exists unless this string establishes a relation or connection between two "somethings." Syntactic information is *in the symbols*, in the form of an expressed relationship.

Semantic information is purely conceptual; it comes into being when "meaning" is assigned to a pattern of symbols. Semantic information is created through an act of interpretation. It is created as an interpreter interacts with the data, and exists in the mind of the interpreter. The information contained in the words on this page is pure syntax until you read and understand them. At that point, the information becomes pure semantics.

Syntax asks, "What does it say?" and semantics asks, "What does it mean?" Said another way, syntax connects things, and semantics connects connections. "We want to maximize revenue," and "Saturday is our best business day" are both simple syntactic relations: "goal = maximize revenue," and "Saturday = best business day." The implication, "Because our goal is to maximize revenue, and Saturday is our best business day, we ought to stay open on Saturday" is semantics.

Because semantics is interpretive, it always carries information brought to the analysis by the interpreter. Some of semantics is in the eye of the beholder. This introduces a collaborative element into the data mining process, making it a cooperative and iterative exercise carrying both man and machine on many passes through the data. This collaboration, involving as it does a variable human element, can be subjective. The automated part of the team can help here by introducing some consistency.

Conventional data-analysis tools are sometimes touted as "knowledge discovery" tools if they provide excellent intuitive views of data that let a human user easily infer previously unknown relationships. But, where did this "discovery" take place? In software? No, it takes place in "wet-wear," between the user's ears. Authentic knowledge-discovery tools formulate an interpretation themselves, and present it to the user for evaluation. The discovery occurs in the machine, and is validated by the human user.

Data by itself is pure syntax. The information it contains is represented in patterns that may or may not have "meaning." All data analysis must begin on the syntactic level. For example, it might be noted that a certain sales pattern occurs regularly in some sales volume data. This is a syntactic fact. If correlation with data in the general ledger shows that this sales pattern explains certain revenue peaks, a semantic fact has been discovered. Syntax precedes semantics, because knowledge precedes understanding.

The distinction between syntax and semantics marks the difference between conventional data-analysis tools, like spreadsheets, and true data mining tools, like rule induction engines. Conventional data-analysis tools are syntactic. They translate data from one syntax (e.g., a database) into another syntax (e.g., a colorized scatter plot). They offer essentially no interpretation, impressions, evaluation, hypotheses—no semantic content. The act of interpretation is left entirely to the user. In contrast, data mining tools may perform syntactic transformations, but their principal purpose is to add semantic content: to offer with the data an interpretation for consideration by the user.

12.4 Population Imbalance

Within a population, the class having the most members is called the *majority class*. All other classes are called *minority classes*. Among airline pilots, males are a majority class and females a minority class.

Population imbalance is a problem for data mining and predictive modeling, because patterns in the population are often conditioned primarily by the properties of the majority class. Patterns among minority classes can be "lost in the glare" of the majority class. Visualization tools are particularly vulnerable. This can be quite a problem when, as is often the case, it is the minority class that is of greatest interest (e.g., fraud, churn, etc.).

A savings bank, for example, might notice that most purchasers of its certificates of deposit are men. It would like to increase sales of these instruments to women, and decides to use data mining to determine what inducements have had a good response from women in the past. Population imbalance will be a problem if this bank's CD holders are 99 percent male, because CD purchase-triggers found from this population will be driven by historic male behaviors. And in this case, *stratification* (splitting a population into groups based upon member attributes, like gender) might not yield a sufficiently large sample of female CD purchasers.

Addressing the data volume problem by appropriate sampling or stratification suggests two methods for handling population imbalance: decimation and replication. In *decimation*, members of the majority class are removed to restore balance. In replication, multiple "copies" of members of the minority class are added to restore balance. These methods are not equivalent. Decimation can change the distribution (e.g., mean, standard deviation) of the remaining members of the majority class. This change can be significant if the decimation is done carelessly. Decimation can destroy sub-populations. ("We balanced the sample by removing all the good customers from New York!") A population with no duplicated data points (two members at the same location in feature space) will have no duplicates after decimation.

Replication that is carried out uniformly (same number of duplicates of each member) will not change the frequency distribution of the minority class. Replication will not destroy sub-populations, because no data is removed from the sample. Replication will, of course, cause data points to be duplicated, which can lead to misleading data plots, since points in the minority class actually represent several individuals. When replication is not done uniformly, as when some points are duplicated and others are not, the minority distribution can be changed.

Population balance can also be restored by *data synthesis*, in which additional data are created from existing data. The number of minority data points can be boosted by introducing new minority members. These new minority members are slight modifications of existing minority data, or averages of existing groups of minority data. This is a reasonable approach to population balancing when some *a priori* rules are known that allow validation of the artificial data. Data synthesis is a risky technique requiring care and insight, because it amounts to the introduction (perhaps concoction) of data, which was never observed, and could confound subsequent mining work. If synthesis is used, the artificial data should be tagged as such in the data store.

12.5 Missing or Unreliable Ground-Truth

The "noise" problem described in the previous section applies to ground-truth as well as feature data. Sometimes, data is made available for the analysis of some problem, but no ground-truth is provided. Or, the ground-truth available is unreliable. In an instance like this, it is difficult to complete the construction of an effective predictive model. Even if such a model can be built, there will be no reliable data for its validation.

There are two approaches to mining data in the absence of reliable ground-truth. One is to synthesize ground-truth, and the other is to rely entirely on unsupervised learning techniques (e.g., auto-clustering). Each technique has its strengths; selection of one or the other depends upon the requirements of the problem.

Ground-truth synthesis generally requires expert knowledge, or a collection of valid ground-truth data from which other examples can be generated. Approaches that sometimes work are to use expert knowledge to create a few examples with valid ground-truth, and then generate other, similar examples by slight modification of the original examples. Or, if it appears that the ground-truth classes are convex sets, additional examples can be generated by forming weighted averages of existing examples.

This synthesis of additional feature vectors is carried out for the feature vectors depicted in Figure 12.1.

Figure 12.1

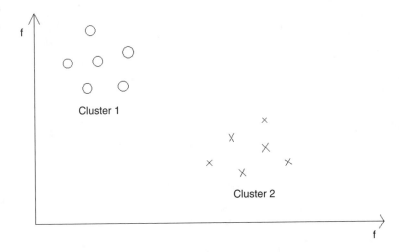

To synthesize feature vectors, the pair-wise averages of existing vectors are computed (denoted by little boxes, Figure 12.2). These averages are then included as new vectors.

The synthesized feature vectors have been added to the population, increasing each class from 6 to 16 feature vectors (see Figure 12.3).

Unsupervised learning techniques allow the analysis of data "as is," since no use is made of ground-truth assignments. Patterns discovered using these techniques cannot be tied to ground-truth classes, but they can be used to aggregate data into sets having similar properties. The properties of such natural aggregations are often the basis for important discoveries (see the section on link analysis, discussed in Chapter 8).

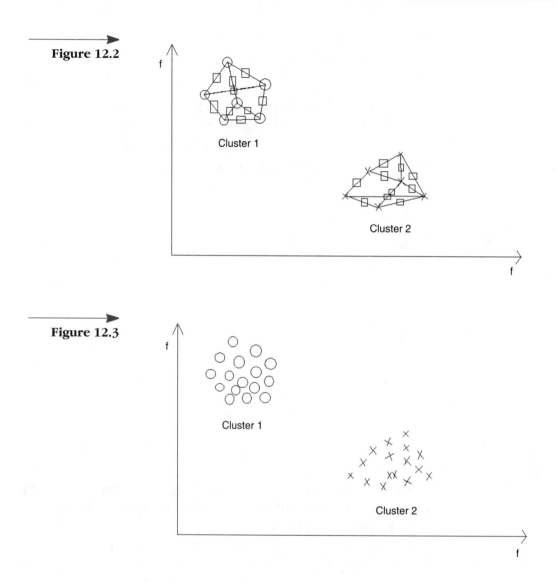

Figure 12.2

Cluster 1

Cluster 2

Figure 12.3

Cluster 1

Cluster 2

12.6 Making Good Feature Sets from Bad Ones

There are two general approaches to enhancing feature sets. One is to improve the features themselves; the other is to improve the feature mix. A carefully selected mix of weak features may outperform a randomly selected mix of strong features, and is often less demanding of collection and processing power.

12.6.1 Optimizing Features: Conventional Methods

Numerous mature, conventional feature-enhancement techniques exist. These include Principal Component Analysis (PCA, viz Karhunen-Loeve, which linearly optimizes for representation), Independent Component Analysis (ICA, which linearly optimizes for discrimination), genetic algorithms, adaptive quantization/ coding methods, etc. Some or all of these can be used during a single development effort.

12.6.2 Optimizing Feature Mix: Co-Selection Methods

Given that many parametric feature sets can be generated, the question becomes, "Which feature(s), when used together, provide effective classification with reasonable processing effort?" This is the "credit assignment problem" for general multiple regression. We refer to the selection of effective subsets of a large group of available features as the "co-selection" problem.

Three straightforward approaches to co-selection are:

1. **Bayesian Co-Selection**—Bayesian co-selection identifies statistically optimal subset(s) of a suite of features, subject to the assumption that all goal classes are normally distributed in feature space. The assumption of goal class normality is fairly stringent; nonetheless, it often holds approximately for some classes even in difficult problems, making Bayesian co-selection a generally useful indicator of feature salience.

   To carry out Bayesian co-selection, each feature separately is used to build a classifier for a collection of feature vectors. The features are then ranked in order of their ability to classify these vectors. The correlation matrix for the features provides a measure of feature independence. Co-selection may then be performed based upon the combination of salience and independence: Features with high classification power and low pair-wise correlation are selected.

2. **Co-Selection by Classifier Inversion**—In this co-selection method, a classifier is trained on the entire feature set. It is then "run in reverse." That is, an output is run backwards through the classifier to determine the "prototypical features" that lead to its selection as the correct class. Most

classifiers cannot be inverted in this way, so this is a limited technique.

3. **Co-Selection by Rule Induction**—When rule induction algorithms are available, they can be applied to a data set to generate heuristics. Analysis of these heuristics to determine which features are used most frequently, or are given greatest weight by the induced rules suggests which features to select. Ineffective features presumably will not be used by induced rules, and can be "weeded out."

12.7   Associative Feature Selection

Associative memories are applications that learn patterns by internally constructing abstract prototypes. A particular type of neural network, called the Hopfield Net operates using this principle. Hopfield Nets are usually trained by a process called simulated annealing.

Once an associative memory has had many patterns of each ground-truth class stored in it (a little over-training is usually good in this case), retrieval of a ground-truth class brings back a "prototypical" feature vector (an archetype, or profile) for that ground-truth class. These "class profiles" can be converted to rules, or used as templates for matching against vectors to be classified.

12.7.1   Classifier Orthoprojection

This is a big name for a simple idea. Many data mining applications run into performance and storage problems because the number of features is large. Classifier orthoprojection is a technique for reducing the number of features in a data set without losing too much information. This allows mining or modeling to proceed more efficiently.

Classifier orthoprojection is a method for finding a subset of the existing features that contain much of the information in the entire feature set.

In this method of feature selection, a classifier of some sort (it doesn't really matter what type) is constructed using the entire set of features. The classifier need not be optimized, but should have at least a modest level of accuracy (e.g., better than random guessing).

Once the classifier has been trained to a modest level of performance, it is modified so that features can be "switched on and off" inside the model. This is often accomplished by assigning weights of zero inside the model to features not to be used, and weights of one to features that are to be used. The modified classifier is then used to classify a test set with various combinations of features set "on and off." The combinations of features that give the best results as a group are selected as the final set. This is essentially a "genetic algorithm" for feature selection.

12.7.2 A Word of Caution

Techniques from linear algebra, probability, and information theory can often be used to reduce the dimension and preparation cost of a feature set, but not always. The parity-n problem (also called the "exclusive OR" problem) is an oft-cited example. In classifying an n-bit string for parity (even/odd number of "1's"), *no* proper subset of the features by itself provides *any* information to support classification. Unless *all* the features are known, *nothing* is known about a bit string's parity class. Said another way: For this problem, we do not incrementally accrue information as we collect features. *All* the classifying information arrives with the final feature, whichever that happens to be.

12.7.3 Automating Feature Synthesis

Successful automation of feature synthesis requires four capabilities:

1. Acapability to automatically and parametrically (defined below) extract a variety of potentially salient features

2. A capability to effectively compute intermediate performance measures for feature sets

3. A capability to determine which features in which combinations are most salient

4. Most importantly, a capability to automatically adjust feature extraction parameters and mix to improve salience and independence

12.8 Class Collisions

It is not unusual during data mining to find among the data two or more feature vectors from different ground-truth classes, but with identical components. For the purposes of data modeling, these vectors (and the individuals they represent) are indistinguishable, since their attributes (features) are the same. This occurrence is called a *class collision*. Class collisions tell your data mining tools that there are points in feature space that have ambiguous class assignments. A feature vector at these locations can be in one of multiple classes. The presence of class collisions indicates that the ground-truth classes defined during model specification overlap *under the representation given by the current feature set*.

Class collisions cause data mining problems because some feature vectors from different ground-truth classes cannot be separated. This leads to situations where collided vectors are counted multiple times (e.g., once for every class they hit), collided vectors are not counted at all (e.g., because they aren't in any one class), etc., resulting in confused statistics and misleading analyses. Worse, when predictive models are being built, collisions cause training software to repeatedly learn, and then unlearn information about the population. In the parlance of adaptive systems, this is an instance of *destructive interference* where facts learned about a feature vector at one time during training are corrupted by learning that occurs later.

Class collisions are sometimes the result of over-zealous quantization of the data. For example, if both salaries and ages are quantized to decades, a 20 year-old making \$30,000 is indistinguishable from a 29 year-old making \$39,000. Should the first be in class 1 (say, "high-risk"), and the second in class 2 (say, "moderate risk"), an ambiguity results. Two feature vectors with location (2nd decade age, 3rd decade salary) exist in feature space, but one is in class 1 and the other in class 2. If there are many instances of class collision, data mining tools may have difficulty detecting patterns. In this sense, quantization "blurs" data by obscuring differences. Too much blurring can obscure significant details.

Class collisions can be handled in several ways, depending upon the type of work being done. One approach is to use more discriminating features: using finer quanta on quantized features, or adding new features that distinguish between colliders. Both of these approaches have costs (e.g., more reconstruction values, more precise measurement methods, higher dimensional feature spaces).

Another approach is to remove feature vectors that participate in collisions. This is an easy remedy to automate, but it has two serious drawbacks:

1.   Excision reduces the number of feature vectors and can selectively destroy a large percentage of a minority ground-truth class. Data mining is often conducted to search for important minority classes (e.g., fraudsters, churners). You don't want to remove any of these, because examples of rare, high-interest feature vectors are hard to come by.

2.   Excision hides the existence of class ambiguity from your data mining activity. Class collisions are troublesome, but they are real. "Fixing the data" by removing feature vectors that you don't like is a heavy-handed way to seek the truth.

Sometimes class collisions can be effectively handled by moving the collided vectors a little bit. This is actually a reasonable approach when the features are floating-point numbers measured by some physical device that is subject to noise anyway. Very small random numbers are added to one of more of the features of the collided vectors, moving them slightly apart.

Often, though, the best approach to handling class collisions is to do nothing. Many data mining tools handle ambiguity in feature space using the "probability rule." A collided location in feature space is said to have a mixture of ground-truth classes, according to the relative proportion of class examples colliding there. That is, if a particular location in feature space is occupied only by class 2 examples, there is 100 percent certainty that a vector at that location should be assigned to class 2. But a location occupied by three class 1 examples, and two class 2 examples will be assigned to class 1 with 60 percent certainty, and class 2 with 40 percent certainty. More sophisticated formalisms, such as Bayes' Theorem, can be used to refine these assignments.

12.9   Summary

Even with careful adherence to data mining methods and the most powerful tools available, significant obstacles may still be encountered, particularly as limitations of the source data. Several of these include: correlated or irrelevant features, diluted information, syntax and semantics, population imbalance, and missing or unreliable ground-truth. Several techniques for enhancing or optimizing feature sets were presented that may be useful in overcoming such obstacles. When such techniques are not successful, it is generally best to consider revamping the project and investigating alternative data sources.

13

Successful Data Mining Project Management

The development of data mining applications has many facets, including representation of the extracted knowledge, selection of appropriate data mining methods, reducing search complexity, the use of prior knowledge to improve the discovery process, controlling the discovery operation, statistical inference, prototyping, and evaluation. Successful integration of these components into a system requires a development methodology and appropriate analytic techniques. While a data mining methodology supports the engineering and scientific aspects of a project, as described in Chapter 4, project management methods are also important.

Data mining projects are no different from other projects in that a clear vision of the expected results of the project needs to be common among all of the concerned parties. In other words, the goals and objectives need to be clearly defined and well understood. This is true for all projects, not just those involving IT, engineering, and other departments. The activities that would apply to any project would apply to data mining projects, be they planning, organizing, directing, communicating, infrastructure implementation, software development, process improvement, or training design and delivery.

As in all project management efforts, a significant portion of the project manager's effort is in the early part of the project in defining the project scope, estimating effort and cost, planning, scheduling, staffing, and so on. Of course, data mining can be conducted as part of a larger project that involves some or all of the following activities: system engineering, specification, architecture, design, application development, unit test, system test, site integration, site test, training, or maintenance. Although similar project planning, organizing, directing, controlling, and communicating activities apply to such projects as well, for our purposes, we focus primarily on data mining model development (vs. deployment).

Data mining projects are different from typical IT development projects, in the aspect of on-going control. Data mining projects frequently call for creativity and innovation as part of the Prototyping/Model Development phase (Step 5). And, due to the spiral nature of the "mining" activity, additional cycles may be necessary in order to satisfy the objective, or answer the problem statement. This characteristic provides many challenges to the project manager in terms of managing cost and schedule performance and customer expectations. Of course project control is important, but it must be applied judiciously.

A data mining project can be completely successful in terms of conducting all of the right processes correctly, and even so, yield no usable results. In some cases, the available data simply does not support the goal of the project, in others it may not be adequate to provide the required level of performance.

There are several component aspects of project management, a discussion of each follows:

- Project delivery concept
- Project analysis
- Project staffing
- Project schedule
- Cost
- Methodology
- Project delivery

13.1 Project Delivery Concept

The key to success is starting with the end-goal in mind or a vision, if you will, of the successful project. The vision will certainly include satisfaction of key objective(s) or fulfillment of purpose.

The project delivery may also include some tangible and measurable results. The project manager or technical leader (often both) must work with their client(s), be they internal or external, to determine precisely what "products" will be delivered as a result of each data mining project, and when the results will be made available. The results can include such items as:

- Feature analysis report

- Preliminary model performance as a set of confusion matrices

- Report of key findings

- Model deployment

- Tools deployment

- Application software implementation

- Complete turn-key functional application system

- Documentation

- Training

- On-going system maintenance

Whatever the case, the overall goals and objectives and all of the specific deliverables should be defined in a project concept document. This can also be called a Project Scope document, a statement of work, or several other names. The critical aspect is that the document provides a contract between the data mining team and the ultimate users of the system, be they internal or external "clients."

13.2 Project Analysis

Once the project concept and deliverables are well defined, the project manager needs to start thinking like a journalist. In other words, he or she needs to provide answers to the "Five W's and an H" question, which are who, what, where, when, why, and how. And for project managers, there's usually one additional question: "How much?" Also, while a journalist answers these questions during or after events occur, the project manager must make the best possible attempt to answer them in advance. The process of formulating the answers to these questions is essentially the planning process.

- The project delivery concept description provides an answer as to *what* will be delivered and provides information that is useful in staffing and schedule planning.

- Project staffing assignments provide an answer as to *who* will perform the work, and frequently also provides the answer as to *where* the work will be performed.

- The project schedule provides an answer as to *when* tasks are planned to be performed, or the duration of each activity, as well as information on delivery and other milestones.

- The cost estimate provides an answer as to *how much* the project will cost.

- Methodology provides an answer as to *how* the effort will be performed.

- The problem definition, as described below under methodology should provide at least a partial answer as to *why* the project is being performed.

Some additional questions should be answered as a byproduct of answering the significant questions listed above. The project manager should document any assumptions and communicate them appropriately, within the planning documents, which include staff, cost, and schedule information as described below.

13.3   Project Staffing

As with any project, the staffing requirements for a project depend on the scope and magnitude of the project, the effort required at various states of the methodology, as described briefly later in the chapter, and so on. For example, if a reliable data source such as a well-thought out mature data mart, is available to provide features to be mined, simply through queries; significantly less staffing effort will be required during that phase of the methodology than if features must be derived from a deep and wide collection of archive files.

For most data mining projects, there are typically four key roles that may be performed. A single person may perform these on a very small project, but even then it might be unusual for one person to have all of the skills, abilities, and interests to carry them out appropriately. Most often several people are needed to accomplish the necessary tasks:

- Lead scientist (e.g. mathematician)

- Technical lead

- Project leader/manager

- Domain expert

For example, the technical leader and scientific leader may be the same person, working with a project leader that tracks progress against the project plans, and a domain expert that can assist with interpretation of the discoveries found through the data mining experiments. It really depends on the nature of the project. The level of staffing required to perform a data mining project depends on the goal, problem statement, the tools, and project concept (scope). These key staff members may be assisted by software engineers, mathematicians, technical writers, etc., as dictated by the project concept.

13.3.1 Lead Scientist (e.g., Mathematician)

The scientist brings advanced knowledge of scientific concepts to bear on the solution of a problem. This person may serve as a consulting resource to several projects simultaneously, and can be particularly helpful in identifying problems or alternative approaches, if the techniques that normally produce results fail to do so for a particular problem.

13.3.2 Technical Lead

The technical leader, by whatever name, serves as the technical focal point for the project with emphasis on the methodology and results.

13.3.3 Project Leader/Manager

The primary purpose of the project leader is to manage the project to achieve its technical and business goals. In addition to developing the project plans being described here, the project leader ensures that appropriate communications are taking place to avoid any surprises.

13.3.4 Domain Expert

Domain expertise is key to the success of any development project, but this is particularly true in data mining activities. The data mining team may believe it is making progress, only to find out that it is misusing the data or misinterpreting the results of its modeling activities. Access to domain expertise throughout the project is essential.

13.3.5 Location, Location, Location

The location where the data mining activities will be carried out may be a function of the location of the team members who are assigned. Considerations include access to tools, access to the data, and access to domain experts. Today, in the authors' experience, access to the data is the easiest to solve, in a purely logistical sense. Today's high-bandwidth networks and transmission protocols, make it easy to access or transport enough data to satisfy the modeling requirements for many of data mining knowledge discovery and preliminary modeling projects. There is a vast array of tools that are available for a variety of platforms, so tool availability often becomes a financial rather than a logistical issue. This leaves the ever-challenging people issue. We have found that communication between the technical/scientific team and the domain experts can often be the difference between success and failure. Frequent teleconferences are helpful, but working together side-by-side is often best.

13.4 Project Schedule

Standard Gantt charts such as those created by Microsoft Project (as in Figure 13.1), Primavera, and other project management tools are very helpful for developing and communicating project plans.

Figure 13.1

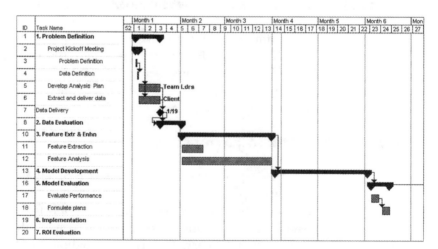

While this plan indicates a six-month schedule to accomplish the first five phases that we have been focused on, there can be a wide variance in the amount of time required to conduct a data mining project depending on the complexity of the data and the difficulty of the problem. This plan relates closely to the data mining methodology discussed throughout the book, and in detail in Chapter 4. What is lacking in the sample illustration is a plan for multiple prototyping cycles, which are common to this type of project.

1. Problem Definition

It is imperative for the data mining team members to understand the objectives for the data-mining project, as well as the subject data. These are the key topics that are covered in depth during the kickoff sessions. Following the kickoff meetings, the data mining team formulates its analysis plan while the client team prepares the subject data. Close contact with the content expert(s) is very beneficial to developing an understanding of the data attributes, ranges, coding values, business rules, and so on. In some cases, external research such as literature searches and interviews is also beneficial. The plans for data preparation and analysis are developed based on the number and types of data features and ground truth being provided by the customer.

2. Data Analysis

Feature analysis is the first critical research phase in the data mining process, wherein data analysis tools are used to analyze features. The result of the analysis is the determination of which individual features and which combinations of features are expected to perform best for satisfying the objectives (problem defined) of a project. These tools may include visualization, as well as a variety of mathematical and data-analysis tools. This data mining activity is an iterative process. Numerous tests are conducted and hypotheses tested.

3. Feature Extraction and Enhancement

Feature extraction and enhancement tools will be used to analyze, and when possible improve, the "salience" of manually selected, intuitive features. Part of the feature extraction phase includes the application of these powerful tools to automatically identify, extract, and validate salient features from inscrutable data sets. These tools (e.g., parametric analyzers, PCA engines) facilitate the selection of salient feature sets.

4. Model Development

Predictive, classification, or other models are developed using an iterative process based on the objectives of the project and findings of the feature analysis phase. These models may be encoder-decoder networks, invertible BAMs, TRBFs, etc. Models are developed through a machine "training" process and their performance is tested using blind-data.

5. Model Evaluation

Typically on-going evaluation of models is conducted as a byproduct of the training process. Confusion matrices are produced that indicate the precision and recall capabilities of each model. At the end of the model development cycle, it is appropriate to consider the best single or best combination of models in addressing the problem(s) at hand and satisfying the objective. At this point there may be a decision regarding whether to proceed with further development or model implementation.

6. Implementation

Implementation of a data mining solution can require a minimal or massive amount of effort and investment, as is illustrated by several of the case studies that follow. However for the purposes of this book, the focus remains on the first five phases of data mining projects.

7. ROI Evaluation

Often companies desire to evaluate the return on investment of a project some period of time following its implementation to determine whether the results that were used to justify the project implementation were actually realized. Again, some of the case studies that follow provide examples of projects with excellent ROI.

13.4.1 Project Cost

Labor costs typically account for the majority of the total cost for data mining projects focused on generating a predictive model, for example, as a proof-of-concept, before investing in a full-scale system. However, for large efforts that may involve implementation of a complete application system that employs models at the heart of the system, there might also be significant expenditures relating to packaged software, computer platforms, communications equipment and application software development. In addition to labor and capital estimates, travel, other expenses and contingency estimates should be factored into the total project cost estimate.

Experience on prior projects can be useful in estimating or evaluating project cost estimates, but depending on the project delivery concept, the costs can range dramatically. For example, for the case studies described in this book, the actual project costs range from approximately $30,000 for a "proof of concept" modeling task with no deliverables (except for applicable confusion matrices to document model performance) to $18 million for the United Airlines Orion system.

13.4.2 Project Delivery

The actual delivery is where many projects falter. Sometimes, the team members start to relax once the difficult research and development phases have been completed, and then the "95 percent syndrome" takes over. It is important for the team to stay focused on resolving all of the open issues and ensuring that the project reaches 100 percent of its delivery goals.

13.4.3 Business Intelligence Preparedness

Many readers may hold the misconception that a data mart or data warehouse is necessary to conduct data mining. While such repositories can be useful, even more important is the understanding of the source data that is essential to the process of developing such a data repository. Business Intelligence, and data mining in particular, clearly provide the best capabilities to realize the potential Return-on-Investment that is anticipated when an organization undertakes the substantial development effort for a resource such as a data mart or repository.

The information technology aspects of business intelligence were discussed in Chapter 5, and the mathematics and science of data mining were covered throughout the remainder of Part II.

There are several considerations that contribute to an organization's readiness to exploit the advanced capabilities offered by data mining techniques. They include:

- Well-defined data elements (accurate meta data)

- Domain expertise that can participate in the project
- Sufficient historical data and outcomes
- Organization climate that supports risk taking
- A well-defined problem
- Capable staff
- Capable tools

Although data mining and Business Intelligence have become closely associated with data warehousing, for good reasons, both can be accomplished by organizations with various levels of maturity of information management and data warehouse implementation.

13.5 Summary

As described thus far, the development of data mining applications has many facets. As is generally true for all projects, a clear and common vision of the expected results needs to be documented. Data mining initiatives are often conducted as part of a larger system development effort. A data mining project can be completely successful in terms of conducting all of the right processes correctly, and even so yield no usable results. In some cases, the available data simply does not support the goal of the project, in others it may not be adequate to provide the required level of performance. The project sponsors must determine whether the mining exploitation (model) performance provides an adequate Return-on-Investment.

Part IV

Data Mining in Vertical Industries

- Industry Descriptions
- Industry Challenges
- General Data Mining Applications by Industry
- Industry Case Studies

14

Data Mining in Practice

One of the most attractive facets of data mining is the development of insight into a business process. This enables the development of predictive models. In competitive markets, there are numerous areas that can benefit from the use of predictive models, for example: niche selection, product release timing, and marketing focus. Predictive models can be based on conventional methods or on advanced predictive modeling capabilities, such as neural networks, radial basis functions, decision trees, fuzzy-logic, time series, or other techniques.

In Part I, the value of Business Intelligence and specifically, data mining, was discussed. In Part II, the information technology and mathematical techniques involved in Business Intelligence applications and data mining were covered. Here in Part IV, several case study examples demonstrate ways that data mining is providing valuable benefits in various industries. Because custom Business Intelligence applications provide high-value key insights that can be used to enhance an organization's competitive position, many organizations are unwilling to divulge the secret details of their projects. Some are not even willing to have their name published along with the type of application. All of these organizations recognize the competitive value of their systems and would prefer to keep the benefits for themselves, particularly in today's competitive e-commerce economy.

Powerful customer profiling techniques are at the heart of many such applications. The value is derived both from the advanced predictive models, as well as from the databases of historical information that empower them. The organizations that develop and acquire such intelligent system assets use them to both build and retain market share.

As discussed in Chapters 2 and 3, there is a wide range of behavior-profiling examples, including:

- Customer profiling for acquisition, retention, winback and value maximization
- Job applicant profiling for employers to identify candidates who are most similar to their company's proven winners
- Web-prospect profiling
- Patient profiling for wellness, treatment, or recovery
- Consumption or utilization profiling

Other examples of high value data mining applications include:

- Staffing level prediction
- Inquiry routing
- Automated response
- Scenario notification

In subsequent chapters, data mining is discussed as it applies within various industries. In several examples, even the authors' own customers elected to remain anonymous. Although specific details of data features, algorithms, and return-on-investment calculations are not available in many of our examples, these cases still demonstrate the value and sheer necessity of advanced data mining applications. They are essential for companies who are striving to be ahead of their competition.

Some industries started applying pattern recognition and predictive algorithms about 20 years ago. Although they weren't called data mining at the time, and certainly not business intelligence, such applications are the precursors of today's commercial applications. In government, the intelligence community continues to apply such techniques, in ways we have no choice but to leave to your imagination—James Bond and Austin Powers, notwithstanding.

The general maturity of data mining deployment by industry is a function of the magnitude and type of information available. For example, the financial services industry has been one of the leading adopters of data mining techniques. Perhaps it is related to their overall lead in information technology adoption. When talking about financial services we mean banks, brokerages, investment and finance companies, and so on.

Data mining has created a revolution in the way businesses analyze their data to find previously unknown patterns and relationships among the data. Direct marketing is one of the most popular applications of data mining because the results can be readily applied to obtain a better campaign response and a higher return on investment. For example, a trained statistician or consultant can develop a response model using data from a past direct marketing campaign to predict those most likely to respond to the next campaign. By contacting only those most likely to respond, that marketer can substantially increase the percentage of responses and generate higher profits.

Direct marketing campaigns extend beyond the retail merchandising industry to other consumer and business services. The convergence of direct marketing and Internet-based electronic commerce provides a rich resource for future applications of data mining in this burgeoning arena.

Customer churn is a significant problem in many industries. It is generally considered to be far more cost-effective to retain existing customers than to secure new ones. Thus, it is desirable to identify customers who are at risk of changing their service to a new provider and offer them incentives to retain their existing service.

Identifying customers who are at risk of changing their service, and subsequently determining the appropriate actions to take that will encourage customers to retain their service, presents a significant challenge to organizations responsible for customer care and customer retention. It is often unclear exactly what characteristics dissatisfied customers' exhibit and, therefore, difficult to predict exactly which customers will not renew their service. In addition, even when it is known that a specific customer is dissatisfied, it is very difficult to determine what incentives can be offered that will encourage him or her to retain his or her service. Of course, it is desirable to offer these dissatisfied customers incentives in as cost-effective a manner as possible.

Customer historical data frequently contains information that can be extremely valuable to retention specialists. Historical data holds usage patterns and other important customer characteristics that, when discovered, can be used to identify satisfied and dissatisfied customers. Combined with historical information identifying which of those customers renewed their service, which did not renew their service, and what incentives were offered to both groups, a predictive model can be built to predict which customers will not renew their service as well as make recommendations as to the most effective incentives to offer them.

However, the correlations between historical data values are often extremely complex and represent a potentially impossible task for humans to determine. Modern pattern recognition technologies, such as neural networks, have the ability to recognize complex correlations and patterns within historical data, consistently distinguish between almost identical patterns, accurately reduce these complex relationships to a level which is understandable to humans, and predict customers who are at risk of changing their service to another provider with a relatively high level of accuracy.

14.2   Case Studies

In subsequent chapters, case studies are provided for a selection of industries, along with a general discussion of data mining applications in those industries. The industries selected for discussion are customer service, retail, insurance, financial services, health care and medicine, telecommunications, transportation and logistics, energy, and government.

The case study format follows the methodology described throughout the book, according to the following stages:

1.   Problem definition

2.   Data evaluation

3.   Feature extraction and enhancement

4.   Prototyping/model development

5.   Model evaluation

6.   Implementation

7.   Return-on-Investment evaluation

Not all of the stages are indicated for all of the cases. For some, it is due to a lack of available information. For most, we are not concerned with the implementation details, but place more emphasis on the model development activities. Since direct marketing is of interest across most industries, we begin with a related case study, here.

14.3 Summary

Some may be surprised at the extent to which Business Intelligence and data mining applications have been deployed. Each of the chapters that immediately follow discusses characteristics, needs, and problems that relate to a specific industry; and challenges the industry faces, general data mining applications, and one or more case study examples.

15

Data Mining in Customer Service

15.1 The Industry

Customer service initiatives continue to increase in scope and perceived organizational value. As discussed in Chapter 1, CRM encompasses the processes of finding, reaching, selling, satisfying, and retaining customers. Although until recently customer service initiatives were focused solely on customer satisfaction (e.g., problem resolution) issues, for many organizations today, customer service has expanded to support the entire CRM life-cycle. Customer Interaction Centers are now concerned with each and every customer contact as an opportunity to enhance customer satisfaction and optimize the financial value of the customer to his or her organization. As discussed earlier, optimizing customer relationships may not only entail maximizing the financial value of each individual customer over time, but may mean optimizing an organization's customer mix.

15.2 Challenges in Customer Service

The key to satisfying customers, optimizing their experience, and thereby quite possibly their loyalty, lies in understanding their individual preferences. As Dorian Pyle so eloquently notes in the Foreword, customers have become a critical resource. Twenty-first century customer relationships are based on mass customization rather than mass production. What one customer may consider to be "attentive" customer service, another may deem "oppressive." Being able to recognize the differences between these two types of customers and making effective use of such information remains a challenge, but a challenge that data mining techniques are uniquely well suited to address.

15.3 General Data Mining Applications

As discussed in Chapter 2, there are many data mining applications that can enhance an organization's products and services. They include:

- Customer acquisition profiling
- Customer retention profiling
- Customer-centric selling
- Inquiry routing
- Online shopping
- Scenario notification
- Staffing level prediction
- Targeting market
- Web-mining for prospects

15.4 Case Study: Effective Customer-Centric Marketing

For this case study, Rhonda was in contact with Richard J. Selmeier, vice president and general manager of CustomerLinx Data Services in San Francisco. CustomerLinx was founded in 1997 as Plus Communications International and acquired DTS Decision Support, Inc., in 1998, which had originated in1986 as Data Tel Services. The January 2000 renaming of PCI was intended to more accurately reflect the company's strategic mission of, in its words, "Combining the best in technology with the best of people to help our customers gain the competitive edge through superior CRM methods." It calls itself an "Internet e-Customer Care Company (IC3)."

CustomerLinx's suite of customer care services includes interactive chat, live operator support, e-mail response, e-commerce push marketing, and Fax. It provides market research, database creation, lead generation, list generation, and data warehousing. It conducts campaigns that include market research, polling, sales, cross-selling, retention, loyalty, house holding, profitability, product audits, customer service, customer support, and collections.

CustomerLinx considers data mining technologies critical to providing its customers with CRM services that "build customer loyalty and generate new sales so a one-time buyer is converted into a lifetime customer." CustomerLinx provides centralized data collection, mining, and analysis of customer interfaces information.

Historically, CustomerLinx' mission has been to help its clients implement successful acquisition, usage, and retention marketing campaigns in telecommunications, financial services, catalog, retail, and e-commerce industries. Its new vision is a logical extension of its experience. It has a history of providing customer-tailored knowledge-based marketing services including inbound and outbound Fax, IVR and Internet response services, providing the related technology, tools, and staff. Its client list is quite impressive, including the product and marketing managers of such prestigious organizations as Bank of America, Charles Schwab, Bell Atlantic, Qwest Communications, Wells Fargo, Bancorp, Pacific Telesis, Oracle, Prudential Insurance, as well as those from many other smaller and not-so-small companies. Its primary services have included modeling, scoring and analytical services, campaign management and modeling, response processing, direct marketing, and Web-based and fulfillment services.

The following case study describes an innovative business model that CustomerLinx implemented for direct marketing campaigns called "In Campaign-Modeling." Traditionally, clients had been billed based on the number of staff hours that were expended to conduct a specific customer acquisition or customer retention campaign. Since only a small percentage of the overall customer population is interested in such offers, the sponsoring companies fund large, costly campaigns targeting masses of people, hoping to get even a small response. The new model changes the payment scheme to a performance-based scenario whereby its clients are only billed fees for the actual sales that are made. Since this case study covers recurring services, more so than a specific case, we deal in generalities more than in our subsequent case studies.

15.4.1 Problem Definition (Step 1)

Each campaign may be for a different sponsor, and certainly each campaign focuses on a unique offer, or set of offerings. So, CustomerLinx must develop the model that targets the high-probability prospects for each individual offer. The problem statements would appear to be something like:

> *Identify the set of prospective customers who are most likely to pur-*
> *chase _____ (the specific current offer).*

15.4.2 Data Evaluation (Step 2)

For services that CustomerLinx provides, there could be a range of demographic data that might apply. This type of data can be purchased from Dun & Bradstreet or similar database services. In some cases, clients provide a customer or prospect list. Often such data can be problematic, because it can seldom be expected to satisfy the objectives of being comprehensive, correct, and complete. In the past, statisticians, rather than marketing professionals, have been the ones with access to vast stores of consumer data. They sample the large databases and run complicated statistical programs. Marketing professionals were unable to benefit from the vast repositories of consumer data.

From a field of 25–30 software products evaluated, CustomerLinx selected Quadstone's product, Decisionhouse, to access and analyze its consumer information and develop applicable models. Now the marketing staff of CustomerLinx has the capability to continually model, test, and update consumer information. The software provides an integrated platform to apply those aspects of segmentation, OLAP, query, reporting, statistics, and visualization necessary to analyze consumer behavior. They are now able to access and analyze clients' customer databases across all channels and develop customer profiles that identify those customers with the highest propensity to accept a specific offer. Large volumes of data are vital to building accurate models such as these. The mathematical details of the analytical techniques are transparent to the managers and business users who analyze customer behavior data across multiple channels, mailing and control cell lists, and even click-stream data.

15.4.3 Feature Extraction and Enhancement (Step 3)

Feature extraction and enhancement is a function of the specific campaign and application. Some of the features that may or may not be applicable for a specific campaign might include: age bracket, household income, residence type (apartment, condo, single family, etc.), residence location (city, suburb, rural), number of children by age bracket, gender of children by age bracket, recent purchase information, known hobbies, and so on.

15.4.4 Prototyping/Model Development (Step 4)

CustomerLinx' aggressive business model forces it to scrutinize customer data and analyze behavior patterns quickly so it can effectively solve each campaign's problem statement and identify, and then act on, the set of prospective customers who are most likely to purchase the specific current offer. CustomerLinx uses Decisionhouse to develop models that identify only the most likely candidates for programs and therefore, more effectively target its marketing campaigns. In addition to multi-dimensional visualization, the modeling environment supports cross-tabulated reports, decision tree segmentations, and response models.

Since modeling tools are now in the hands of the marketing decision makers, it is able to answer questions in real time that apply to rapidly changing commercial markets. It now has the business knowledge that helps it find answers that make statistical as well business sense. CustomerLinx is now able to perform analysis during campaign execution to refine or redirect resources within that campaign. The speed of modeling performance, combined with the flexibility to change and redefine customer behavior provides CustomerLinx with a distinct advantage against its competitors. Dick Selmeier, president of CustomerLinx, indicates that customer-profiling activities now take about 25 percent of the time they used to.

15.4.5 Model Evaluation (Step 5)

Data regarding evaluation of individual profiles or models was not available as of this writing.

15.4.6 Implementation (Step 6)

Since CustomerLinx employs commercial off-the-shelf data analysis and data mining products, the resulting profile models can be stored as data, and updates can be implemented on a continuous basis.

15.4.7 Return-On-Investment Evaluation (Step 7)

In a recent campaign, CustomerLinx was able to increase the response rate from 0.8 percent to almost 4 percent. This represents five times as many successful customer contacts. In other words, to yield the same number of sales, CustomerLinx only had to make 20 percent of the contacts that would otherwise have been necessary to yield similar results.

CustomerLinx's ability to succeed with a business model wherein it accepts the risk, and virtually guarantees success, provides great value to its clients. This is clearly a win-win proposition whereby CustomerLinx can garner larger fees by assuming risk from its clients, which the clients should be willing, if not eager, to pay because they are no longer paying by the hour for open-ended campaigns that may yield negligible results.

CustomerLinx considers the modeling capability of its marketing professionals as a real advantage over its competition, in that it now has the flexibility to handle larger campaigns and scale to add clients in traditionally highly competitive markets. The models that it has developed on its clients' behalf have resulted in increased profitability. The combination of saved time and increased revenues have caught the attention of industry leaders who constantly search for innovative best practices in the emerging Customer Relationship Management (CRM) industry.

15.4.8 Future Directions

CustomerLinx is continuing to extend its CRM capabilities and client offerings, and is now providing online reporting and analysis to its customers through "Knowledge Metrics Dashboards." The "dashboard" format facilitates decision-making of CustomerLinx' clients, based on real-time information, such as marketing sales results, customer satisfaction and emerging customer care issues, service quality levels, and market opportunities. CustomerLinx will continue to use predictive modeling to improve customer care and reduce attrition through customer profiling. According to Richard Selmeier, "The overall process is one of turning data into information, information into knowledge, and applying the knowledge to reduce key customer concerns, improve product and service satisfaction and loyalty and increase revenue."

15.5 Summary

Some of us want to celebrate the advent of such innovative applications, as CustomerLinx' "in campaign modeling." There are people who may respond positively to e-mail, "snail mail" (that's post office mail), or Web-based offers, that virtually *never* respond to telemarketing offers. For some it goes back to the behavioral psychology of deliberately not rewarding behavior that is considered undesirable. For readers in database marketing programs, if Rhonda is in your database, please indicate that she conforms to such a profile. (She wants to be part of the "80 percent" that are not contacted for a specific offer.)

Data Mining in Retail

16.1 The Industry

"Money makes the world go around," and a great deal of that money is generated through consumer sales channels. According to Hoover's Online Web site, "U.S. retail cash registers ring up about $2.7 trillion annually in sales, and of that, about a quarter comes from general merchandise, apparel, and furniture (GAF) sales."[1] For our purposes, we define all consumer sales channels including durable goods (e.g., automobiles) as retail sales. Traditional retail sales channels include department stores, high-volume stores, specialty stores, and mail-order catalogs. Home shopping television channels, infomercials, and Web sites, such as BottomDollar, Gomez, mySimon, and many others have resulted in increases in "armchair" and "desktop" shopping. Although such sites are primarily targeted at GAF sales currently, people can already shop for cars, houses, insurance products, and other products and services, on the Internet.

16.2 Challenges in Retail

People, in general, are spending smaller amounts of their discretionary time shopping. "Brick and mortar" retailers are losing market share to other retail sales channels, while the number of e-commerce sites targeted to consumers is exploding.

---

1. GAF: Industry acronym for general merchandise, apparel, and furniture sales, measured apart from other retail items such as food, building supplies, and cars. GAF is the gauge of non-durable consumer retail sales.

16.3 General Data Mining Applications

For retailers of all types, the capability to understand and predict their customers' buying habits is critical. Direct marketing applications of data mining are very widespread to make such programs more cost effective. Market basket analysis is important in virtual as well as physical storefronts, as described in the Amazon.com example in Chapter 1.

16.4 Case Study: Catalog Retailer Database Marketing Program

For this case study, Rhonda interviewed Randy Erdahl, group manager of Corporate Research and Analysis for Fingerhut Companies, Inc., and Tom Ebling, CEO of Torrent Systems. Fingerhut is one of the largest consumer catalog companies in the United States, with annual sales of $1,609.2 million.[2] It provides consumers with a range of specialty, as well as general merchandise catalogs. It has expanded from catalogs and direct mail to include several robust Internet shopping sites. At the time of this writing, Fingerhut owns and operates eight Internet retail sites, and has equity positions in several others. Fingerhut's pre-existing "direct-to-consumer fulfillment capabilities" are a tremendous asset, due to the growth of consumer electronic commerce. Owned by Federated Department Stores, who also owns the prestigious Bloomingdale's and Macy's chains, Fingerhut provides a vehicle for Federated to increase its emphasis on direct retailing.

Fingerhut sends out an astounding number of catalogs on a daily basis, an average of one million per day, at a total annual cost of $600 million. Fingerhut utilizes a massive data warehouse containing up to 1,400 attributes for each of seven million active customers. It includes such information as payment preferences, product purchases, product interests, important dates (e.g., birthdays), etc. The data warehouse provides an essential resource to support Fingerhut's extensive use of database marketing in its campaigns and mailing, which together have contributed significantly to the company's growth.

---

2.   Fiscal Year-End: January 1998 Sales per Hoover's online Web site, www.hoovers.com.

16.4.1 Problem Definition (Step 1)

Fingerhut originally relied upon a Promotional Scoring System (PSS) to score the value of customers, based on the information contained in its vast data warehouse, and to create distribution lists for individual catalogs based upon the scores. The weakness of the PSS was that multiple catalogs were being sent to individual households. Due to its huge direct marketing expenditures (hundreds of millions of dollars), Fingerhut needed to optimize its customer selection over multiple catalogs. Specifically, its problem statement could be stated as:

> *Identify the optimum (set of) catalog(s) to send to the optimal set of customers for today's mailing.*

16.4.2 Data Evaluation (Step 2)

A significant amount of data was already in place to support the marketing process for Fingerhut's 120 independent catalogs in direct marketing to 6–7 million customers. Additional data was captured to support the new Mail Stream Optimization (MSO) process. Most of the features in the models are RFM (Recency, Frequency, Monetary) behavior data-driven.

16.4.3 Feature Extraction and Enhancement (Step 3)

There are 30 attributes that are used to measure the similarity among any pair of catalogs. These are particularly useful in the new MSO application.

16.4.4 Prototyping/Model Development (Step 4)

Fingerhut developed 24 unique models to support its MSO program across its 120 catalogs. For some catalogs, unique demographic features apply (e.g., special interests such as kids, sports, etc.). The level of performance is predicted for each calendar for each customer and then the combination is determined in order to maximize the total predicted profit. Regression models are used to compare saturation between catalogs. For example, the customer may not be sent the catalog with the highest predicted profit, because a higher total profit can be expected by sending a different combination of catalogs. Linear programming optimization techniques are used to evaluate all combinations of catalogs.

16.4.5 Model Evaluation (Step 5)

To evaluate MSO performance, a 9-month trial was run for 10 percent of the total customer base, against a 10-percent control group. Although some revenue was lost, it was significantly less than the reduction in advertising expense.

16.4.6 Implementation (Step 6)

The computing environment for the system includes a distributed memory parallel system with four processors. Without such a powerful system, the system was initially projected to take 22 days to execute the processing for Fingerhut's weekly reporting. The only way to process the entire warehouse of data and make weekly reporting a reality was to run the business application in parallel, using the power of all four processors at once. However, the Business Intelligence application was designed to run sequentially, on one processor at a time, even on multiprocessor systems. The company began the search for a solution.

Fingerhut chose Torrent Systems, Inc.'s Orchestrate system. This system enables sequential applications to process significantly more data in less time by partitioning data across multiple processors and then streaming the data through multiple, parallel instances of each application step. Initial tests were conducted on a 10-percent sample of MSO data, as described under model evaluation. In September, 1998, Fingerhut rolled out the Orchestrate-enabled MSO against 100 percent of the data.

Today, Fingerhut's system crosschecks the needs of 7 million customers that are scored against 20-40 catalogs each week. The scoring process produces over 700 million scores each week and the optimization process must find the single best solution from more than one trillion possible candidates. The scoring process runtime is less that 12 hours or one-sixth of the time that the company anticipated (72 hours). "With results like that," Erdahl said, "We now handle problems that were too big to even think of solving before."

The elapsed time for the MSO project was approximately six months.

16.4.7 Return on Investment Evaluation (Step 7)

Since the system has been in full-scale production, Erdahl estimates that the company has saved approximately $5 million (over the first 18 months, or about $3.5 million per year). As for future uses, Erdahl stated, "We foresee other ways that we could reap benefits from our infrastructure investments that were related to MSO." Some examples include: prospecting with new rented lists using the same principles, optimizing across multiple channels (for example including Internet and targeted e-mails), expanding to include additional brands, and overall contact optimization.

Fingerhut's Web site even touts its MSO accomplishment as providing "fewer and more precisely targeted catalog mailings." In addition to the financial advantages, there are obvious customer relations advantages of sending more precise mailings.

16.5 Summary

The Internet and e-commerce are having a profound impact on direct marketing. The expense of direct mailing must be weighed against the ability to compete with e-tailers, so more effective mass marketing techniques are mandated. Fingerhut seems to be on the right track with its plans to eventually expand its optimization programs across multiple channels. Data mining techniques are clearly important in this environment.

17

Data Mining in Insurance

17.1 The Industry

Insurance is a system for protecting individuals against financial loss, whereby contributions, known as premiums, are collected to share the risk across many insured individuals. Actuaries calculate the probability of loss and determine the premiums that must be collected. Thus, each insurance holder is protected against the burden of an actual loss.

The insurance industry is very broad. Businesses and consumers purchase insurance to provide financial protection against a range of unfortunate circumstances, ranging from minor maladies to catastrophic events, including accidents, theft, natural disasters, illnesses, and even death. Life, property, automotive, and health insurance are common to most consumers. There are many additional types of coverage, including those that businesses require (such as liability and worker's compensation insurance), as well as many specialty insurance offerings including specific health coverage (i.e., cancer insurance) or air travel insurance. Insurance is also available for large or unusual assets such as those insured by Lloyd's of London.

17.2 Challenges

Beyond the obvious concern for correct actuarial information and calculations, one of the industry's major difficulties is fraud. Although insurance may be intended to protect purchasers against catastrophic losses, many seem to expect their insurance to protect them against any loss at all. Fraud takes many forms.

17.3 General Data Mining Applications

As in all other industries being considered herein, customer retention, or loyalty enhancement programs are equally important within the insurance industry, due to the ever-increasing competition in the global insurance marketplace.

Insurance scoring algorithms are somewhat equivalent to credit scoring algorithms, in that profiles are applied and a rating is assigned to each customer, which represents a measure of the risk associated with that customer.

Liability prediction applications, such as the one described in the case study below, can be used in order to (a) take action to mitigate the extent (or financial damage) of the liability, or (b) to identify funding to be held in reserve to satisfy such liabilities.

Fraud detection is clearly one of the industry's most significant challenges, and it takes many forms including claim fraud, premium avoidance fraud, and indemnity fraud, with claim fraud being of greatest concern.

Claim fraud can occur in virtually any type of insurance. Medical claim fraud occurs when medical providers provide unnecessary treatments and services or file claims for treatments and services that are not actually performed. Similarly, other types of property and casualty fraud (i.e., automotive or homeowners) occur when claims are submitted for repairs that are not actually performed. Even life insurance is not immune to the possibility of claims for death benefits for people who are not actually deceased.

Premium avoidance fraud can occur under a variety of circumstances. Some examples include:

- A policyholder attempts to reduce premiums by providing misinformation to the insurance carrier, such as fewer employees or lower payroll.

- A policyholder submits incorrect business classification to qualify for lower premium rates (e.g., for workers compensation).

- A policyholder changes insurance to cover injured employee and falsifies accident date.

Indemnity fraud occurs when claimants receive indemnity benefits, when they are no longer qualified. For example, a worker capable of returning to work or discontinuing medical treatments would commit indemnity fraud by continuing to receive workers' compensation.

17.4 Case Study: Workers' Compensation Liability Prediction

State-operated workers' compensation programs provide financial assistance to injured workers. One of the most difficult administrative problems such benefit programs face is the efficient management of liquidity: having exactly the right number of "reserve dollars" on hand to pay this month's benefits—no more, no less.

The substantial assets that back these programs are held in long-term instruments, so as to optimize use of funds that would otherwise stand idle. Premature withdrawal of assets from these long-term instruments reduces return, and may incur penalties. Late withdrawal of assets may result in inability to make benefit payments, incurring political and legal liability.

17.4.1 Problem Definition (Step 1)

The liability prediction problem is to predict as accurately as possible, based upon workers' compensation claims already filed, how many reserve dollars to have available for payment of benefits at some specified future date. This amounts to constructing a predictive model that uses demographics (claimant age, occupation, etc.), and financials (pre-injury wage, type of injury, etc.) to predict future fund liability.

- Predict the total cost of an individual worker's compensation claim based on the information contained in the applicable claim form.

- Predict the medical expense related to an individual worker's compensation claim based on the information contained in the applicable claim form.

- Predict the duration of disability related to an individual worker's compensation claim based on the information contained in the applicable claim form.

17.4.2 Data Evaluation (Step 2)

The training data covered four years of workers' compensation claims for a southwestern state. Data mining applications based on features that have been extracted from forms which were manually completed face daunting data quality problems. The person filling out the form may have an "agenda," which influences his or her responses. Many fields may be left blank, or contain garbled data. In many cases, the only approach open to the miner is to disregard fields that are ignored by many respondents, which greatly reduces the set of features available for analysis.

Another characteristic of data that is gathered from manual input forms is that it tends to be largely nominal, containing few numeric fields. Form designers have discovered that respondents give more complete responses if all they have to do is check a selection of boxes. For data mining techniques that require numeric data, such nominal data must be coded, which can require considerable effort.

In our case study, the limitations of the manual input data were compounded by the lack of precise information regarding the severity of the injury, or a professional prognosis. The available data was primarily demographic in nature, making accurate estimation of individual claim costs unlikely.

Over 10,000 workers' compensation claims, along with their ultimate costs, were collected for the study effort. These records contained scores of fields describing various characteristics of the claimant and the injury. As expected, most of the data was nominal (body part codes, injury type codes, etc.). There were many missing fields (left blank by the respondents).

Conventional statistical analysis was used to determine general population parameters. The distribution of ultimate claim values (in dollars) was heavily skewed to the low end: Over 99 percent of the claims had final valuations under $100,000.

Single-factor Bayesian analysis was applied to determine the most salient features for claim value prediction. Visualization techniques and correlation measures were used to verify that these features were independent.

The data had many missing fields. In order to ensure that any results obtained could be applied in practice, attention was restricted to only those fields present in virtually all records. This reduced the number of available salient features to fewer than 20.

It was determined that too few records (~12 percent) had the information required to address litigation probability. However, it was possible to build a predictive model using the extracted features that correctly predicted the likelihood of the involvement of an attorney over 80 percent of the time. This indicates that the involvement of attorneys in workers' compensation cases is systematic, and correlated with demographic features. (For example, in this data set, young males were the demographic group most likely to retain legal council in support of a claim.)

One of the data fields provided was a manually derived estimate of future medical costs. It was hoped that this field would be accurate enough to serve as ground truth for the model, but such was not the case. Auto-clustering showed that the manual estimates did not occur in clusters using the available data. Since the goal of the study was to look for improvements in current estimation techniques rather than replicate their shortcomings, only closed cases with true-valuations were used for mining.

17.4.3 Feature Extraction and Enhancement (Step 3)

The salient features selected during analysis that were identified as being correlated with the ultimate total claim value were selected as the basis for predictive modeling. Also, some features were synthesized from the best features. The final set consisted of the following twelve features:

1. Type of injury

2. Part of body

3. Person's age at time of injury

4. Gender

5. Marital status

6. Age of policy at time of injury

7. Employment status at time of injury

8. Retained attorney?

9. Claim ever contested by carrier?

10. Type of employment

11. Traumatic, occupational, or cumulative injury?

12. Pre-injury weekly wage

Only features 3, 6, and 12 were originally numeric; all others were nominal. The other features were manually coded to numeric values. The features were statistically normalized (using z-scores) Principal component analysis was applied. The data set was divided into two smaller sets: A and B. Each of these smaller sets held approximately 2000 case records.

17.4.4 Prototyping/Model Development (Step 4)

A radial basis function neural network was applied to the feature sets A and B. This was performed in both supervised and unsupervised training modes.

For set A (the feature vectors used in training), individual case valuations could consistently be predicted to within $1000 over 98 percent of the time. The predictive model was applied to the entire training set, and the predicted valuations summed. The model predicted the total medical expense for the training set to within 10 percent.

The predictive model was then applied to the entire blind set B (which was NOT part of the training data), and the predicted valuations were summed. The model predicted the total medical expense for the blind set to within 15 percent, a modest degradation from the training data. Results on individual cases in the blind set, however, were very poor: In only 30 percent of the cases were the predictions within $1000 of their actual valuations.

Bayesian analysis showed that the natural patterns of the data were disrupted when records for claimants having attorneys were present. A simple stratification was performed to remove cases involving attorneys and contested claims, and the procedures above repeated

After removal of cases involving attorneys followed by retraining, the blind test set results improved to estimation of claim valuation for the whole population to within 0.5 percent on the training set, and to within 7 percent on the blind-set. But estimates of individual claims were still poor.

17.4.5 Evaluation (Step 5)

Results during this prototyping effort suggested that more could be done with the supplied data set, particularly in additional stratification and feature enhancement. The twelve features studied do support the estimation of gross population parameters, but they do not by themselves support the estimation of the future values of individual claims. For this kind of point-estimation, additional data on the claimant is required.

The data available for this study was limited in terms of its predictive power. Missing values in the supplied data set forced consideration of only a small subset of the collected features. Aggregate results were consistently much better than individual results. These facts, coupled with the high resolution ($1000 bins) desired for the output prediction, indicate that the supplied data set did not adequately cover the universe of discourse.

17.5 Summary

Fraud provides a significant target for data mining applications in the insurance industry, be it claim fraud, premium avoidance fraud, and indemnity fraud, or of some other form.

18

Data Mining in Financial Services

18.1 The Industry

All companies that were incorporated before the computer age started out with paper-intensive maintenance of their financial records on a series of ledgers. The thought of it brings visions of Ebenezer Scrooge and Bob Cratchet to mind. With the advent of computers, financial record keeping became the first business application. The computer departments of most companies started out reporting to the position we know today as the Chief Financial Officer in the corporate hierarchy. Hence, the foundation of information technology to support financial record keeping has a long history.

Laborious manual record keeping was especially true for banking organizations. Here too, it became the initial target for computer systems. But gradually, the computer systems applied to financial record keeping have been extended to support far more than "bean-counting" activities. The advent of the automated teller machine (ATM) during the 1970s changed the landscape for such organizations. Information on customer activities (behavior) has become of critical importance. Financial services corporations continue to invest heavily in information technology. Estimates of the industry average IT expenditure are consistently about 15 percent of revenue.

Today's financial services industry encompasses a variety of commercial entities including investment banks, brokerage houses, merchant banks, investment companies, finance companies, credit card banks, and a variety of service providers. These entities typically generate their revenue by collecting very small fees on very large volumes of transactions, in a fiercely competitive market.

Due to their IT leadership as well as this competitive environment, financial services organizations are among the early adopters of data mining technology, which they consider a distinct competitive weapon. They apply it so extensively, that they are even offering data mining-based information products to their customers. Chase Manhattan Corporation's Web site provides an example. It displays the slogan "the right relationship is everything" and provides a service offering that "enables a customer to store and retrieve financially related documents and data." i-VAULT! provides a powerful index/data mining tool and other services. This is merely one example of many that could be cited.

18.2 Challenges

The extremely competitive nature of the financial services industry stems not only from the "bank on every corner," but now from e-commerce Internet services that compete as well. Retaining customer loyalty is of the utmost importance to retaining market share, and is currently the key business challenge.

Due to the myriad of general and specialized tools, techniques, and applications available to the financial services community, identifying and effectively using the best one is a critical technical challenge.

18.3 General Data Mining Applications

The financial services industry is a leader in applying data mining applications, where a range of solutions and tools apply. Statistical tools such as SAS and SPSS are widely used, and these are frequently supplemented by multiple selections from a range of modeling environments. In addition, very focused statistical and data mining application-specific solutions are prevalent risk management for all types of credit, and fraud detection are but a few examples. Fair, Isaac is a credit scoring application that is quite pervasive throughout the financial services industry. HNC's Falcon product, based on neural network techniques, is used to detect credit or debit card fraud. It too, has been widely adopted.

Specific custom solutions are also applied. For example, CSI developed an application to detect fraud within international fund transfers. The application system determines whether transactions are allowed to process, based on user-defined thresholds for the confidence ratings generated by the application software, and enables financial institutions to avoid large fines that can be levied on individual banks by the Office of Foreign Assets Control (OFAC). Since transaction review was a labor-intensive process before the application was implemented, both labor savings and the avoidance of fines contribute to the ROI for this application.

The current emphasis is on customer acquisition and retention, including direct marketing applications of data mining technology. For example, in October 1998, two of the United States' largest financial institutions joined to form the financial services giant known today as Bank of America. The merger between NationsBank and Bank of America leaves one company with responsibility for managing the financial affairs of one-third of America's households and 80 percent of *Fortune* magazine's Global 500 companies—approximately $614 billion in total assets.

Bank of America uses SAS Enterprise Miner™ to support several CRM initiatives. With more power and responsibility come bigger problems. "In the banking industry, there's about a 20 percent annual customer attrition rate," says Chris Kelly, senior vice president of database marketing for Bank of America. "It costs us considerably more to attract new customers than it would to retain the current customers," explains Kelly, "so we try to focus our sales force on those customers that are likely to attrite and are highly profitable as well."

Determining which customers to target, however, was no easy task for Bank of America. The bank's primary customer database consists of 2.6 terabytes of data located in an NCR/Teradata data warehouse. "On that corporate data warehouse we keep a marketing data mart for analytic purposes—roughly 18 months of customer data at a detailed transactional level," says Kelly. "Our biggest problem working with such large data sets was our ability to move the information out of the data warehousing environment into the analytic environment."

In order to accurately analyze customer data and predict not only which customers were more profitable, but also which of those were likely to move their business elsewhere, Bank of America executives needed a powerful solution to help them implement an effective Customer Relationship Management (CRM) strategy. So, Bank of America worked with SAS Consulting Services to expand its modeling environment into an all-encompassing CRM solution. Bank of

America uses SAS Enterprise Miner to access and analyze data as well as to generate detailed reports.

Bank of America's CRM strategy is enabling the bank to manage customer relationships in a variety of areas. "One of the challenges of CRM is managing the communications flow to ensure that all customer contacts are relevant," explains Kelly. For instance, some customers prefer telephone calls to direct mail, while others prefer online banking to direct mail. The only way to learn about each customer's preferred means of communication is by keeping a detailed history of involvement with the customer. Bank of America uses the data mining techniques including decision trees, neural networks, associations, and data mining regression. The bank also uses its CRM application software to analyze life events of customers in order to make communications more relevant. Customers who have married recently, for example, receive a different set of communications from customers who have just retired.

"The goal of our CRM program is two-fold," says Kelly. "One is to ensure that we are communicating to the customer in the proper tone with relevant products and services. The other goal is to improve the retention rates of the company. We feel that by being timely and communicating with our customers, we can effect a change in the number of customers who leave every year." Bank of America can also flag customer files so that when a file is accessed, the teller can know what marketing segment the customer belongs to, and what kind of services will most likely generate a customer response.

When implementing its customer retention program, where timeliness is a key factor, Bank of America saw dramatic improvements in time to market. "We were able to reduce our time to market from approximately a six-week process to a six-day process, including extracting customer information, scoring files, and making that information available to our associates," says Kelly. Customer relationship management is often about contact with individuals. Bank of America's CRM solution has helped it improve the quantity and quality of the personal contact with its customers.

The CRM system has provided significant ROI for Bank of America. As one example, "The retention program we ran in California had a return on investment of about 10 to 1, and our first-year profit saves were in the neighborhood of (U.S.) $10 million," says Kelly. "With the continued rollout of this program to other states, we estimate that we can save in the neighborhood of (U.S.) $30 million in profits. Our CRM solution has not only helped us to optimize our marketing expenditures, but also to provide customized and differentiated service that will enhance our customers' experience with Bank of America."

Rhonda also interviewed Don Cozine, who works in the U.S. modeling and analytics department at American Express and writes frequent product reviews for *Data Mining Review*. American Express Company provides travel and network services in addition to financial services such as charge cards, travelers checks, investment products. Don uses Salford Systems Classification and Regression Trees (CART) tool to develop customer classification models, and considers it particularly effective when working with "dirty data." CART is a memory-based reasoning technique built on a sound theoretical foundation.

18.4 Case Study: Direct Marketing Profiling

For this case study, Rhonda interviewed Joseph Somma, who has been vice president and director of customer acquisition and research at HSBC Bank in Buffalo, New York, since 1996 and had considerable prior database research experience in banking. Mr. Somma is responsible for the design and development of customer databases and response models and the design of direct marketing programs for consumer, investment, and commercial business applications. His responsibilities also include the development of market channel strategies for direct banking, Internet, PC Banking, and other electronic channels.

HSBC Bank USA describes itself as "a New York State banking institution with over 450 branches in New York, seven branches in Florida, three in California and two in Pennsylvania. . . . [It] is the third largest depository institution with the largest branch network in New York State. The bank serves more than 2 million New York State households, more than 800,000 personal customers in other states, and more than 200,000 commercial and institutional customers nationwide." HSBC Bank USA is a member of the global HSBC Group. HSBC Bank USA serves more than 1.4 million retail banking customers, providing a variety of checking, investment, loan, and other financial products, as well as serving business and commercial customers.

Consistent with our description of the extreme competition in financial services, a typical branch of a neighborhood HSBC Bank might have a half dozen or more competitors in close proximity. This generates continuous competition to attract potential and retain existing customers in the surrounding area. In order to maintain high customer acquisition and retention rates while maintaining profitable operations, the goals of a bank often include: expanding relationships with current customers, keeping marketing costs low to maintain margins, and moving to market quickly with new intelligence. These are true for HSBC; however, the specific case study examples deal with selling stock index certificates of deposit (CDs).

18.4.1 Problem Definition (Step 1)

Selling stock index CDs is part of a rebranding effort HSBC is undergoing from "bank" to "investment company." Its goal with this financial instrument is to penetrate the top 30 percent of its customer base, which is a profitable segment. Focusing on the best prospects for each product helps maximize sales and minimize marketing costs; for this specific case, HSBCs problem definition is:

> *Identify current HSBC households who are most likely to purchase our stock index CD product.*

18.4.2 Data Evaluation (Step 2)

HSBC Bank USA uses SPSS on an on-going basis to mine its evergrowing repository of customer data. Its frequently develops predictive models for cross-selling and "roll over" sales applications. As with any cross-selling application, demographic data is important, but the data used in the stock index CD analysis also included purchase history, balance increases and decreases, current balance, and usage patterns. In addition, the product had been sold previously and customers with prior purchase history were identified.

The data used for the evaluation included 300,000 households. All of the analysis was conducted at the household level. A sample of 150,000 households was selected for model development and verification. Features that were found to be useful for identifying households who would be most likely to purchase stock index CDs included:

- How recently they purchased anything
- How recently they invested

- How recently they took out a loan

- Over $10,000 on deposit

- A profitability measure

- Frequency at which they bought investment products over the last 12 months

- Frequency at which they bought investment products over the last 18 months

- Age

- Income

- Other demographic variables

HSBC also considered using gender as a feature. The demographic information that it had purchased for its analysis included three values for gender: male, female, or unknown. Its analysis identified the value of "unknown" to have the best predictive salience. However, since there were so few unknowns, the feature did not provide much lift to the overall model.

18.4.3 Feature Extraction and Enhancement (Step 3)

Considerable effort went into the process of identifying the best RFM features. RFM is commonly used in direct marketing efforts to represent recency, frequency, and monetary factors, which are often key to direct marketing analysis and data mining programs. This effort involved creating categories and then evaluating their effectiveness to find the best levels using a Chi-Squared Automated Interaction Detection (CHAID)-oriented approach. CHAID is a stepwise statistical method for splitting data into groups based on attribute values. It can be used to induce rules and build decision trees. Discriminate models were used to evaluate continuous data.

18.4.4 Prototyping/Model Development (Step 4)

Since this was the first data-mining project to be presented to HSBC's senior management, Joe elected to use a decision tree model so that he could demonstrate the use of "management intuition." This avoided the intimidation that might have resulted from a neural network approach.

As is common, the modeling effort involved several iterations of model development. Although the micro-vision code and cycle code features were expected to provide some lift, they didn't actually help. These features worked well for acquisition programs, but didn't provide the information needed for this cross-selling application.

The entire model development effort took only three weeks, with 70 to 80 percent of the effort expended on data cleansing, scoring, verification, and building of variables, and only 20 to 30 percent of the effort expended on hard-core analysis. HSBC considers SPSS to be an effective tool for researchers to quickly deliver business intelligence to decision makers.

18.4.5 Evaluation (Step 5)

Joe described the performance of the end product model as "very good" because it explained over 80 percent of household purchasing behavior.

18.4.6 Results (ROI)

The entire file was scored, and 60,000 households were identified to receive the direct marketing mailing for the stock index CDs. Without the predictive model, 160,000 pieces would have been mailed. The marketing ROI was significantly better at 310 percent.

Since this project over two years ago, HSBC has used decision trees frequently in developing models. Recently, it has been using neural networks in combination with decision trees yielding very good results. On average, its models result in 50-percent better response rates combined with 30-percent reduction in related marketing costs. Its data mining programs also provide a better capability to create and deploy timely marketing strategies.

HSBC has plans to develop a data warehouse to support mortgage, equity, and other list selection activities. The results will be made available in the individual branch Customer Information Systems, so when customers are at their location, the bank employees know the best sales objectives. Data mining for direct marketing is a critical aspect of what the data warehouse will be used for to provide return.

18.5 Summary

Financial services companies typically generate their revenue by collecting very small fees on very large volumes of transactions, in a fiercely competitive market. Applied data mining techniques can help these companies compete.

19

Data Mining in Health Care and Medicine

19.1   The Industry

The health care "business" has changed dramatically during the past decade with financial risk being shared by providers as well as payors (employers and insurance companies) and patients. Cost factors, government regulations, and technology advances all drive the pace of change in health care. The Health Insurance Portability and Accountability Act of 1996 (HIPAA) has been a recent factor. Making high-quality health care available in a cost-effective manner is a common goal. Changes in the health care industry may be considered even more dramatic with emphasis shifting from reactive treatment of patients to proactive "wellness" programs, and payment for services changing from "fee for service" to "managed care" or even "capitation" models.

Under "fee for service," health care providers submit claim forms for services rendered, and are reimbursed up to the amount considered "reasonable and customary" for the location where the service is rendered. Preferred Provider Organization (PPO) plans are a special type of fee for service plan that features pre-negotiated rates for providers (physicians and others) that are members of the applicable PPO network. This is sometimes referred to as "Managed Care." The providers accept a smaller fee in exchange for access to the patient population covered by an employer or health care administrator. Under "capitation," a provider organization agrees to provide health care services for a monthly fee per member. In other words, if the members are healthy, the providers get to keep the fees while providing little service, but if the members are less healthy than the providers expect, they can be in a losing proposition. These programs are often referred to as Health Maintenance Organizations (HMOs).

At the same time the picture of health care "business" has been changing, advances in medical treatments have been dramatic. Diseases that were terminal illnesses 20 years ago can now be routinely treated. Many treatments are less invasive, such as those utilizing minute remote-controlled robotic devices, and therefore pose less patient risk. The pharmaceutical industry continues to provide a wider range of more effective drug therapies. With the current levels of investment in biomedical research, the prospects for treatment of our aging population are continuously improving.

Traditionally Information Systems in health care have focused on reimbursement for services rendered. But today, clinical information systems are making significant strides in supporting caregivers, and collecting patient care information. The resulting clinical data repositories provide a rich field where data mining can be applied for both patient profiling and research applications. As a result, there is increasing emphasis on measuring the effectiveness of treatments, or what is commonly referred to as "outcomes measurement," which in turn requires increased collection and dissemination of clinical information.

As the health care industry continues to increase emphasis on clinical applications, multimedia data types are also sometimes stored in clinical data repositories. Such data types include audio, video, graphical representations (such as EKGs), and diagnostic images. These multimedia data can also be the subject of data mining activities.

Medical research and development have recently been well funded by venture capitalists. There can be issues pertaining to the ownership results of their research results, when making the results available could enhance the well-being of the general public and advance other research endeavors.

19.2 Challenges

As in other industries, keeping pace with the rate of technological and medical advancement provides a significant challenge. Researchers at the Food and Drug Administration must be concerned with quickly making advanced new medical treatments available to those who suffer from chronic and serious medical problems, but not so quickly as to endanger patients with unproven treatment protocols.

Cost is a constant issue in this ever-changing market, described above.

19.3   General Data Mining Applications

Consistent with other industries, early data mining activities have focused on financially oriented applications, such as the actuarial cost-risk models used by HMOs, medical claim fraud, etc. Predictive models have been applied to predict length of stay, total charges, and even mortality. Such models can be applied to the individual hospital information based on actual experience and can take severity adjustments into account.

Similar to other types of human behavior profiling models that are discussed herein, patient profiles can be developed for wellness, treatment, or recovery, based on individual diagnosis or risk category.

Health care information pertaining to the treatment of individuals is separate from information pertaining to medical technology. Data mining in medicine applies to pharmaceutical and biotechnology information. "Bio-informatics" applications are used in the analysis of genetic sequence data and other types of analyses.

Analytical tools are at the heart of outcomes improvement, providing the ability to correlate differences in treatment with significant impacts on clinical outcomes, cost outcomes, and/or patient satisfaction outcomes. Such tools can automatically identify subgroups (or clusters) within a population, and provide descriptive statistics regarding how each sub-group compares with the population as a whole or other sub-populations. Rule induction can be used to provide descriptive statistics regarding how a user-specified sub-population (e.g., all those patients with a specific diagnosis) compares to the population as a whole or other sub-populations.

At the fundamental level, analytical tools can be used to monitor patient care and outcomes to identify variations (both positive and negative), and determine whether these variations are significant. This information is often depicted graphically over time with various charting techniques. Beyond this basic tracking capability is the profiling capability that represents various providers' treatments and outcomes. Further statistical analysis is required to determine whether any variations are of statistical significance.

Interactive data mining "knowledge discovery" tools can be used to identify critical variations and define priorities for further analysis. Pattern recognition tools can also be used to identify significant variations. For example, identifying the types of drugs that are associated with a majority of adverse drug effects could be determined interactively or through pattern recognition techniques. Visualization tools such as N-dimensional graphics capability provides the capability for analysts to visually interact with and discover patterns in data that would otherwise be too complex for humans to recognize. Hypothesis testing and evaluation tools are required to provide the capability to improve clinical outcomes. Clinical process improvements are identified, deployed, and evaluated through the comparison of risk-adjusted outcomes of well-defined population and process samples.

The growth in the volume of information available, along with managed care concerns, have complicated the caregiver's decision-making process. Organizations are increasingly demanding that their processes become more consistent and accurate while being less dependent on experts or specialists. Intelligent information systems that address knowledge management and decision making are being developed and implemented to perform functions that have traditionally been performed by specialists.

What is a medical diagnosis, if not a pattern-recognition problem, albeit a very complex one. In spite of the wide-ranging variation from case to case, classifying features (e.g., symptoms and history) with salience (classification power) clearly exist. The complicating factor in medical diagnosis is the high number of possible outcomes. Nevertheless, pattern recognition is applicable to patient analysis whether for diagnostic or health maintenance purposes.

We believe that a wide range of predictive models could be developed for diagnostic purposes. These models may well utilize data that is not traditionally used in developing diagnoses, and may perhaps require less effort and cost to acquire.

In support of the goal of improving long-term outcomes, pattern recognition techniques could be applied to patient risk reduction or "wellness" strategies, e.g., to recognize patients that conform to various risk profiles based on clinical information collected in a clinical data repository (CDR). Rule induction could explain why the patient's "risk profile" is high, and might even suggest improvements to life style factors along with confidence factors relating to the impact such improvements would have on a patient's wellness likelihood.

19.4 Case Study: Predicting Patient Diagnosis for PVD

Monte was involved in a study at CSI that was conducted on behalf of a managed care group in the western United States. This could be regarded as a simple experiment in "evidence-based medicine."

19.4.1 Problem Definition (Step 1)

The goal of this study was to determine whether and to what extent weakly related factors might be able to suggest the presence of a putatively unrelated disease. The purpose was not to replace or enhance standard diagnostic techniques, but to investigate the possibility of using patient medical records to estimate the likelihood that certain co-morbidities not noted by caregivers in the record might be present.

Specifically, it was desired to investigate the effectiveness of hematologic and demographic facts as indicators of peripheral vascular disease (PVD). The problem definition could be stated as:

Identify the diagnostic hypothesis (relative to PUD) that is most likely for each patient based on the information available.

19.4.2 Data Evaluation (Step 2)

The data consisted of 2,018 usable cases provided by the client. The measurements, or features, provided included several "flags" indicating the presence of certain hematological facts, for example blood viscosity, as well as demographic data including age, gender, and so on.

19.4.3 Feature Extraction and Enhancement (Step 3)

There was no special feature extraction and enhancement for this modeling activity. Most of the data was represented as binary indicators (zeros and ones). Additional numeric data was used without coding of any kind.

19.4.4 Prototyping/Model Development (Step 4)

A predictive model was developed to estimate the likelihood of concurrent peripheral vascular disease (PVD). PVD is typically diagnosed by "differential blood pressure," which is the difference between the blood pressure measurements taken in an arm and a leg.

This example serves to illustrates the power of data mining. Data mining has the capability to utilize data that is not usually regarded as diagnostic to estimate the likelihood that a disease may be present. In other words, there is often predictive power in features thought not to possess it.

The prototype that was developed for this study accepts the feature data provided by the client as input, and generates one of the following diagnostic hypotheses, as output for each subject patient:

- Arterial insufficiency
- Arteriosclerosis obliterans
- Decreased circulation
- Intermittent claudication
- No indication in chart
- Peripheral vascular disease

This software prototype produces its diagnosis in a fraction of a second, and provides a confidence factor indicating its certainty.

19.4.5 Evaluation (Step 5)

The prototype was developed using 1,009 case files. When applied to these same cases, it gives a correct diagnosis regarding the presence or absence of PVD 961 times, or an aggregate correctness of 95.24 percent. Many of the "missed" cases have low confidence indicators, as of course is desired.

When applied to a "blind-set" of 1,009 cases the neural network has never seen before, the prototype provides the correct diagnosis 714 times, for an aggregate correctness of 70.76 percent. Once again, many of the "missed" cases have low confidence indicators, which the system could indicate as "no diagnosis offered." The prototype was not optimized for accuracy, and additional effort could improve the performance. In addition, using a larger number of cases could also increase the prognostic power of the system. Other areas could also be addressed, given additional data, include estimating outcomes and developing "episodes of care."

19.4.6 Results (ROI)

The primary value of this study is that it demonstrates a capability to predict the likelihood that a specific disease is present in a patient. Such capabilities could be applied to enhance early diagnosis of certain conditions and ultimately reduce treatment costs for a population.

19.5 Summary

Health care organizations retain vast repositories of patient data that are virtually untapped as a source of information to improve patient care.

20

Data Mining in Telecommunications

20.1 The Industry

The telecommunications industry has experienced dramatic growth and evolution with today's systems. The industry delivers multimedia data through a variety of methods including traditional wiring, wireless, and satellite communications networks. Annual global spending on telecom services, already $726 billion, is expected to grow to $1 trillion by 2001.[1] It is not uncommon for households that only had one telephone number a decade ago, to have five or more today. These lines service personal computers, FAX machines, cellular telephones, and pagers. At the same time the industry has been deregulated. This has fostered greater competition. Household Internet access is driving increased demand for bandwidth, causing competition to extend to cable and satellite channels.

It's difficult to imagine that we will continue to experience the revolutionary change and explosive growth that we've seen recently. Perhaps going forward we can expect evolutionary changes, continued dynamic growth, and innovative applications that make use of enhanced communications bandwidth.

20.2 Challenges in the Telecommunications Industry

Keeping in pace with the rate of technological change provides a significant challenge to businesses throughout the telecommunications industry, as demonstrated by the Iridium collapse. The Iridium project began in the early 1990s, but by the time its network of 66 satellites was in place and its telephone network was operational,

---

1.   Hoover's online Web site, www.hoovers.com.

cellular telephone networks had become widely available on an international level. These networks were able to offer distinct price advantages and a smaller, more convenient device. Change is certainly not limited to voice networks. The Internet is causing dramatic growth in data communications. "By 2001 some analysts think that 90 percent of the traffic carried on telecommunications networks will be data."[2]

At the same time the industry faces dramatic technological change, deregulation is changing the business landscape resulting in competition from a wide range of service providers.

As in other competitive industries, finding and retaining customers is important to telecommunications providers. Since the business model in telecommunication services involves subscribing customers who pay for services after they are rendered, fraud is also a significant issue.

20.3   General Data Mining Applications

In addition to customer profiling applications, subscription fraud and credit applications are utilized extensively throughout the industry. Serious concerns about privacy and security, which are magnified by the Internet, are likely to result in data mining applications targeted to these areas in the near future.

20.4   Case Study: Modeling Direct Marketing Response for a Communication Service

Direct marketing response modeling identifies the characteristics of potential customers for a product or service that make those prospects actual buyers. Thus, this is another very specific example of a customer profiling application. The cost of any direct marketing campaign is directly proportional to the number of prospects being targeted. Each contact, whether by telephone, direct mail, or a face-to-face interview, increases cost. However, only those prospects that actually purchase a product or service contribute to revenue. Reducing the number of prospects to contact, while at the same time

---

2.   Hoover's online Web site, www.hoovers.com.

increasing the response rate, results in reduced marketing expenses and increased profit, and therefore provides a distinct financial advantage.

Cactus Strategies, a consultancy that specializes in heuristic business tools and models, is developing a customer care and acquisition system for an anonymous client communication services company. Cactus Strategies uses PolyAnalyst Pro software from Megaputer Intelligence.

20.4.1 Problem Definition (Step 1)

The communication services company is focused on introducing a suite of new products to the market and is seeking to improve its direct marketing performance. The problem statement for this case is:

Identify those prospects for our new service that are most likely to purchase.

20.4.2 Data Evaluation (Step 2)

The subject data set consisted of information for approximately 6,000 companies that expressed an interest in products that are similar to the new product being offered. Since information about non-buyers of the new products was not available, Cactus Strategies added an equal number of records for randomly selected businesses that were purchased from an independent vendor of business data. A total of 53 information attributes, or features, was available for each company including: the size, location, business classification, operation type, and time period the company was tracked.

20.4.3 Feature Extraction and Enhancement (Step 3)

The first step of the analysis was to transform the data into a form suitable for analysis by aggregating the values of some variables and substituting some original variables by their more predictive combinations. Then, two rounds of the Find Dependencies algorithm facilitated quick identification of the set of variables that had the greatest influence on the purchase decision. The time taken by elaborate machine learning algorithms depends on the number of variables investigated, so eliminating redundant variables greatly improves the speed of analysis.

The data was analyzed using a suite of data mining tools that provides a wide selection of exploration tools for predicting values of continuous variables, explicitly modeling complex phenomena, determining the most influential independent variables, and solving classification and clustering tasks. A preliminary analysis resulted in the selection of 12 attributes thought to be most predictive.

20.4.4 Prototyping/Model Development (Step 4)

The classification algorithm was run to analyze only those variables found to be important. PolyAnalyst's classification algorithm uses fuzzy logic to develop a continuous function modeling the probability that a record represents buyers/nonbuyers. Then, it selects a threshold for minimizing the number of incorrect classifications. The PolyAnalyst Find Laws exploration engine, chosen to power the classification, allowed for the fast production of a viable and explicit model. After about eight hours of model prototyping, the system found a classification rule that is capable of estimating the probability that a potential customer will be a buyer, predicting with 81 percent accuracy, based on only three of its characteristics (features).

Later, the clustering algorithm was applied to enable the model to be refined even further. The resulting business model had the advantages of being descriptive and easily applied to the bulk of the data, and of satisfying the client, particularly interested in predicting buyers using categorical variables. Discovered rules can be deployed in external data scoring applications which provides immediate business benefits. The client can now score all its potential customers by their likelihood of purchasing new products, and direct market only to likely buyers.

The heuristic tool at the heart of the customer care and acquisition system predicts which prospective customers have actual demand for the introduced products and which are most likely to become buyers. The system assesses the probability that a potential customer needs the promoted products and might choose a particular class of service, based upon its business profile. The key data mining elements of this project are the identification of a business rule that predicts demand for the client's services and the continuous improvement of this profile. The data mining algorithms are at the heart of the heuristic tool, providing key insights.

20.4.5 Model Evaluation (Step 5)

A joint application of PolyAnalyst algorithms resulted in a model that was capable of accurately predicting purchase decisions.

20.4.6 Results (ROI)

The business value of the discovered model is readily visualized by PolyAnalyst's Lift and Gain charts. The Lift chart evaluates the benefits of performing a model-based vs. random marketing campaign. The Gain chart illustrates the dependence of dollar-based profit on the number of model-suggested prospects contacted. It allows the company to optimize the number of prospects contacted to achieve a balance between the maximum profit and exposure. For a Gain chart, the cost per contact, profit per response, and maximum number of prospects for the marketing campaign are entered. For the selected parameters the profit peaks when 1,500 best prospects are targeted.

With a response model at hand, the client can identify the most likely buyers prior to spending time and money communicating with prospects. Contacting only a fraction of prospects—those most likely to purchase—results in lower direct marketing expenses and better response rate, and therefore increases profit.

20.5 Case Study: A Predictive Model for Telecom Credit Risk

Monte was instrumental in the development of credit risk assessment models for the telecommunications industry, in the spring of 1999. Due to the volume of customers processed, the service provider has a performance requirement sustained at 1,000 customers per minute.

20.5.1 Problem Definition (Step 1)

Specifically, we consider the design and construction of a predictive model to mitigate subscription fraud. This model applies business intelligence, and exploits historical customer behaviors to predict which potential customers are good credit risks. The prediction accuracy of the model had to be a substantial improvement over the existing technique (a conventional regression method). (The formal problem statement for this case is included in section 20.5.6.)

20.5.2 Data Evaluation (Step 2)

Cellular phone credit applications for 120,000 customers were available for analysis along with the associated credit report information. For the risk assessment application, an initial review of the data disclosed that "empty" fields constituted approximately 50 percent of the data. These data gaps were unsystematic. There was no pattern to the presence or absence of particular data fields. This meant that the development of Business Intelligence from this data faced a daunting data quality problem.

20.5.3 Feature Extraction and Enhancement (Step 3)

During feature extraction, data fields are selected from those available for use in a predictive model. Sometimes these "raw features" are used as is. However, often they are combined with other features, normalized, or otherwise transformed to maximize the impact of their information content.

One data-mining truism is that "the best feature set is not the set of best features." A mistake commonly made by novice data modelers is to collect those features containing the information most directly bearing on the solution of a problem, and ignore "weaker" features. While it may seem desirable to have many features directly relevant to a problem, it is frequently the case that these powerful features are not independent. For example, "sales" and "revenue" are probably two good features for predicting changes in a company's stock price, but they are certainly not independent (as discussed in Chapter 6).

In our study, we tabulated the abilities of each feature separately to correctly classify customers as good or bad using a simple Bayesian classifier. Feature number three did the best job, at 75.2 percent, feature four was next at 73.55 percent, and so on. "Salience" is a numeric measure of how well each feature does in preserving the identity of small classes:

Table 20.1 *Feature Effectiveness and Salience*

Rank	Feature Number	% Accuracy	Salience
1	3	75.2890173410405	.443517509452841
2	4	73.5549132947977	.535473414280081

Table 20.1 *Feature Effectiveness and Salience (continued)*

Rank	Feature Number	% Accuracy	Salience
3	9	71.0982658959538	.453013339865345
4	8	65.7514450867052	.486195012363272
5	2	64.1618497109827	.496983733844041
6	5	62.1387283236994	.590529027809203
7	1	61.7052023121387	.694308274257602
8	7	59.393063583815	.442620607605822
9	10	46.6763005780347	.481392968626008
10	6	41.0404624277457	.499437989430928

Based upon the information in the table, it looks like a good feature set would contain both features three and four. When we compute the correlation coefficients of all features with each other (see below), we discover that (fortunately for us) our features are largely independent of each other (correlation close to zero), so they all give us independent information.

Table 20.2 *Correlation Matrix of Features Sorted by % Bayesian Accuracy*

	3	4	9	8	2	5	1	7	10	6
3	+1.00	-0.07	+0.00	-0.02	+0.00	-0.03	-0.06	+0.04	-0.03	+0.03
4		+1.00	+0.00	-0.01	+0.01	+0.06	+0.02	+0.03	-0.05	+0.03
9			+1.00	-0.01	-0.03	-0.04	+0.01	+0.04	-0.00	+0.05
8				+1.00	+0.01	+0.01	+0.00	+0.03	-0.04	+0.03
2					+1.00	-0.01	-0.05	-0.02	+0.03	+0.02
5						+1.00	+0.05	-0.00	+0.02	+0.04
1							+1.00	-0.01	-0.03	-0.10
7								+1.00	+0.03	+0.01
10									+1.00	+0.06
6										+1.00

In general, it is desirable to use as few features as possible. This reduces processing cost and model complexity. The analysis above addresses features individually. But it must still be determined which collection of features is best *as a set*. A more sophisticated analysis of the salience and correlation of the features determines which subset of each size (one feature, up to all 10) should be used for maximum success. Feature salience is the primary factor.

Table 20.3

Dimension	Efficiency	Feature Mask	Feature Mask Interpretation
1	.694308274257602	1000000000	"If you can only use 1 feature use #1"
2	.624339853856034	1000100000	"If you can only use 2 features use #1 & #5"
3	.591335886395776	1001100000	"If you can only use 3 features use 1, 4 & 5"
4	.566443612276951	1101100000	
5	.550976454738736	1101100100	
6	.539218778420057	1101110100	
7	.529108108875373	1101110101	
8	.519007898340901	1101110111	
9	.509911922836751	1101111111	
10	.502145165688368	1111111111	

The efficiency measure penalizes large feature sets, even though large sets might do a better job of classifying the data. The general rule is to use the largest set in the list that returns some benefit over its smaller successors. In our case, by the time we are up to seven or eight features, most of the benefit has been derived.

Preparation of the data for analysis began with randomization of the record order. This was done to remove "co-location bias": sampling bias that arises as a result of the order in which records are stored. Once this step had been completed, records could be selected for analysis by simple linear resampling, since every such sample would be a random sample.

To begin the feature analysis, descriptive statistics were computed, visualization was used, autoclustering was performed, and other data mining techniques were applied. The purpose of this analysis was to determine which features were information bearing for the application at hand. Feature analysis was followed by feature extraction, during which data items were selected from the data store and conditioned for ingestion by the predictive model. Feature analysis and extraction typically consume approximately 80 percent of the effort involved in developing a predictive model, as they did for this effort.

Missing data fields were consistently filled using two different (proprietary) techniques, and analysis tools were applied to check for "reasonableness."

20.5.4 Prototyping/Model Development (Step 4)

A rapid prototyping sequence was then conducted, which resulted in the predictive model development over the course of several days. An objective function for prediction accuracy was created. An objective function is the mathematical expression that assumes an optimum value when the problem is solved. A simple objective function might be "classification accuracy." If our model's determination of the credit-worthiness of potential customers is correct 100 percent of the time, for example, we may regard our problem as solved. For this case study, a complex multi-factor objective function was developed to control different aspects of the problem. The driver though, was "model cost," which is described below.

20.5.5 Evaluation (Step 5)

Model validation was performed using blind testing. The model was used to process data that was not used for feature conditioning or model construction. An accuracy score was computed for the blind testing predictions.

The entire development cycle, from first receipt of the data to final validation of the completed model, consumed approximately five weeks. A team of one full-time and one part-time data-mining engineer performed the work.

20.5.6 Results (ROI)

Building a customer profiling system provides financial value, only if the long-term return (net of operation and maintenance costs) exceeds the development cost within a reasonable time frame.

Customer profiling can be performed with various objectives in mind. In our telecom subscription fraud case study, service providers enter into service agreements with customers who may or may not pay their bill. Service providers assume an up-front risk, because they don't bill for service until the end of the billing cycle (typically a month). Specifically, the goal is to discover patterns in business data that will enable limitation of loss due to this type of fraud.

The subscription problem is faced by all businesses engaged in providing service for credit. Such businesses don't know in advance who's going to pay their bill. Many businesses operate at-risk for some period of time, because they are providing service and incurring cost under the assumption that the customer will pay for services rendered.

In the cellular telephone business, customers walk in the front door, wanting to purchase a cellular telephone and arrange for services. There's likely to be a variety of telephones and service plans available. After some discussion and explanation, a service contract is signed, and the customer leaves with the equipment. In many cases, customers could be making long-distance phone calls by the time they reach the parking lot. The service provider is at risk.

In deciding whether to offer a service agreement, it is customary to assume initially that the potential customer is acting in good faith. Based upon his or her credit application and credit report, service providers must decide whether this assumption is warranted for this particular customer. There are two components of risk in the subscription problem: lost opportunity cost and fraud cost. If a customer is one who would pay her bill, but is turned away as a bad risk, the revenue that would have been generated is lost. This is lost opportunity cost. In statistical terms, it amounts to a "type I statistical error." On the other hand, if the applicant is a deadbeat, and a contract is let, the service is given at the provider's expense. This is fraud cost, and a "type II statistical error" has been made.

Data mining analysts represent this kind of decision in a diagram called a confusion matrix. In the subscription problem, there are two kinds of customers, "good" and "bad," and two choices open to the service provider, which will be called "sign" and "don't sign." There are two right decisions: Sign the good customers, and don't sign the bad customers. There are too wrong decisions: Sign the bad customers, and don't sign the good customers. The confusion matrix for a hypothetical business day during which a provider made a few right decisions, and a few wrong decisions, might look like:

Table 20.4   *"100 people knocked on my door today..."*

	Signed Up	*Turned Away*
Will Pay	75	10
Won't Pay	5	10

The confusion matrix says that experience will later show that, of the 80 customers signed up on this day, 75 will turn out to be good, and 5 bad. Of the 20 customers turned away (either because we rejected them or demanded an exorbitant deposit), 10 would have turned out to be good and 10 bad.

Things would be simpler if both kinds of errors had the same cost, but frequently they don't. In most situations, some types of errors are more expensive than others. In the case of telecom subscription fraud, accepting a bad customer is usually several times more expensive than rejecting a good customer. Also, in accepting a bad customer, the loss is incurred in real dollars, while rejecting a good customer costs only market share, measured in potential dollars.

Different types of losses can often be quantified based on historical data. Knowing the relative size of the error costs can be very helpful in making business decisions about how to manage them. An essential part of problem formulation for the subscription problem is estimation of the various error costs.

For the sake of our analysis, suppose that it is determined by looking at historical data that the average annual profit on a good customer is $100, and the average annual loss on a bad customer is $300. Looking at the confusion matrix above (for which the correct decision was made 85 percent of the time), the "cost" of my current decision model is:

Table 20.5

Cost	= (loss from turning away good customers) + (loss from signing up bad customers)
	= (10 × $100) + (5 × $300)
	= $2500

Spread over the 75 good customers I acquired, this gives an average annual per customer model cost of:

Annual Average Model cost per paying customer = $2500 / 75 good customers

= $33.33 per average paying customer per year

Now if, for example, expenditures improve model accuracy, reducing the model cost by 10 percent, the ROI is $3.33 per paying customer per year.

Does the current "85 percent" model have any value? Compare it to the egalitarian "all comers" approach: Everyone is signed up. If *all* potential customers are signed up, revenue increases by 10 × $100, but model cost increases, too:

Table 20.6

Cost	= (loss from turning away good customers) + (loss from signing up bad customers)
	= (0 × $100) + (15 × $300)
	= $4500

Today's "all comers" model cost is $4500, while today's "85 percent" model cost is $2500, a difference of $2000 a year for each day that the current model is used. This is $2000/75 equals $26.66 per paying customer per year that the current model puts into the provider's pocket.

Assuming 250 business days a year, this amounts to $500,000.

After consideration of all these factors, the problem can be stated:

"Based upon the information available at the time an offer decision must be made, which customers should be offered a service contract, and which customers should not be offered a service contract?"

Using a predictive model as my customer profile, I can answer this question.

Certain facts can be ascertained when a potential customer walks in the front door. Some will be helpful in making a credit decision, while some are just collected to support administrative processes. Not all of the information collected will be relevant to the contract offer decision. (In fact, there are some factors, such as race, gender, religious affiliation, age, etc., which generally cannot legally be used in a credit decision. These must be excluded from consideration.) In some cases, additional data may be collected from outside sources.

20.6 Choosing Features for Profiling

As the previous case study demonstrates, customers can be expected to have certain characteristics in common. For example, good customers: have adequate incomes, pay their bills on time, have a good employment history, have successfully carried other credit accounts, have a checking account, and so on. When these factors are present in combination, confidence that this will be a good customer is increased. Likewise, customers can be expected to have certain characteristics in common. They have marginal incomes, a spotty payment history, change jobs frequently, credit accounts in default, etc. When these factors are present in combination, confidence that this will be a bad customer is increased.

Considering all of these factors, information should be collected which gives insight into income, payment history, job status, credit accounts, and so on. This can begin with a standard credit application that the potential customer fills out. Since the information collected using such a "volunteer" format cannot be expected to be completely reliable and objective, it might be augmented with a second, more objective source, such as a credit report. For the model under discussion, it was determined that information taken from a credit application, supplemented by a report from a credit bureau, would be used to estimate the likelihood that a customer would be good or bad.

Using information from previously collected credit applications and credit reports, data mining techniques were used to build a predictive model that ingests this information, and produces a classification result of either "good," or "bad." Credit managers use this classification to support their final decision . . . a decision that they still make themselves.

20.7 Summary

Telecommunications is among the most advanced industries in applying data mining for credit, fraud, and customer retention applications.

21

Data Mining in Transportation and Logistics

21.1 The Industry

The transportation and logistics industry encompasses a range of companies that provide logistics and other transportation services. The industry covers movement of packages, cargo, or passengers over land, sea, and air, and includes companies such as: Federal Express, United Parcel Service, Airborne Express; Trans World Air, Delta Airlines, Northwest Airlines, United Airlines; Carnival Corporation; Avis, Enterprise, and Hertz Rent A Car; CSX Corporation; and Norfolk Southern Corporation.

21.2 Challenges

Some segments of the industry are geared to consumers-only, while others cater to businesses. Many companies in the industry offer their services to both consumers and businesses. Hence, they may face the challenge of separate pricing for each target market, while all face concerns relating to competitive pressures. For many consumers, thoughts of the transportation industry bring to mind visions of travelers stranded at cold, crowded airport terminals during inclement weather. Unfortunately, many consumers don't recognize that FAA regulations, limited infrastructure, weather, collective bargaining, or other circumstances that are out of the carriers' control, may be the cause of the service disruption. Certainly, customer acquisition, service, and retention are challenges for transportation carriers.

Other challenges relating to the transportation industry are based on both huge capital and infrastructure investments (think airlines and railroads), as well as significant operating expenses for fuel, skilled staff, taxes, and so on. Continuous improvement of operational efficiencies is essential for business viability in this industry.

21.3 General Data Mining Applications

As in all other industries, customer-profiling applications apply within transportation. But transportation also has its own specific type of objective functions to maximize or optimize, such as route optimization for all types of carriers, fitting cargo to containers, or passengers to vehicles, etc. As in the financial services, direct marketing and telecommunications industries, many transportation companies work with vast accumulations of data.

21.4 Case Study: Maximizing Revenue Through Forecasting

For this case study, Rhonda interviewed Bob Bongiorno, director of research and development in United Airlines' Information Services Division, and Tom Ebling, CEO of Torrent Systems. United Airlines Inc., is the world's largest airline, serving over 130 cities on 5 continents,[1] and with annual revenue of over $18 billion in 1999.[2] Other airlines share its problem of needing to maximize the value of each and every flight made by one of their airplanes.

It's a common practice among airlines, even within a single class of service (e.g., economy vs. first class) to charge a variety of fare prices for virtually the same service. Considerations include how far in advance the reservation was booked, when it was paid for, which days of the week and times of day are involved, routing, length of stay, round-trip purchase, and so on. According to Alice Lesch Kelly, writing for *CIO* magazine, "What sounds like a disservice to full-fare passengers is actually a shrewd strategy that airlines use to maximize profits by forecasting customer demand and charging multiple fares on single flights. Airlines hold as many seats as possible for last minute, full-fare business travelers, but if they miscalculate demand they end up with empty seats."[3]

1.   United Airlines Web site, www.ual.com
2.   Hoover's online Web site, www.hoovers.com.
3.   http://www.cio.com/reprints/070199_torrent.html

Conversely, overbooking averages about 15 percent of the total number of seats for every flight. Some flights have as many as 30 percent "no shows," while others have none. Airlines utilize powerful passenger-demand forecasting systems to determine what prices to make available and when. "Most airlines' systems work reasonably well but don't have the power necessary to mine all available passenger data."[4]

21.4.1 Problem Definition (Step 1)

The Orion system is concerned with yield optimization for all United flights that are scheduled within the next 330 days. The airline industry utilizes three key metrics to track their performance.

- Load factor is the percentage of seats filled (i.e., for a single flight, load factor would be the number of passengers divided by the number of seats).

- Unit revenue is the revenue per seat mile (for filled and empty seats).

- Yield is the revenue per passenger seat mile.

The individual metrics relate to each other as illustrated by the following formula:

$$\text{Unit Revenue} = \text{Load Factor} \times \text{Yield}$$

In other words, averaging all of the revenue for all of the flights over the number of seats that move from one destination to the next, be they filled or empty, multiplied by the number of miles per leg, results in the unit revenue metric. The higher the (average) unit revenue per seat mile, then the higher the total revenue.

The critical requirement for a Passenger-Demand Forecasting System is to maximize the total value of seats sold. This requires an appropriate trade-off of yield and load factor. Prior to Orion, close to 30 percent of United's seats were unsold on any given flight. United's previous passenger-demand forecasting system provided the capability to forecast demand for individual flight "legs."

One requirement for the new system was the ability to model entire paths (e.g., for a cross-country flight), rather than individual

---

4.   http://www.cio.com/reprints/070199_torrent.html

legs, which enables appropriate allocation of seats to various fare classes. The flight path modeling can contribute significantly to revenue optimization. Additionally, the new capability to model flight paths facilitates United's planners' capability to consider potential impacts of overbooking.

The problem statement for United's Passenger-demand Forecasting System would be:

Determine the optimal pricing mix for each airplane flight, including the number of full-fare seats that should be maintained.

21.4.2 Data Evaluation (Step 2)

United's previous Passenger-Demand Forecasting System encompassed 4,000 daily flights, times 330 days, for a total of 1.4 million passenger "legs" forecast daily. Orion processes 350,000 logical possible flight paths every day times 330 days, for a total of roughly 120 million possible combinations. Additional information that Orion takes into account includes the most recent prices at which tickets were purchased, historical travel patterns (e.g., seasonality), holidays, conventions, special events, etc.

United shuttles millions of passengers every month throughout the world. On a daily basis, the company has millions more seats for sale across an 11-month period. "We have to analyze this massive amount of data to determine the optimum mix of 'seat classes' representing various fares," Bob Bongiorno explains.

As with any predictive model, Orion can only perform as well as the supporting data that it has available. For example during Spring Break 2000, there was a strike threat by US Airways flight attendants. Consequently, there were more oversold seats than would have been desirable. Similarly, the new millennium (1/1/2000) holiday traffic was much softer than anticipated.

21.4.3 Feature Extraction and Enhancement (Step 3)

Typical ETL functions are performed in preparing data for Orion processing. Several forecasting calculations provide additional input information.

21.4.4 Prototyping/Model Development (Step 4)

There are three key models that comprise the Orion system. The forecasting model was developed by United using moving averages, adjusted for seasonality, holiday, special events, etc. It is based on the previous Passenger-Demand Forecasting System, but expanded to consider logical flight paths. The net value per passenger model calculation is based on passenger revenue less marginal costs (commissions, meals, etc.).

The optimization model provides the significant advantage of the Orion system over its predecessors. The previous Passenger-Demand Forecasting System optimized individual flights. Orion optimizes the entire network revenue in one pass. There are now individual flight legs where revenue is sacrificed to support the overall optimization. United uses CPLEX mathematical programming software for its resource optimization model development. It includes linear, mixed-integer, and quadratic programming capabilities.

Some of the algorithms are self-learning. Planners can provide input and adjust results. (For example, if they become aware of an unusual circumstance for a location such as a convention.) The results of the modeling process are sent to the Apollo flight reservation system, where inventory planners can fine-tune the results.

21.4.5 Model Evaluation (Step 5)

Orion's results are evaluated against the results of a simulation that evolved over a four-year time period.

21.4.6 Implementation (Step 6)

The Orion system was implemented in three phases. In 1997, the first phase was implemented, which encompassed the historical database that was necessary to support the path-based modeling. Initially, the contents of the database (flight path data) were converted back to "leg-based" to support the old Passenger-Demand Forecasting System. A year later, during the second phase, the new computing platform was implemented. It is an IBM RS/6000 SP2 "Deep Blue" platform with four terabytes of disk space, running Torrent Systems' Orchestrate middleware product. Orchestrate manages all the lower-level communication to enable the Orion system to take advantage of the parallel processing capabilities of the hardware platform. The middleware enabled United to scale its system up from 16 to 47 processors.

In May of 1999, the network-based optimization models were implemented with an expected return of between 100 and 200 million dollars per year. As of this writing, United's revenue has been better than the industry average for every month it has used the new network-based optimization models, except one. And, that difference can be explained because the predictions were based on historical information from a year earlier that reflected a strike faced by a competing airline.

The Orion system runs on a nightly basis. Orion's large data and complex optimization algorithm required an advanced hardware and software solution to meet the throughput requirements.

21.4.7 ROI Evaluation (Step 7)

United Airline's Orion system, which was implemented over two years ago at a cost of $18 million, including system infrastructure and development costs, is fully deployed and is helping United's planners to make better pricing decisions. In general:

- Load factor, the percentage of seats, dropped slightly.

- Unit revenue, per seat mile, increased significantly.

- Yield, revenue per passenger seat, increased slightly.

United Airlines "expects its 24-node IBM® RS/6000® SP®-based system, called Orion, to boost its annual revenues between $50 million and $100 million by allowing revenue management analysts to quickly make much-more-informed decisions about passengers' flying behavior and then charging optimum fares to different categories of travelers."[5]

Following on the heels of Orion, United has a new project under way called Atlas, which features a 300-gigabyte database to enhance its pricing analysts capabilities even further. Future applications that are anticipated for the new platform include aircraft and crew scheduling. The system provides better yields per seat mile.

---

5.   "Flying High" by Joanie Wexler reprinted with permission from RS/6000 Results. International Business Machines, 1998, Torrent Web site www.torrent.com.

21.5   Case Study: Vehicle Tracking Optimization

This case study describes the application of genetic algorithms to an optimization problem in the transportation industry. Genetic algorithms create models whose parameters are bit strings (strings of zeros and ones). Genetic training typically begins with the creation of a collection of randomly generated parameter sets, giving a population of useless models.

Genetic algorithms have two components: a reproduction component, and a selection component. The reproduction component merges the parameter strings of two or more existing models *(sexual reproduction)* to obtain a new string. Sometimes, this merging is done with random mutations allowed. Sometimes, the parameters of a single model are just pseudo-randomly altered *(asexual reproduction)*.

After reproduction has occurred, the selection component applies "natural selection" to the new, larger population. Selection is based upon the score assigned to each individual model by a "fitness function." Weaker models are discarded, and stronger models are allowed to reproduce, beginning the next cycle in the genetic sequence.

Over the course of many iterations, effective predictive models can be "evolved" by this unsystematic manipulation of their "genetic material" (bit strings). While this whole approach may seem far-fetched, genetic algorithms produce excellent solutions to many combinatorial optimization problems.

The analysis and development for this study was conducted by Computer Science Innovations, using a rapid prototyping methodology in 21 calendar-days.

21.5.1   Problem Definition (Step 1)

The Signpost Problem arose as part of a vehicle tracking system being developed for a large western city. Part of the control system for this network was a subsystem to accurately track the location of each of hundreds of city buses, and measure their adherence to schedule as they moved along a total of 65,000 miles of assigned routes.

The developers of the vehicle tracking subsystem decided to use a signpost system in which transmitters are installed in specific locations along routes. Each transmitter has a unique identification number, which it continually transmits. Transmission frequency and power give each signpost a range of a few hundred feet.

Each bus in the system has an on-board transponder, which picks up the identification number of the signpost it just passed, attaches a time tag to it, and forwards it to a central command post. This gives a precise time and location for that bus. The question is where to put the signposts. With 65,000 miles of road including a mix of high and low traffic routes, some signpost locations can be expected to service traffic more effectively than others. The problem definition for this effort might be stated as:

Identify the optimal combination of locations for vehicle tracking signposts.

The problem was analyzed manually (at great expense) by a team of experts, who formulated a placement of signposts that met accuracy specifications, and required 436 signposts. Each signpost cost $500 for installation and maintenance over the life of the contract, for a total signpost cost of $218,000. Since this was a fixed-price contract, every penny of this $218,000 that could be saved by more efficient signpost placement would go directly to the bottom line.

One approach to finding an optimal signpost placement would be to write a computer simulation, and try all possible combinations of locations. Municipal surveyors had determined that there were 1,800 feasible signpost locations. A little computation shows that 400 signposts can be distributed in a number of combinations that is written as a 2 followed by 412 zeros. This is, according to Einstein's General Theory of Relativity, roughly equal to the number of atoms in the entire universe raised to the sixth power. Clearly, a brute force search cannot work.

21.5.2 Data Evaluation (Step 2)

The data available to support this work consisted of detailed bus routes and schedules for about 2,000 buses, and an annotated city map, all in digital form. This amounted to about 100 megabytes of spatio-temporal data. Conventional data mining techniques showed this data to be of very high quality, though some subtle errors were discovered and corrected in the supplied data. Manual spot checks were conducted using a sample of the data.

21.5.3 Feature Extraction and Enhancement (Step 3)

Each bus route was reduced to a sequence of "segments." A segment was a small linear stretch of road having a unique designator. The map of the city was given in a form that allowed the computation of distances between segments. Bus schedules consisted of absolute arrival and departure times from special locations along the routes called "time-points."

Visualization was used to actually display the map data, and over-lay animations of buses moving along their scheduled routes. This allowed visual validation of the data by domain experts. This visualization was supported by a simple simulation engine that just updated the display at discrete intervals.

21.5.4 Prototyping/Model Development (Step 4)

Because only three weeks were available to build and apply the model, it was decided to use a genetic algorithm to optimize the placement of the signposts. The simulation engine was attached to a genetic algorithm.

The reproduction function applied a simple numeric test to the current suite of signpost locations, and removed, moved, or swapped signposts based upon their score (asexual reproduction). The numeric test assigned to each possible signpost location a numeric estimate of how much benefit a signpost there would provide (in terms of spatio-temporal accuracy). Components of this value function were such factors as vehicle density within that location's range, number of routes that passed that location, proximity of already assigned locations, etc.

The selection function then ran (at high speed) an entire 24-hours worth of bus routes, computing a location accuracy and schedule adherence score. If the new signpost locations were better than the former, they were retained. If not, the old set was restored, and the process repeated.

The computer in this study is just playing a board game. The board is a city map, the signposts are game pieces, and the computer must use the smallest number of pieces that satisfies an accuracy score (computed by running the buses). This process was initiated, and the computer was then left unattended for the remainder of the study effort (about two weeks).

21.5.5 Evaluation (Step 5)

At the end of the study effort, the machine running the genetic optimization was pulled out of the corner, and asked to display the smallest set of signpost locations it had encountered that still satisfied the accuracy specifications of the program.

The machine displayed a suite of 176 sensors, which it could prove satisfied the specification (because it could run the simulation and compute the accuracy). The total cost savings to this fixed-price program was $130,000.

Additional value was derived, because the city was able to use this model to plan signposts for future routes.

21.6 Summary

The case studies for transportation demonstrate solutions for two very different applications, while at the same time both address operational efficiencies.

22

Data Mining in Energy

22.1 The Industry

The power we use in our daily lives originates primarily as oil, natural gas, and coal. Our electric utility providers handle the conversion for most of our uses. They also generate power through nuclear plants, but operational and disposal problems don't bode well for the expansion of nuclear energy. The future, albeit distant, is likely to be in renewable sources, including water, solar power, and "biomass."

As in the telecommunications industry, deregulation of energy utilities offers expansion opportunities at the expense of increased competition. As the world population and economy continue to expand so will demand for energy continue to increase.

22.2 Challenges Faced by the Energy Industry

Some of the key challenges faced by the energy industry in general include the depletion of resources that are necessary to generate energy, and environmental concerns relating to byproducts of energy product processes.

22.3 General Data Mining Applications

Similar to other industries that carry customer accounts, customer profiling applications and fraud detection are quite applicable to the energy industry. Another application that is more industry-specific is consumption prediction.

22.4 Case Study: A "Shocking" Problem— Hypothetical Prototype Iterations

An electric utility company has hired a software-engineering firm to develop a model within a computer information system to help it make a complex business decision. This decision requires analysis of available evidence, and the use of probability to recommend the best course of action. The company has two power generation plants: One is a modern, high-capacity facility, and the other an older, low-capacity plant. The modern plant produces enough power to meet the daily power demand about 35 percent of the time. The other 65 percent of the days, both plants must be activated.

Peak demand always occurs in the late afternoon. It takes two hours to activate the second plant, so the activation decision is made each day at noon. If the second plant is activated, and the extra power is needed, the utility makes money. But if the second plant is activated, and the extra power is not needed, the utility loses money. This is because it costs money (in fuel and labor) to produce electricity, but there is no economical way to store "excess" electricity. For this reason, the decision to activate the second plant has immediate and significant financial implications.

There is also a downside to deciding not to activate when the extra power is actually needed. When this happens, brown-outs occur. Customer goodwill is affected, but more is at stake. As a protected monopoly, the company could face stiff fines and additional regulation if it fails to satisfy demand.

22.4.1 Problem Definition (Step 1)

For this problem, then, we expect the computer program to recommend activation of the second plant about 65 percent of the time. This kind of figure is called a "prior probability," because it represents how likely something is "without conditions," that is, prior to consideration of evidence that might be available at the time a particular choice must be made. The performance specification requires that the decision about noon activation of the second plant be made every day, and be correct most of the time. The problem definition for this case could be stated as:

Based upon the weather and other factors, identify whether the second plant should be activated at noon today.

22.4.2 Data Evaluation (Step 2)

Assuming our hypothetical situation occurred a few years ago, the weather data needed by the computer program was collected by a service bureau that fails to consistently provide complete, reliable predictions, so weather information is regularly unavailable or out-of-date. Alternative data sources are expensive, and not significantly better. As a result, the computer program will only have reliable weather data some of the time. Historic utilization data relative to weather conditions is also available.

22.4.3 Feature Extraction and Enhancement (Step 3)

Since this is a hypothetical case, we will assume that the raw weather and history data is sufficient without feature extraction and enhancement processing.

22.4.4 Prototyping/Model Development (Step 4)

A smart young engineer proposes to solve the problem in the following way:

"When the data we need for the noon decision is unavailable," she says, "why don't we just randomly recommend activation of the second plant 65 percent of the time? Guessing can be done with no data at all, and requires almost no effort. This matches the prior probability; won't this meet our spec?"

Question: Is the young engineer right? If you know that there is a probability of 65 percent that the right thing to do is activate the plant at noon, and you randomly decide to activate 65 percent of the time, what percentages of the time will your decision be correct?

22.4.4.1 *The First Prototyping Cycle: Using Prior Probabilities to "Guess Well"*

For simplicity of analysis, we will assume that the probability of activation on a given day is independent of the activation outcomes for other days: Every day is "a new ball-game."

We make a table of the four possible cases (guessed "activate" and was right, guessed "activate" and was wrong, guessed "don't activate" and was right, guessed "don't activate" and was wrong):

	should activate	shouldn't activate
guessed "activate"	Guessed correctly!	Guessed incorrectly!
guessed "don't activate"	Guessed incorrectly!	Guessed correctly!

This representation of choices and their probabilities is called a "confusion matrix." Correct choices are on the "major diagonal," and incorrect choices are on the "minor diagonal."

Because our guesses are independent of the actual conditions of the problem, we can compute the probabilities of our guesses being correct by multiplying probabilities:

	should activate	shouldn't activate
guessed "activate"	0.65×0.65	0.65×0.35
guessed "don't activate"	0.35×0.65	0.35×0.35

For example, the probability that we guessed "activate," and the correct answer actually is "activate," is the product of their prior probabilities: 0.7×0.7. The rest of the confusion matrix probabilities are computed in the same way.

We see that the probability of making a correct choice by guessing is:

Probability that we guessed "activate" and were right

+

Probability that we guessed "don't activate" and were right = P(guessed "activate" and correct decision was "should activate")

+

P(guessed "don't activate" and correct decision was "don't activate")

$= (0.65 \times 0.65) + (0.35 \times 0.35)$

$= 0.4225 + 0.1225 = 0.545 = 54.5$ percent

22.4.4.2 Evaluation of the First Prototyping Cycle

So, we will be correct 54.5 percent of the time by guessing, which satisfies the requirement that the choice is correct "most of the time."

22.4.4.3 The Second Prototyping Cycle: Using Conditional Probabilities to Guess Better

The guessing solution meets the specification of the problem, but just barely. With only 4.5 percent margin over the required 50 percent accuracy, some uncomfortably long "runs" of bad recommendations can be expected. We need to identify an approach to refine the guessing strategy, for example, by applying additional information.

There are several ways that additional information can be brought to bear on the activation decision. All require that some ad-hoc facts be known or assumed. These additional facts, or "conditions," can be used in combination with our "unconditional" prior probabilities to compute "conditional probabilities." The conditional probability of an outcome is the probability of that outcome given that some specified condition holds.

For example, it might be noted that, while the probability of second plant activation on any given day is 65 percent, the probability of second plant activation on any given Friday is 80 percent. The first probability is the prior probability for any day (probability in general, without other conditions being specified), while the second probability is the conditional probability ("the probability of second plant activation today, given that today is a Friday"). Conditional probability provides an objective, mathematical way to "weigh evidence" during the decision-making process.

Whatever we might discover about Fridays, the prior probability of second plant activation for all days is still 0.65. If we remove "high-Fridays" from our population, we have to recompute the prior probability of second plant activation for the other days. The prior probability of second plant activation for non-Fridays must be P, where:

$$[(6 \div 7) \times P] + [(1 \div 7) \times 0.80] = 0.656P + 0.80 = 7 \times 0.65 = 4.556P$$
$$= 3.75P = 0.625 = 62.5 \text{ percent}$$

Our discovery about Fridays being "high demand" days, and the other days being, on average, lower demand days lets us refine our strategy: "If it is Friday, randomly recommend activation 80 percent of the time. Otherwise, randomly recommend activation 62.5 percent of the time."

Using confusion matrices with the refined prior probabilities, we see that the probability of our new strategy giving a correct recommendation on Fridays is:

$$(0.80 \times 0.80) + (0.20 \times 0.20) = 0.68, \text{ or } 68.0 \text{ percent.}$$

The probability of our new strategy giving a correct recommendation on non-Fridays is:

$$(0.625 \times 0.625) + (0.375 \times 0.375) = 0.53125 = 53.125 \text{ percent.}$$

The new strategy makes us "53.125 percent right" on non-Fridays, and "68.0 percent right" on Fridays. Our overall accuracy, then, is:

$$[(6 \div 7) \times 53.125 \text{ percent}] + [(1 \div 7) \times 68.0 \text{ percent}] = 0.552499 = 55.25 \text{ percent}$$

22.4.4.4 *Evaluation of the Second Prototyping Cycle*

We have gained three-quarters of a percentage point by using the new information about Fridays. This might not seem like much, but consider this: If we have to apply our "guessing strategy" 133 days during a year, we can expect to avoid one wrong recommendation each year with the new strategy (because three-quarters of a percent of 133 recommendations is one recommendation). This could amount to a savings of many thousands of dollars each year in fuel and labor costs.

22.4.5 The Real Answer: An Intelligent Data Mining Solution

The preceding analysis suggests that we look for other "rules" about our utility's operation. We can interview plant engineers and budget analysts, look through the production records of the utility, create plant simulators; all are potential sources of useful rules that can infer conditional probabilities that will improve our ability to make correct recommendations. What are the conditional probabilities for the other days of the week? For "hot" or "cold" days? Holidays?

Expert systems in use today sometimes contain many thousands of rules, each contributing to the accuracy of the final result.

Computer systems that use rules to make decisions usually made by humans are called "Expert Systems." These systems frequently rely upon empirical estimates of conditional probabilities derived from historic records (or human experience) to make objective decisions of quantifiable accuracy. These systems put valuable human expertise wherever it is required, 24-hours a day, seven days a week. It will never ask for a raise, retire, or allow subjective factors to influence its decisions.

Even more exciting than the prospect of building sophisticated expert systems to attack intractable decision problems is the following: If we can compute the use of known facts for decision making, shouldn't it be possible to reverse the process and use mathematics to discover, directly from historical data, previously unknown facts? In other words, can probability be used to program computers to learn?

The answer is yes. Machine learning technology, whose theoretical foundation was laid by Alan Turing, John Von Neumann, and others in the 1940s and '50s, is moving full-steam ahead, with some impressive results. Underlying it all is mathematics, with probability one of the central components.

22.4.6 Evaluation (Step 5)

We began with the apparently silly suggestion that a complex prediction algorithm be replaced with a properly tuned random number generator; we have arrived finally at expert systems, which can objectively make complicated decisions at super speed by emulating the intelligent behaviors of human experts.

Chains of creation are often like this: They begin with a novel association of basic ideas, which is then formalized, tested, and refined. But a chain can only be built by those who possess the links. If we can agree that "creativity" is putting together basic knowledge in new and useful ways, we come immediately to the realization that creativity without basic knowledge is impossible. Those without mastery of the fundamentals of mathematics are at risk of finding themselves spectators in the creation of the technological society of the third millennium.

22.5   Case Study: Forecasting Energy Consumption

CSI was engaged to develop a data mining system to predict electrical load profiles for the electric utility industry. The return on investment for this application is based on a utility's ability to manage unit commitment, off-system sales, and costing decisions.

22.5.1   Problem Definition (Step 1)

This case study describes the application of radial basis function networks (RBFs) to the "long-term" (next year) forecasting of hourly demand for electric power. This is called the *load forecasting problem*. An RBF was created that performed hourly load prediction based upon annual average loads, date-time-for-prediction, and forecast weather. This RBF was followed by a conventional smoothing operation to regularize the model's output.

Weather forecasts months in advance are not likely to be accurate, so the real utility of the long-term model is to allow simulation planning of "what-if" scenarios. It was found that weather forecasts out to about 10 days were accurate enough to support load prediction results having operational value. A naïve model using only monthly average values for each hour gives predictions that have a relative error of about 12 percent (RMS). This gives a rough performance target.

Twelve months of hourly meteorological data and the corresponding hourly load data were obtained from commercial electric utilities. Each year of historical data provides 8,760 data points (the number of hours in a year).

Long-term load forecasting is the prediction of load at an arbitrary future time. No "previous day" actual load data will be available to support such conventional time-series prediction techniques. Long-term load prediction must be based exclusively on temporal factors and predicted weather.

The analysis and development for this study was conducted under a rapid prototyping methodology in 30 mandays.

22.5.2   Data Evaluation (Step 2)

A regional utility provided the hourly load data. Historical hourly weather data was provided by a government meteorological station in the service area. The data from these two sources was used to train the predictive model. Weather forecasts by a commercial service were used for later model operation.

The weather data consisted of:

Wet-bulb temperature (degrees Celsius)

Dry-bulb temperature (degrees Celsius)

Relative humidity (percent)

Wind direction (degrees of bearing)

Wind speed (knots)

Cloudiness (numeric rating from 0 to 9)

Statistical data mining of the 365 days of available feature vector revealed 14 days with corrupted data (typically, drop-outs resulting from sensors going offline). These days were not considered during exemplar selection, leaving 351 days of data, having a total of $24 \times 351 = 8,424$ feature vectors.

22.5.3 Feature Extraction and Enhancement (Step 3)

Cloudiness was a frequently and systematically missing field, and removed from consideration as a feature for this reason. The correlation coefficient of wind direction with load was very low, and the correlation coefficient of dry-bulb with wet-bulb temperature was very high (0.94). Therefore, wind direction and wet-bulb temperature were deemed irrelevant and redundant, respectively, and not selected as features for the model. This left a set of meteorological features consisting of dry-bulb temperature, relative humidity, and wind speed.

Visualization of load data versus time showed that days of the week during a given month had consistent "profiles." Three fundamental "day types" were observed: weekdays (Monday-Friday); weekend-days (Saturday and Sunday); and holidays (e.g., Christmas Day). "Day type" became a synthesized feature for the predictive model. Computation of correlation coefficients showed that month and hour-of-day were correlated with load, so these were selected as features.

Hence, the feature selection process resulted in a final set of six temporal-meteorological features: month, day type, hour-of-day, dry-bulb temperature, relative humidity, and wind speed. For this application, the month, day, and hour are nominal features, and were numerically coded. Principal component analysis (PCA) was not applied, because it was deemed desirable to retain the identity of the original features.

22.5.4 Prototyping/Model Development (Step 4)

A sample of 20 percent of the hourly feature vectors was extracted and used for training. A radial basis function (RBF) classifier was trained using a modified reinforcement learning technique (Chapter 10). The classification results of the RBF were passed through a "filter" to smooth the load predictions. Standard spatial techniques were used for the smoothing. Several iterations of the prototyping activity were required to determine proper filtering parameters for the post-process. Some adjustments were made to the coding scheme for certain features.

22.5.5 Evaluation (Step 5)

The final prototype required about 2 hours to train, and performed the prediction of an hour's load in about 300 milliseconds (i.e., 7.2 seconds to predict a 24-hour day's worth of loads). The completed model was evaluated by processing the entire 365 days of feature vectors (including the 14 "bad" days), constituting a test that was about 80 percent "blind," with 4 percent "real world" anomalous input.

The RBF was trained to perform load prediction for data consisting of both residential and commercial customers. The overall performance on the 80-percent blind test set was about 6 percent error (RMS). The performance of the model on the part of the data used for training was considerably higher, at 0.2 percent error (RMS). This suggests that the model was probably over-trained to some extent.

22.6   Summary

Deregulation of energy companies offers expansion opportunities at the expense of increased competition, at the same time the industry faces the depletion of resources that are necessary to generate energy. Consumption prediction is a useful data mining activity in the energy industry.

23

Data Mining in Government

23.1 The Industry

If anyone has vast collections of data, it's the United States government. Whether Defense, Intelligence, NASA, Internal Revenue, or Health and Human Services, each and every government agency collects masses of various types of data to support its mission. The data ranges from leading-edge scientific research data such as that collected by space probes, medical research, and the like, to mundane demographics describing individual citizens or various populations. An entire industry of contractors and consultants provides services supporting the various missions and information systems requirements.

23.2 Challenges

In years past, much of the government contractor focus was on aerospace and defense. Here, the information technology focus was on developing advanced communications and information systems to support defense and intelligence missions. The stringent security requirements are becoming even more important with the explosion of the Internet. The peacetime reduction of the government's emphasis on defense missions has necessitated aerospace and defense industry's diversification into new markets, including both non-defense government areas such as medical and health care, as well as commercial markets. On a recent visit to the National Institutes of Health, Rhonda was told that government contractors are vigorously pursuing opportunities to migrate their defense-related advanced technologies to healthcare. These include advanced pattern recognition technologies as related to data mining.

23.3 General Data Mining Applications

Extensive research and development efforts have been funded by the U.S. government and Department of Defense that have enabled many contractors to develop advanced pattern recognition technologies. Such technologies have been applied in a variety of defense-related problem domains. Over the years, contractors have refined their capabilities with successive projects incorporating enhancements that continuously improved the capabilities of their techniques.

23.4 Pattern Recognition Study

Monte participated in a government-funded study at Computer Science Innovations, Inc., to evaluate how learning machine development occurs in the "real world": The Pattern Recognition Study (PRS), a comparative, empirical study of the applicability of several learning machine paradigms to a difficult pattern classification problem.

Using special equipment and manual techniques, one of our customers detected a phenomenon of great interest. The occurrence of this "PRS event" could not be predicted, and the event itself was brief. Customer personnel had been manually scanning the collected data sets looking for the PRS event, but this required many hours of intense labor and was prone to error. Small-scale in-house attempts at automating the search were partially successful, but yielded a false alarm rate that still left the users with an extended manual search to perform.

To support supervised learning, the customer provided a collection of example waveforms, some of which contained the PRS event, and some of which did not. Customer experts identified each waveform by type ("event" or "non-event"). The study team constructed several training sets from the supplied waveform data. These training sets contained thousands of waveforms, both "event" and "non-event," which served as the basis for all pattern recognition experiments for the study.

Two categories of investigation were pursued during the study: an empirical comparative investigation of classical techniques, and an empirical comparative investigation of non-classical techniques.

The techniques evaluated were:

- Classical:

  1. Bayesian Classification

  2. Nonlinear Multiple Regression

  3. Fast Fourier Transform (FFT)

  4. Visual Cluster Detection in N-dimensional Space

- Non-Classical:

  1. Neural Networks

     a. Multi-layer, Feed-Forward (trained by genetic algorithm)

     b. Multi-layer, Feed-Forward (trained by back-propagation)

     c. Multi-layer, Feed-Forward (trained by a hybrid technique)

  2. Boltzmann Machines (BAM, trained by simulated annealing)

  3. Knowledge-Based Expert System (KBES) Classification

Experimental work demonstrated that the "best" classical technique was Bayesian classification. In a blind test, the Bayesian classifier was able to correctly classify 85.0 percent of the waveforms. The "best" non-classical technique was a 2-layer, feed-forward neural network trained by back-propagation. In a blind-test, it was able to correctly identify 98.8 percent of the PRS events present, and 96.1 percent of the non-events. This neural network requires only a few milliseconds to process a feature vector.

23.4.1 How Do Trained Learning Machines Compare with Human Experts?

To determine how the neural network's performance compared to that of human experts, four human analysts were allowed to classify a test set consisting of 1592 waveforms. Of these waveforms, 199 contained PRS events. For each waveform, the humans, working individually, estimated their belief that a PRS event was present by assigning a numeric score in the range zero to ten. A score of zero indicated that the analyst was absolutely sure that a waveform did not contain a PRS event; a score of ten indicated that he was absolutely sure that it did contain a PRS event; and, intermediate scores indicated intermediate beliefs. The decision threshold between non-event and event was set at a score of five. The neural network also classified this same test set, producing for each waveform a score in the range zero to ten, as above. The network gave most waveforms that contained a PRS event a score of eight. For PRS event detection, the overall detection accuracy for human and machine was about the same.

The customer's false alarm problem was due to the fact that when faced with "close calls," humans are uncertain. The network, on the other hand, is much more certain about its conclusions. For this experiment, the human analysts average score correctly identified only 40 percent of the non-event waveforms, while the network's score correctly identified 85 percent.

Overall, the network outperformed the human analysts. It equaled their PRS event detection accuracy, exceeded their non-event rejection accuracy, and is about 100 times faster when processing single waveforms.

Based upon these results, we recommended that PRS implementation proceed using a feed-forward, back-propagation neural network, which was developed during a follow-on effort.

23.4.2 Other Work

Several learning machines can be integrated to solve different parts of a difficult, multifaceted problem. In 1990, we built a learning machine that ingests the digitized instantaneous frequency (IF) of manually keyed Morse code transmissions, and translates them directly to text at 20 words per minute (essentially real time). This is a difficult problem, because human telegraphers are not consistent in their keying. This system is PC-based, consists of 30,000 lines of code in "C," and integrates two KBESs, a Bayesian classifier, and a neural network. For this problem, no single learning machine was adequate, but the combination was shown to be reasonably effective. Under poor signal-to-noise conditions, the accuracy of this system exceeded that of human operators.

For another application, a KBES was built to identify and classify twelve different types of radio signals to modulation type. After standard expert system development and manual tuning, the KBES was able to correctly classify 78 percent of the signals. It then underwent a one hour supervised training session, and its performance was improved to 86 percent. After a signal has been reduced to a feature vector, this PC-based learning machine can classify it in 10 milliseconds.

In another effort, prototype neural networks were built to distinguish tanks from trucks based upon their radar profiles. These machines, while limited, are sometimes able to classify vehicles that humans cannot. In fact, one of the machines could correctly determine the model of the tank/truck observed over 60 percent of the time. Other applications we investigated included optical character recognition, route scheduling, voice identification, and specific emitter identification.

23.5 Summary

For problems too hard to attack directly, learning machines provide an implementation strategy that yields results that are as good as the developer's ability to collect examples.

Glossary

These are terms frequently encountered in the data mining literature.

3D Space: Three-dimensional space, consisting of the set of all 3-tuples of values satisfying certain mathematical requirements (i.e., a vector space). If the values are real numbers, 3D Space is the space of everyday human experience.

24 by 7: 24 hours a day, 7 days a week.

Actionable: Having characteristics (e.g., adequate information content) in a form that can be practically applied to achieve a desired result.

Adaptive Algorithm: An algorithm whose behavior is modified during operation by the adjustment of algorithm parameters. Typically, this adjustment occurs only during algorithm creation, and not in an "online" operational mode.

Adaptive Logic Network (ALN): A powerful, trainable, piecewise, linear regression function.

Attribute: A characteristic of a member of a population (e.g., weight, height, income, gender, etc., in a population of humans; revenue, P/E, sales, etc., in a population of retail businesses, and so on.)

Auto-clustering: Automatic discovery and characterization of collections of similar objects in a set; finding clusters in data automatically.

Backpropagation (Backprop): A learning algorithm that uses a gradient method to extend the Delta Rule for training multi-layer perceptrons (MLPs). Published by Paul Werbos in 1975, this was the first systematic technique for training non-trivial neural networks. It decisively overcame the weaknesses of the one-layer perceptron cited by Minsky and Papert in their 1969 book, *Perceptrons*.

Backward/Forward Chaining: The two principal inference methodologies used by expert systems. In backward chaining, reasoning begins with effects, and proceeds backwards toward possible causes. In forward chaining, reasoning begins with causes, and proceeds forward toward possible effects. Each method is appropriate to particular types of inference.

Bagging: Combining the results of more than one predictive model to obtain more certain or accurate results.

Bidirectional Associative Memory (BAM):A regression method that operates by learning and exploiting associations between patterns.Typically implemented as a variant of a Hopfield net, and trained using simulated annealing.

Bit: Acronym for "binary digit."The smallest piece of data that can be stored in a digital computer, having one of two possible values: zero or one.

Blind-Set:A data set none of whose members were used to train a predictive model.This set is held in reserve and used to validate the trained model.

Blind-Testing: Validating a predictive model by measuring its performance on a blind-set.

Boosting: Applying one predictive model to the output of another to obtain more certain or accurate results.

Business Intelligence: Integrated actionable information that offers insight into enterprise operation and market behaviors, giving a competitive advantage; processes methods for creating, using, extending, and preserving such information.

Byte: The fundamental unit of storage in a computer, usually consisting of 8 bits. An 8-bit byte can assume 256 different values.

Categorical: See *Nominal*.

Classification: As a verb, refers to the act of assigning a symbol to a member of a population.As a noun, refers to the symbol assigned.These symbols can consist of numbers or letters. For exam-ple, assigning the symbol "churn" to a customer is a classification; assigning the symbol "23 percent" to a customer's credit score is a classification; and assigning the symbol "12018" to tomorrow's stock market closing index is a classification.

Cluster:A coherent subpopulation; a collection of members of a population that are similar enough that they can be regarded as "going together," to forming a "cluster."

Clustering: The process of assigning data to clusters.When done automatically and no ground-truth classes have been defined, it is called auto-clustering.

Cognitive Engineering (CE): The use of computer science and data mining to build applications having embedded intelligence.

Cognitive Engineering Methodology (CEM):A systematical methodology for cognitive engineering. CEM typically involves rapid application development (RAD) according to a spiral methodology.The "CRISP" and "SEMMA" methodologies are examples.

Coherent: Having consistent properties, or showing little variation. Geometrically, coherent populations consist of a few "tightly grouped" parts. Non-coherent populations are diffuse scatterings of members.

Confusion Matrix:A matrix showing the class counts given by a classifier in relation to the true class counts.A way of tracking misclassifications for a predictive model.

Customer Relationship Management (CRM): The discipline of optimal management of all phases of the relationship between provider and consumer through systematic analysis of provider-consumer interactions.

Data: Consist of values obtained from a population sample. Data express in symbolic form attributes of members of the population being sampled. Up until a few years ago, formal treatments of data were careful to distinguish between the singular, "datum," and the plural, "data." This convention has pretty much disappeared; the term "data" will be used here for both.

Data Mining: The detection, characterization, and exploitation of actionable patterns in data. Data mining has two components: Knowledge Discovery and Predictive Modeling (see definitions).

Delta Rule:A learning algorithm for training one-layer perceptrons. Many variations of this rule exist; it is fundamentally equivalent to using a linear approximation to an error function to compute and apply a correction factor.

Dimension: Is "the cardinality of a minimal spanning set." Intuitively, dimension is "the number of coordinates of a point in space." This is different from "VC Dimension," which expresses the complexity of a classification problem.

Element: Also called *data element.* See *Attribute*.

Embedded Intelligence: The ability to automatically (without human involvement) perform functions normally done only by humans, such as pattern recognition, decision making, planning, and the like.

Enterprise Resource Planning (ERP): A business and information technology term for robust enterprise-level application systems with shared databases that support financial, human resources, order processing, and other standard business functions.

Feature Space: The set of all feature vectors viewed as a mathematical space.

Feature Vector: The representation of a member of a population as an ordered tuple of its features.

Features: Symbolic representation of the attributes of a member of a population (weight in pounds, revenue in dollars, gender as M/F, etc.)

Field: See *Attribute.*

Fuzzy Logic:A mathematical extension of set theory and propositional logic allowing computation with generic, imprecise descriptions of attributes. For example, a "crisp" classifier wants a precise expression of the temperature outside ("99 degrees"), while a "fuzzy" classifier wants to know that it's "hot."

Genetic Algorithm:A learning algorithm that operates by combining the parameters of several existing learning machines to obtain a "daughter" machine superior to its parents.

Goal Class:A ground-truth class. For example, the "churn" problem might be characterized as having two goal classes: "churn" and "non-churn." Essentially a synonym for ground-truth.

Gradient Method: A method that uses the techniques of differential calculus to compute directions and rates of increase and decrease of functions. When applied to the objective function being used to train a learning machine, gradient methods give the changes in machine parameters that will yield maximum improvement in the machine's capability.

Ground-Truth: The classification assigned to a datum as its "actual" class.

Heuristic: Synonym for rule.

Histogram: A bar chart showing the number of members of a population that fall into each of the groups denoted along the horizontal axis.

Inference Engine: An implementation of an inference methodology.

Inference Methodology: A systematic, context-sensitive method for applying knowledge to solve a problem.

Inselberg Parallel Coordinates: A visualization method that depicts many dimensions simultaneously on parallel vertical axes.

Knowledge Base: An organized collection of heuristics relevant to a particular problem domain.

Knowledge-Based Expert System (KBES): A predictive model that applies codified expert-level human knowledge in a particular problem domain according to an appropriate inference methodology. KBES are typically built for forensic applications (diagnostics, planning, classification).

KBES are architecturally primitive, and strictly segregate heuristics (their knowledge base) from the inference engine.

Knowledge Discovery: The first component of data mining. Systematically using manual and automated tools to detect and characterize actionable patterns in data.

Learning Algorithm: An algorithm that adjusts the parameters of a learning machine to enable it to better perform desired tasks, such as predictive modeling.

Learning Machine: A mathematical model having parameters that can be adjusted by a learning algorithm to enable the machine to perform desired tasks, such as predictive modeling.

Leave-One-Out Validation: One-fold cross validation.

Lossless Compression: Conversion of a data set to a smaller data set from which the original can be perfectly recovered.

Lossy Compression: Conversion of a data set to a smaller data set from which the original cannot be perfectly recovered.

Machine Space: The set of all possible assignments of parameters for a predictive model, viewed as a Euclidean Space. Training a learning machine can be regarded as a search of machine space looking for the best vector of parameters.

Maximum: The largest value in a set. (If the set has no largest value, the maximum is the least upper bound.)

Mean: A single value that represents a set of values as an "average" of some type:

- Arithmetic: the sum of N values divided by N is their arithmetic mean

- Geometric: the Nth root of the product of N values is their geometric mean

Median: The datum that is in the middle after all data have been put into an ordered list. If there is an odd number of data values, the median is the middle value. If there is an even number of data values, the median is the average of the two middle values.

Midrange: The average of maximum and minimum values of a set.

Minimum: The smallest value in a set. (If the set has no smallest value, the minimum is the greatest lower bound.)

Mode: Strictly speaking, the data value that occurs most frequently in a set. (This definition is often extended to include all local maxima of the probability distribution.)

Multi-Layer Perceptron (MLP): A type of artificial neural network consisting of interconnected elements called neurons. These neurons are simple elements that perform a weighted average of their inputs, and apply a "response function" to the result. Neurons in an MLP are arranged in layers, the output of each layer being forwarded to become the input of the next.

Multimodal: A probability distribution having more than one mode. (In this case, the distribution will have multiple "humps.")

N-Dimensional Space: Set consisting of the set of all N-tuples of values satisfying certain mathematical requirements (i.e., a vector space).

N-fold Cross Validation: A technique for estimating the blind performance of a predictive model when no blind set is available. N data points are "held out" of the training set, the model is trained on the remainder, and blind tested on the N "hold outs." This is done multiple times, holding out a different set of N values each time. The results of all these blind runs are combined (usually averaged) to give a performance estimate for the model when trained on all the data (no "hold outs").

Neural Networks: Mathematical transform whose values are computed through the cooperation of many simple transforms. Usually a synonym for "multi-layer perceptron."

Neuron: Also called artificial neuron. A processing element in an artificial neural network. Neurons come in many forms, the most common being some variation of the elements proposed by McCulloch and Pitts in the 1940s.

NN: Neural network.

Nominal: Named. Sometimes called "categorical." Nominal values are names of attributes, rather than numbers. Height expressed as "tall," "medium," or "short" is nominal, because different heights are expressed as categories rather than quantities. See *Numeric*.

Non-Parametric: Refers to statistical methods that are not based upon population parameters (mean, variances, etc.).

NP-Hard: Intuitively, a class of "decision problems" for which no computationally effective models are known. (Related to the computational power of "deterministic Turing Machines." The details are beyond the scope of this book.)

"N-tuple" (pronounced "en toop-uhl"): A set of N values in order, e.g. (1,4,2,9) is a "four-tuple." This is different from the 4-tuple (4,9,1,2) because the order is different. 3-tuples are often used to represent points in 3-dimensional space by giving their x, y, and z coordinates.

Number Line: One-dimensional Euclidean space; e.g., the "x-axis."

Numeric: Having a numeric value. Numeric features express the values of attributes as meaningful numbers, rather than names. "Height in inches" is numeric, because different heights are expressed as quantities rather than categories. See *Nominal*.

Objective Function: A function that measures the performance of a learning machine. Learning occurs by optimizing the objective function. For example, the objective function for training a classifier might be "percent accuracy of classification."

Online Analytical Processing (OLAP): Conventional data aggregation and representation for the support of (mostly manual) data mining by an analyst: "retrieve, segment, slice, dice, drill-down, count, display, report."

Over-training: Occurs when a learning machine is allowed to learn information from a training set that doesn't generalize. For example, a learning machine might think that a customer whose name beings with "A" should be classified as "churn," because that was coincidentally true in the training set. Over-training usually occurs in one of three ways: A training set is used that isn't representative of the real-world population; training is continued beyond the point at which the machine begins "memorizing" idiosyncrasies of the training set; or, the learning machine is much too powerful for the problem, and learns only idiosyncratic details of the training set rather than generalizable knowledge. Learning machines that have been over-trained give excellent results on the training set, and poor results on blind-sets.

PAC Learning: A theoretical formalism for assessing the representational power of classification algorithms. (PAC is an acronym for "probably approximately correct.")

Parameter: As used in statistics: the value of an attribute of a population. The average income of Florida families is a population parameter. As used in Predictive Modeling: a value that controls the operation of a model. The slope of a regression line is a model parameter.

Parametric: Refers to statistical models based upon population parameters (means, variances, etc.).

Plane: Two-dimensional Euclidean Space; the set of ordered pairs of real numbers as a real vector space; the Cartesian Plane, spanned by an x and a y axis.

Population: A set, characterized by members having attributes. The fundamental object of investigation in any data mining activity.

Predictive Model: An application that solves a predictive modeling problem. In business, these models are usually classifiers or predictors. They make knowledge actionable. See *Predictive Modeling*.

Predictive Modeling: The second component of data mining: Using the results of knowledge discovery to construct applications (models) that solve business problems. Predictive models are generally classifiers (detect "fraud," categorize customers, etc.) or predictors (estimate future revenue, predict "churn," etc.).

Quickprop: A learning algorithm that is an enhanced version of Backprop. It uses a quadratic rather than a linear update rule, and generally converges in fewer steps than backprop.

Rapid Application Development (RAD): A development methodology driven by the development of broadly functional prototypes rather than a sequence of narrow subsystem integration builds.

RBF: Radial Basis Function. A very powerful "kernel-based" classification paradigm.

Response Function: A function used to scale the output of a neuron in an MLP. Usually a sigmoid based upon an exponential or step function.

Rule: A relationship between facts expressed as a structured construct (e.g., an IF-THEN-ELSE statement in a computing language). The Rule is the fundamental unit of domain knowledge in a Knowledge-Based Expert System (KBES).

Sample: A subset of the population.

Sampling: The process of generating a sample from a population.

Set: A collection. (Left undefined as a fundamental mathematical abstraction.)

Sigmoid: A real-valued function whose graph is "s-shaped." Used to compress a large range of values into a small range of values.

Simulated Annealing: A learning algorithm used to train Hopfield Nets. It is based upon emulation of the thermodynamics of casting metals and glass. This technique is powerful, but practical implementations are generally very slow, and sensitive to how the method is initialized.

Spiral Methodology: The systematic incremental development of an application by constructing a sequence of increasingly able prototypes.

Statistic: A value derived from a sample (e.g., the sample average).

Statistical Inference: The conventional methodology for inferring estimates of population parameters from the statistics of a sample.

Supervised Learning: A training process that uses known ground-truth for each training vector to evaluate and improve the learning machine being trained.

Support Vectors: A powerful predictive modeling technique that creates classifiers by modeling class boundaries.

Time Series: Values arranged in order of increasing time, usually at regular intervals. For example, the output of a "stock ticker" is a time series.

Trojan Horsing: Accidentally introducing the ground-truth as a feature for a predictive model.

Unimodal: Having a single mode.

Unsupervised Learning: A training process that detects and characterizes previously unspecified patterns in data. Auto-clustering is an example of unsupervised learning.

Variance: The square of the standard deviation of a set of values. Measures the "spread" of data. Larger variance implies that data is "spread out," smaller variance implies that data is "packed together."

VC Dimension (Vapnik-Chervonenkis Dimension): A mathematical expression of the complexity of a classification problem for a given population.

Vigilance Parameter: Numeric threshold used by a learning algorithm to determine when two things are "different enough" to be regarded as *different* by the algorithm. Answers the question, "How different is *different*?"

Visualization: Depiction of data in visual form so that quality and relationships may be observed by a human analyst.

Weight: A numeric measure of significance. In neural network parlance, weights are the strengths of the interconnections between artificial neurons. In general, weights can be positive, negative, or zero.

Bibliography

"A Comparison of Neural Network Technology and Human Analysts," CSI, Inc., 1992.

Adriaans, Pieter, and Dolf Zantinge, *Data Mining*, Addison-Wesley, 1996.

Anderberg, David, *Cluster Analysis for Applications*, Academic Press, 1973.

Arbib, Michael, *Brains, Machines, and Mathematics*, Springer-Verlag, 1987.

Barr, A., and E. Feigenbaum, *The Handbook of Artificial Intelligence*, William Kaufmann, Inc., 1981 (3 volumes).

Berry, Michael J. A., and Gordon Linoff, *Data Mining Techniques for Marketing, Sales and Customer Support*, John Wiley & Sons, Inc., 1997.

Bigus, Joseph P., *Data Mining with Neural Networks: Solving Business Problems—from Application Development to Decision Support*, McGraw-Hill, 1996.

"Capitalizing DBMS and Data Warehouse Architecture," Gartner Group: Strategic Forum, Orlando, May 7, 1999.

Cios, Krzysztof J., et al., *Data Mining Methods for Knowledge Discovery*, Kluwer Academic, 1998.

"Computer Science Innovations, Inc. Internal Research and Development (CSI IR&D) Prospectus," CSI, Inc., 1991.

Damper, R.I., *Data Mining Techniques in Speech Synthesis*, Chapman & Hall, 1998.

Dhar, Vasant, and Roger Stein, *Seven Methods for Transforming Corporate Data into Business Intelligence*, Prentice Hall, 1997.

Edelstein, Herbert A., *Introduction to Data Mining and Knowledge Discovery,* Two Crows, 1998.

Fayyad, Usama M., Gregory Piatetsky-Shapiro, Padhraic Smyth, and Ramasamy Uthurusamy, *Advances in Knowledge Discovery and Data Mining,* M.I.T. Press, 1996.

Goldberg, David E., *Genetic Algorithms in Search, Optimization, and Machine Learning,* Addison-Wesley, 1989.

Groth, R., *Data Mining: A Hands-On Approach for Business Professionals* (Data Warehousing Institute Series), 1997.

Hancock, M., *Solving Big Classification Problems with Small Neural Networks,* Proceedings of the Technical and Business Exhibition/Symposium, TABES Paper #91-316A, 1991.

Hancock, M., "Near and Long-Term Load Prediction Using Radial Basis Function Networks," Chapter 13 of *Applications of Neural Networks in Environment, Energy, and Health,* Volume Five of the series, "Progress in Neural Processing," World Scientific, 1996.

Hancock, M., "Estimating Dollar-Value Outcomes of Workmans' Compensation Claims Using Radial Basis Function Networks," Chapter 23 of *Applications of Neural Networks in Environment, Energy, and Health,* Volume Five of the series, "Progress in Neural Processing," World Scientific, 1996.

Hancock, M., and R. Delmater, "Customer Profiling for Financial Services," Chapter 6 of *Handbook of Technology in Financial Services 1999,* CRC Press LLC, 1999.

Hecht-Nielsen, R., *Neurocomputing,* Addison-Wesley, 1990.

Inmon, W., C. Imhoff, and R. Sousa, *Corporate Information Factory,* John Wiley & Sons, 1997.

Inmon, W., *Data Stores, Data Warehousing, and the Zachman Framework: Managing Enterprise Knowledge (McGraw-Hill Series on Data Warehousing and Data Management),* McGraw-Hill, 1997.

Kaufman, Leonard, and Peter J. Rousseeuw, *Finding Groups in Data: An Introduction to Cluster Analysis,* John Wiley & Sons, 1990.

Lavrac, Nada, editor, *Intelligent Data Analysis in Medicine and Pharmacology,* Kluwer International, 1997.

Liu, Huan, and Hiroshi Motoda, *Feature Selection for Knowledge Discovery and Data Mining,* Kluwer International, 1998.

Mattison, Rob, *Data Warehousing and Data Mining for Telecommunications,* Artech House, 1997.

Mena, Jesus, *Data Mining Your Website,* 1999.

Michalski, Ryszard, et. al., *Machine Learning and Data Mining; Methods & Applications,* John Wiley & Sons, 1998.

"N-Dimensional Graphical Representation of Complex Data," CSI, Inc., 1988.

Palaz, Ibrahim, and Sailes Sengupta, editor, *Automated Pattern Analysis in Petroleum Exploration,* Springer-Verlag, 1992.

Pao, Y., *Adaptive Pattern Recognition and Neural Networks,* Addison-Wesley, 1989.

Pyle, Dorian, *Data Preparation for Data Mining,* Morgan Kaufmann, 1999.

Quinlan, J. Ross, *C4.5 Programs for Machine Learning,* Morgan Kaufmann, 1993.

Rich, Elaine, and Kevin Knight, *Artificial Intelligence,* McGraw-Hill, 1991.

Sholom M. Weiss, and Indurkhya, N., *Predictive Data Mining,* Morgan Kaufmann Publishers, 1997.

Silverston, L., et. al., *The Data Model Resource Book: A Library of Logical Data and Data Warehouse Designs,* 1997.

Swingler, Kevin, *Applying Neural Networks: A Practical Guide,* Academic Press, 1996.

Thuraisingham, Bhava M., *Data Mining: Technologies, Techniques, Tools, and Trends,* CRC Press, 1998.

Waterman, Donald A., *A Guide to Expert Systems,* Addison-Wesley, 1986.

Webster, Allen, *Applied Statistics for Business and Economics,* Irwin, 1992.

Westphal, Chris, and Teresa Blaxton, *Data Mining Solutions,* John Wiley & Sons, 1998.

Vendor Information

C

C.1   Directory Web Sites

The following reference sites on the internet provide a range of information including vendor references.

Table C.1

Reference	URL
A Data Miner's Tool	www.byte.com/art/9510/sec8/art8.htm
American Association for Artificial Intelligence	www.aaai.org
Data Warehousing Institute (The)	www.dw-institute.com/
Data Mining News	www.idagroup.com
DM Review	www.dmreview.com/
DBMS Buyers Guide	www.intelligententerprise.com/
Knowledge Centers	www.knowledgecenters.org/dwcenter.asp
Knowledge Discovery Nuggets	www.kdnuggets.com
St@tserv	www.statserv.com

C.2   Vendor Listings

Table C.2

Company:	**Changepoint Inc.**
Address:	1595 16th Avenue, Suite 800, Richmond Hill, ON, L4B 3N9
Phone:	905-886-7000 x479
Fax:	905-886-7023
E-mail:	mgrunstra@changepoint.com
Web site:	www.changepoint.com
Company:	**Codework Italia srl**
Address:	Corso Cairoli 32, 10123 Torino, Italy
Phone:	+39-011-885168
Fax:	+39-011-8122652
E-mail:	codework@inrete.it; sales@codework-it.com
Web site:	www.codework-it.com/
Company:	**Informatica Corporation**
Address:	3350 W. Bayshore Road, Palo Alto, CA 94303
Phone:	800-970-1179
Fax:	650-687-0040
E-mail:	info@informatica.com
Web site:	www.informatica.com
Company:	**InterNetivity, Inc.**
Address:	1545 Carling Avenue, Suite 404, Ottawa, Ontario K1Z 8P9Canada
Phone:	613-729-4480
Fax:	613-729-6711
E-mail:	sales@internetivity.com
Web site:	www.InterNetivity.com or www.databeacon.com
Company:	**KiQ Ltd**
Address:	Easton Hall, Great Easton, Essex, ENGLAND. CM6 2HD
Phone:	+44-0-1371-870-254
Fax:	+44-0-1371-870-254
E-mail:	david.barrow@kiq.com
Web site:	www.kiq.com
Company:	**MarketMiner Inc. (formerly AbTech Corp.)**
Address:	1575 State Farm Blvd. Charlottesville, VA22911
Phone:	804-977-0686
Fax:	804-977-9615
E-mail:	info@marketminer.com
Web site:	www.marketminer.com

Table C.2   *(continued)*

Company:	**Megaputer Intelligence Inc.**
Address:	120 West Seventh Street, Bloomington, IN 47404
Phone:	812-330-0110
Fax:	812-339-1646
E-mail:	info@megaputer.com
Web site:	www.megaputer.com

Company:	**MicroStrategy**
Address:	8000 Towers Crescent Drive, Vienna, VA 22182
Phone:	703-848-8600
Web site:	www.microstrategy.com

Company:	**MINEit Software Limited**
Address:	University of Ulster, Shore Rd, Newtownabbey, Northern Ireland BT37 0QB, UK
Phone:	+44-7715-368683
E-mail:	dave@MINEit.com
Web site:	www/MINEit.com

Company:	**Quadstone**
Address:	286 Congress St., 3rd Floor, Boston, MA 02210-1009
Phone:	617-753-7393
Fax:	617-457-5299
E-mail:	info@quadstone.com
Web site:	www.quadstone.com

Company:	**Salford Systems**
Address:	8880 Rio Dan Diego Dr.
Phone:	619-543-8880
Fax:	619-543-8888
E-mail:	dstein@salford-systems.com
Web site:	www.salford-systems.com

Company:	**SAS Institute Inc.**
Address:	SAS Campus Drive, Cary, NC27513
Phone:	919-677-8000
Fax:	919-677-4444
E-mail:	software@sas.com
Web site:	www.sas.com

Company:	**SIAL Software**
Address:	Av Plinio Brasil Milano 143/403, Bairro Auxiliadora Porto Alegre - RS - CEP 90.520-002
Phone:	55-51-321-2566
E-mail:	info@sial.com.br
Web site:	www.sial.com.br

continues

Table C.2   *(continued)*

Company:	**SPSS Inc.**
Address:	233 S. Wacker Dr., 11th floor, Chicago, IL 60606
Phone:	800-543-2185
Fax:	312-651-3668
E-mail:	sales@spss.com
Web site:	www.spss.com

Company:	**Torrent Systems, Inc.**
Address:	Five Cambridge Center, Cambridge, MA 02142
Phone:	617-354-8484
Fax:	617-354-6767
E-mail:	engelke@torrent.com; mcgrath@collaborative.com
Web site:	www.torrent.com

Company:	**Urban Science**
Address:	200 Renaissance Center, Suite 1900, Detroit, MI 48243
Phone:	313-259-9900
Fax:	313-259-1362
E-mail:	mcyuhn@urbanscience.com
Web site:	www.urbanscience.com

Statistics 101

The population parameters of greatest interest in most applications are the simple intuitive ones: minimum, maximum, midrange, mean, variance, median, and mode. The minimum and maximum are the smallest and largest values assumed by an attribute, respectively. The midrange is the average of the minimum and the maximum. The mean is the average of the attribute value taken over the whole population. The variance is the average square-deviation from the mean, described below. It is a measure of how "spread out" the data values are. The median is the attribute value at the 50th percentile: Half the population has attribute values smaller, and half larger. The mode is the attribute value that occurs most frequently.

The family income example can be used to illustrate the derivation of each of these parameters. Suppose that a sample consisting of seven families has been selected, having the following incomes:

family 1: income = $40,000

family 2: income = $12,000

family 3: income = $36,000

family 4: income = $22,000

family 5: income = $26,000

family 6: income = $37,000

family 7: income = $22,000

The sample statistics are easily computed; sorting the list is helpful:

10,000   22,000   22,000   26,000   36,000   37,000   40,000

sample minimum = $10,000

sample maximum = $40,000

sample midrange = (10,000 + 40,000) ÷ 2 = $25,000

sample mean = (10,000 + 22,000 + 22,000 + 26,000 + 36,000 + 37,000 + 40,000) ÷ 7 = $27,857

$$\text{sample standard deviation} = \{[(10{,}000 - 27{,}857)^2$$
$$+ (22{,}000 - 27{,}857)^2$$
$$+ (22{,}000 - 27{,}857)^2$$
$$+ (26{,}000 - 27{,}857)^2$$
$$+ (36{,}000 - 27{,}857)^2$$
$$+ (37{,}000 - 27{,}857)^2$$
$$+ (40{,}000 - 27{,}857)^2] - 7\}^{0.5}$$
$$= \$9{,}916$$

The standard deviation is the square root of the average of the squares of the differences of the sample values from the sample mean. You can see why it needs its own name!

sample median = $26,000

sample mode = $22,000

Notice that the median, the midrange, and the mean can all be different. These statistics are called measures of central tendency, since they each estimate, in their own way, the "middle value" of the sample data.

The standard deviation measures the variability of the data. For example, if the sample values are all equal (so that there is no variation at all), the standard deviation will be zero. It is an important fact that, for data with a normal distribution ("bell curve," discussed below) that about 68 percent of the data will be within one standard deviation of the mean. We will refer to this as the "68 percent rule" for normal distributions. There are other similar rules, such as the "95 percent rule": 95 percent of the data will be within two standard deviations of the mean; and, the "99 percent rule": 99 percent of the data will be within 2.56 standard deviations of the mean. The standard deviation is typically denoted by the Greek letter sigma (σ). If there is one mode, the population is called *unimodal*. There can be more than one mode, if there is a tie for most frequent value. Such populations are called *multimodal*.

The standard deviation measures how much the data in the population vary from the mean. When the standard deviation is very small, the data is tightly grouped about the mean. When the standard deviation is large, the data is spread widely about the mean.

Histograms provide a familiar example of probability distribution. Also called bar charts, they show the number of occurrences of the various values, or ranges of values in a population. An illustration is contained within Chapter 6 (Figure 6.4).

The horizontal axis is income (e.g., 20K = $20,000), and the vertical axis is the number of persons in each income range, the *frequency*. For ease of use, we have shown the frequencies in the bars of the histogram. Note that the histogram shows that 22 people from the population have an income between $25,000 and $30,000. The ranges specifying the categories define the histogram's *bins*. The boundaries of the bins are called *bin boundaries*. For example, the 25K–30K bin has a frequency of 10.

From the histogram, questions about the probabilities of observing various incomes in a sample drawn from the population can be answered. Because 10 out of 100 people in this population have an income between 25K and 30K, we can say that "the probability that a person selected at random from this population will have an income between 25K and 30K is 10/100, or 10 percent." Other similar questions can be answered from the histogram: For example, the probability that a person selected at random from this population will have an income between 10K and 30K is $(19 + 36 + 13 + 10) \div 100 = 78$ percent.

Techniques Listed by Methodology Phase

E.1   Problem Definition (Step 1)

The problem definition step focuses the effort of the remaining steps on the problem to be solved.

E.2   Data Evaluation (Step 2)

The techniques that support the Data Analysis phase are:

Table E.1

Conventional/ Statistical techniques	• population modeling by statistical moments (means, standard deviations)
	• correlation (testing data for dependence/independence)
	• chi-square analysis (test hypotheses viz data's statistical character)
	• simple visualization (histograms, scatterplots, graphs, charts)
	• time-series analysis (e.g., control charts, linear predictive modeling)
OLAP	• stratification and segmentation ("slicing and dicing" data)
	• roll-ups (summarizing data in various ways seeking explanatory patterns)
	• drill-down (expanding summarized data seeking explanatory patterns)

continues

Table E.1 *(continued)*

	• complex queries and browsing (to uncover complex relationships)
Scientific visualization	• sophisticated feature plots
	• ad-hoc data views
High-end analysis	• auto-clustering (determine natural patterns in the data)
	• rule induction (generate predictive/explanatory rules from data)
	• link analysis (discover significant connections among data)

E.3   Feature Extraction and Enhancement (Step 3)

The techniques that support the Feature Extraction process are:

Table E.2

Elementary conventional methods	• counts, ratios, difference quotients, etc.
Integral transforms	• Fourier Transform (e.g., windowed FFT)
	• wavelets (multi-resolution decomposition)
	• general kernel filters (spectral, spatial, temporal)
Quantization and coding	• MAX quantization
	• histogram equalization
	• view-through-feature coding
Semantic feature extraction	• tokenization (parse tree)
	• bag-of-words
Regression features	• model coefficients (e.g., slope of least-squares line)

Techniques for Feature Analysis and Enhancement are:

Table E.3

Bayesian analysis	• determines how well a linear classifier will do on this problem
Feature registration and normalization	• z-scoring, etc.
Excision/replication/synthesis	• class collisions and population imbalance
Feature correlation and salience	• Do features give independent information?
Principal Component Analysis (PCA)	• Karhunen-Loeve, for example
Independent Component Analysis (ICA)	• filling in missing data fields using a specific correlation technique
Intra-vector regression	• use non-missing values in a vector to consistently fill in missing values within that vector

E.4 Prototyping/Model Development (Step 4)

Techniques for Knowledge Discovery are:

Table E.4

Conventional knowledge engineering	(manual)
Rule induction	
Genetic algorithms	
Fuzzy matching	
Auto-clustering	• K-means, other top-down, centroid methods
	• Region growing, other bottom-up, boundary methods
	• Decision trees
Link analysis	• spatial and temporal
Regression modeling	• linear and non-linear single and multiple

Techniques for Model Construction are:

Table E.5

Model-based ("white-box" techniques)	• hard analytic models (ad hoc mathe-matical)
	• Knowledge-Based Expert Systems (e.g., forward/backward chaining)
	• Decision trees (GINI, twoing, etc.)
Non-model-based ("black-box" techniques)	• Neural networks (backpropagation, reinforcement learning, etc.)
	• multi-layer perceptrons
	• Hopfield Nets (e.g., Boltzmann Machines) • Feature maps (e.g., Kohonen)
	• Adaptive Resonance Theory (ART) machines
	• Regression machines
	• Restricted Coulomb Energy (RCE) machines
	• Radial Basis Functions (RBF)
	• Adaptive Logic Networks (ALN)
	• Hybrid systems ("bagging")

E.5   Model Evaluation (Step 5)

Techniques for Model Validation are:

Table E.6

Blind-Testing
• N-fold cross validation
• Sensitivity analysis
• Application to "use cases"

Index